Bee Nilson's Kitchen Handbook

Also in Mayflower Books

Bee Nilson

Bee Nilson's Kitchen Handbook

MAYFLOWER
GRANADA PUBLISHING
London Toronto Sydney New York

Published by Granada Publishing Limited
in Mayflower Books 1974
Reprinted 1978

ISBN 0 583 19743 4

First published in Great Britain by
Pelham Books Ltd 1972
Copyright © Bee Nilson 1972

Granada Publishing Limited
Frogmore, St Albans, Herts AL2 2NF
and
3 Upper James Street, London W1R 4BP
1221 Avenue of the Americas, New York, NY 10020, USA
117 York Street, Sydney, NSW 2000, Australia
100 Skyway Avenue, Toronto, Ontario, Canada M9W 3A6
110 Northpark Centre, 2193 Johannesburg South Africa
CML Centre, Queen & Wyndham, Auckland 1, New Zealand

Made and printed in Great Britain by
Richard Clay (The Chaucer Press) Ltd
Bungay, Suffolk
Set in Monotype Times

Contents

Foreword

Bee Nilson's Kitchen Handbook gives the essential information on all aspects of good domestic kitchen management. It starts with planning and equipping the kitchen, layout, choice of fittings, and arrangements for easy working. There is an alphabetical list of large and small kitchen utensils with hints on what to look for when making a choice.

Buying and storing food is dealt with in detail. The reader is told what to look out for when shopping for good-quality foods of all kinds, and how to store them to keep them in good condition. Suggestions on how to plan and organise the shopping are also included.

There is a chapter on meal preparation and management which includes a chart of foods in season, how to make your own step-by-step working plan, and what foods it is safe to prepare in advance.

The chapter on food and health includes basic nutrition and how to put it into practice, food hygiene, and a brief look at food laws.

Home preserving of foods is still important to many who have gardens, while others do it to provide the family with something different from the commercial article. This book includes information on how to make different kinds of preserves and how to do home freezing. Finally, there is an A.B.C. of cooking terms and methods, to make it a comprehensive and handy reference.

Chapter One

INTRODUCTION

ABBREVIATIONS

tsp.	*level teaspoon/s*	ml.	*millilitre/s*
Tbs.	*level tablespoon/s*	dl.	*decilitre/s*
c.	*level cup/s*	l.	*litre/s*
pt.	*pint/s*	mm.	*millimetre/s*
qt.	*quart/s*	cm.	*centimetre/s*
oz.	*ounce/s*	in.	*inch/es*
lb.	*pound/s*	min./s.	*minute/s*
g.	*gramme/s*	hr./s.	*hour/s*
kg.	*kilogramme/s*		

TEMPERATURES

° degrees Fahrenheit   E. electric
°C. degrees Celsius   G. gas
Also see Thermometers and Thermostats, pages 41 and 258.

COMPARATIVE WEIGHTS AND MEASURES

British	*Metric*	*Approximations*
1 ounce	28·35 grammes	25–30 grammes
1 pound (16 oz.)	453·6 grammes	½ kilogramme or 500 grammes
2 pounds	907·2 grammes	1 kilogramme or 1,000 grammes
1 fluid ounce	28·41 millilitres	25–30 millilitres
1 pint (20 fluid oz.)	568·2 millilitres	½ litre or 5 decilitres
1 inch	2·54 centimetres	2½ cm. or 25 millimetres
1 cup (½ pt. or 10 fluid oz.)	284·1 millilitres	250–300 millilitres
1 tablespoon	15 millilitres	
1 teaspoon	5 millilitres	

AMERICAN MEASURES

1 cup	8 fluid ounces or approximately 230 millilitres
1 tablespoon	$\frac{1}{2}$ fluid ounce or approximately 14 millilitres
1 teaspoon	$\frac{1}{8}$ fluid ounce or approximately 5 millilitres
1 pint	16 fluid ounces or approximately 455 millilitres

Chapter Two

PLANNING AND EQUIPPING THE KITCHEN

The ideal kitchen is one which is planned especially for the family's needs, but few are able to afford this kind of tailor-made perfection. Most of us have to manage with someone else's design, whether in an old or new house.

Ideas about the perfect kitchen vary widely even on such questions as the aspect. Some insist that it should be on the non-sunny side of the house, while others want the opposite, so that the kitchen is always cheerful and light. Some like a small room just for cooking, and others want space for meals and for the children to play.

Often much can be done to improve existing kitchens simply by rearranging the position of movable fittings and by storing frequently-used equipment in more convenient positions.

If you are buying new kitchen units, be very critical about points such as depth of cupboards and shelves, and the quality of drawers and sliding shelves.

Before buying any kitchen furniture or moving heavy fitments it is wise to draw a plan to scale, on squared paper, showing the kitchen size with all fixtures and projections marked. Then cut pieces of paper to scale to the size of the proposed new units and any fittings you want to move. Move them around on the plan to see how they can be fitted in and still leave adequate space for working and opening doors, both kitchen doors and those of fitments.

If your kitchen is an upstairs one, such as a flat in a converted house, be sure that any equipment is not too big to go up the stairs, nor too heavy for the floorboards. Sometimes the floor needs to be strengthened to take large freezers and washing machines.

Fixtures, including sinks and boilers, can usually be moved if you are prepared to have this more costly kind of reorganisation carried out. Sometimes old and ill-planned kitchens have more doors than are necessary. One of these can often be closed permanently – making more wall-space for storage cupboards or refrigerator.

Many firms selling kitchen units, cookers, and other equipment, offer free kitchen planning advice.

GENERAL LAYOUT

The most convenient shape for working in is either the U-shaped kitchen, or the 'passage' type, with two parallel walls used for the fittings and not less than 4ft. (1¼ m.) clear space down the centre.

As far as large items are concerned, the cooker should be fairly near the sink, and the refrigerator near the main work bench, but not next to the cooker.

With the 'passage' type of kitchen it is possible to have oven, refrigerator and freezer built in along one wall together with storage cupboards and drawers, with one or two conveniently-placed pull-out shelves on which to rest heavy things. The other wall would then provide space for the sink and hob unit, with cupboards or shelves over them. This is also usually the best side for a dish-washing machine.

If space is restricted, a conventional cooker is better than a split-level one, and a refrigerator and a freezer with working tops are better than taller models.

With a square or wide kitchen the use of 'island' working fitments is a good way of getting extra working space. Such a fitment can house the hob unit and provide access to it from both sides.

Avoid putting a cooker in a corner because this makes using the hob and opening the oven door very awkward. If possible, have a metal top to the working surface next to the cooker, for taking hot pots and pans. Laminated plastic tops will stand fairly hot things, but it is nice not to have to worry about possibly spoiling the surface with extra hot pans.

If possible, keep laundry out of the kitchen. The old 'wash house' was a much more hygienic arrangement than using the kitchen, and the modern trend for separate utility rooms or having the laundry equipment installed in the bathroom is a good one. Naturally this depends on where the necessary space can be found. My present utility room is a converted lean-to which opens off the kitchen, and used to house junk and bins for storing the coal and coke which we no longer use.

HEIGHTS AND DEPTHS OF EQUIPMENT

For the average woman of 5 ft. 2 in. to 5 ft. 3 in. (about 1¾ m.), working surfaces are usually most convenient if 34 in. (85 cm.) from the floor. This sort of fitment is often only 18 in. (45 cm.) deep, which is rather narrow for a working top, but it is possible to have them fixed with an overhanging top to a depth of 3 in. (8 cm.) at the front or back to provide a deeper working area. Some cookers are now made for this height of fitment, but they are usually considerably deeper than 18 in. (45 cm.). So, if you want a flush-fitting cooker, the fitments will have to be built out from the wall in the manner I have described.

The taller woman will find 36 in. (90 cm.) from the floor a more convenient height, and these fitments are usually 21 in. (53 cm.) deep, but if necessary, to make them flush with other equipment such as cookers, their depth can be further extended in the same way as the 18 in. (45 cm.) fittings.

Wall cupboards above working surfaces should leave enough space for standing equipment underneath them, and to avoid knocking your head on them when you bend forward over the bench. It is advisable to leave a space of at least 13 in. (33 cm.) between bench top and the bottom of the wall cupboard, and the cupboard should not be more than 1 ft. (30 cm.) deep when fitted above a 21 in. (53 cm.) deep working top. Wall cupboards which are wider at the top than the bottom are very useful. The bottom shelf of these is often an open one, very useful for spice jars and such-like.

WORKING SURFACES

Plenty of work-top space is essential for quick and easy food preparation. Several conveniently placed tops can be more useful than one continuous surface. For example, a working top by the sink bench is important for all sorts of jobs; preferably, have one either side of the sink. Metal-topped surfaces by the cooker have already been mentioned. These are the benches you will probably use most frequently.

A fair-sized top to take mixers and other appliances is needed, and for general mixing and food preparation. Easy-to-clean laminated plastic makes the best surface, with aluminium or stainless steel for the one by the cooker.

The most common depths for these are 18 in. (45 cm.) or 21

in. (53 cm.). This is really too deep for cupboards, but not for work tops. Only a few large items of equipment need this much shelf space. It is inconvenient and time-wasting to stack pieces of equipment one behind the other on deep shelves. If you do have to use such shelves, put the equipment that is least frequently used at the back.

Deep cupboards should either have shallow shelves and then something stored on the back of the cupboard door to use the rest of the space, or, better still, they should have pull-out shelves like drawers. These can be on rollers for easy handling and have a deep front like a drawer.

Units with plenty of drawers are the most useful fitments, provided that they are of good quality and the drawers slide easily. Otherwise, you are better off with cupboards. Drawers are specially useful for all small items, and there should be more shallow drawers than deep ones, although one or two of the latter are useful for larger items such as cake tins, sieves, and strainers. For small equipment allow more drawer than cupboard space, leaving the latter for large items.

Narrow shelves are also more efficient for food storage, but it is now possible to buy sets of individual drawers to hold sugar and other dry goods. These are usually made of clear plastic or glass, so that the contents can be easily identified. They can be purchased in nests or in single rows, and are very useful for fitting under wall cupboards. They are much quicker to use and more convenient than any cupboard storage.

For wall storage, some open shelves are handy for keeping items which are in daily use. This saves a lot of time. Other things can be hung on the walls, or on peg board fastened to the walls at an easy-to-reach height. The things most useful on open shelves or on the walls are saucepans, fry pans, teapot, coffee maker, tea and coffee containers, salt, spices, condiments, measuring jugs, scales, can opener, kitchen scissors, cooking spoons, knives, forks, and ladles.

One or two vertical pull-out drawers are useful, especially under the sink to house swabs, soaps, and other things used at the sink. This is also a useful way of storing tall objects like oven trays and flat cake tins and racks. Another way of storing tall, narrow objects is in a cupboard with vertical divisions like a record filing cabinet.

Awkward corner cupboards or very deep cupboards can be made more convenient by having swing-out shelves or revolv-

14

ing shelves, although the latter must be very well made to be efficient.

ARRANGEMENT OF SMALL EQUIPMENT

For convenience, store equipment nearest to the place where it will be most frequently used.

Near-the-Cooker Store

Saucepans and fry pans.
Wooden spoons and stirrers.
Fish slice and ladles.
Some salt, sugar, flour, herbs, and other flavourings frequently used at the cooker.
A few basins of assorted sizes.
A liquid measure and measuring spoons.
Plates and serving dishes which will have to be warmed for serving food.
Tea, coffee and the equipment needed for making these and other beverages.
Oven cloth and gloves.

Near-the-Sink Store

All washing-up materials.
Vegetables, colander, vegetable knives, chopping board.
Sink tidy, hand towel, and/or a roll of paper towels.
Tea towels.
Equipment for refuse disposal.

Near-the-Refrigerator Store

Jugs to take milk and cream.
Glasses for cold drinks.
The butter dish.
The salad bowl and equipment for making dressings.
Polythene bags and other equipment for storing food in the freezer or refrigerator.

LIGHTING, VENTILATION AND ELECTRIC POINTS

Good, shadow-free lighting is essential for easy and safe working. If a central fluorescent light is not enough, have small lights over awkward places. Hob and oven lights on modern electric cookers are a great convenience in many situations.

Ventilation should be good enough to get rid of all steam. A steam-laden atmosphere is very unpleasant to work in, and steam condenses on walls and fittings which are cold in the winter. An extractor fan is the best way to remove steam and cooking smells, but be sure that it is large enough for the size of the kitchen, that it is correctly sited, and that it has a shutter. Ventilation hoods containing a fan can be fitted over cooking areas.

Have plenty of points at bench-top height for electric appliances, and enough bench space to keep them permanently in position so that time and energy are not wasted on getting them out of a cupboard when they are wanted. Store any attachments nearby.

WALL AND FLOOR COVERINGS

As steam and grease are the two things likely to spoil walls and ceilings in the kitchen, choose something which is resistant to both. You don't only have to consider grease in obvious places like around the cooker. It is surprising how far grease travels when you are frying. It gets carried by currents of air and deposited on walls and equipment at considerable heights.

Tiles are the most durable finish, easy to clean, and come in lovely colours and designs. Part tiling and part paint is less expensive than all tiling, and durable paints can be glossy or matt finish, but must be really washable unless you want to have to redecorate every time the walls become dirty.

Pre-sealed wood panelling can also be used, and so can vinyl wall papers but neither of these is as durable as tiles and paint. Vinyl can be wiped clean but is harmed by grease.

The perfect floor covering for a kitchen has yet to be invented. It has to withstand grease, moisture, heat, not be slippery (especially when it gets wet), and be resilient enough not to make your feet and legs ache.

Quarry tiles are the most hard-wearing, are made in many colours and designs, but they have two disadvantages, they are cold and hard. Some people compromise by having tiles in part of the kitchen and something softer where there is much standing and walking.

A good-quality thick linoleum, sheet or tiles, is a good choice but buy an inlaid one where the pattern goes right through, otherwise it will get shabby very quickly. Floor coverings made of thermo-plastic, vinyl, and P.V.C. are available as sheet or tiles, and are usually colourful, soft, warm for the feet and easy to clean, but some of them stain easily, become slippery when wet and are inclined to be affected by grease and heat. Be careful when choosing them. Buy the best you can afford, and have them properly laid on a smooth, even foundation. Raised joints and bumps in the sub-floor very quickly lead to damage to both these and linoleum coverings.

CARRYING FOOD

A good trolley is an indispensable item for all but the smallest of kitchens. Use it to bring food to and from the dining room (much better than using a hatch), have it by you when washing up to hold surplus dirties and take the clean items back to their storage places. Intelligent use of a trolley saves much time and walking, but you must, of course, have floors which are free from steps or bumpy carpet edges, and the trolley must have good wheels, not toy ones.

You also need to plan a convenient place to keep it out of the way when not in use. I keep mine in the kitchen, just beside the door into the dining room, and use it as an extra place for putting things when I am preparing a meal.

KITCHEN EQUIPMENT

A visit to the kitchen department of any large store will show a bewildering range of kitchen equipment. It is pretty hopeless to go shopping there without some fairly definite idea about what is required. This depends on the kind of cooking which you are going to do, and it is always wise to start modestly, with the bare essentials, and add to them as the need arises. Perhaps the simplest kind of catering is done by the young couple where the wife is working outside the home, the midday dinner is eaten out during the week and often with in-laws or friends during the week-end. All the cooking that is going to be done is for breakfast and a simple evening meal. The following list of equipment will provide the essentials for that sort of catering:

A small cooker of some sort, or separate electric appliances for table-top cooking. These would need to include a grill, a boiling plate, and a kettle.

1 or 2 small saucepans or stewpans to boil and scramble eggs, heat milk, soup, and tinned or frozen foods.

17

1 fry pan for bacon and eggs, omelet, and other fried foods, as well as for egg poaching and other similar cooking.

1 teapot.

1 milk jug and small cream jug.

1 jug for making coffee, or other coffee-making apparatus.

1 vegetable knife.

1 fish slice.

1 tin opener.

1 cooking fork.

1 colander or wire strainer.

2 or 3 basins of assorted sizes.

If an oven is available, 1 casserole and 1 pie dish, or other fireproof dish.

If you are fond of salads, 1 salad shaker for drying lettuce.

1 set of kitchen measuring spoons, and 1 measuring cup or jug.

1 wooden stirrer or spoon.

1 pair kitchen scissors.

1 corkscrew.

1 lemon squeezer.

Salt and pepper shakers or mills.

1 chopping board.

1 holder for and roll of kitchen paper towels.

1 plate-drying rack.

1 oven cloth.

1 swab or washing-up cloth.

Tea towels.

1 packet steel-wool pads for cleaning pans.

ALPHABETICAL LIST OF KITCHEN EQUIPMENT
(with Notes on its Selection and Use)

ALUMINIUM EQUIPMENT

Aluminium and aluminium alloys are used for making a wide variety of household utensils. They resist corrosion and are good conductors of heat. They are capable of taking a variety of finishes, matt, polished, and coloured, but they are relatively soft metals, and scratch easily. Boiling water in aluminium pans causes blackening which is unsightly but harmless. It can be prevented by adding a little vinegar to the water. And sometimes milk sauces and puddings stirred with a metal whisk or spoon in an aluminium pan become discoloured.

The price of aluminium pans is an indication of quality, the heavier pans being the more expensive and the best for cooking. Cast aluminium is the heaviest, and is used for some domestic pans, but the majority are made of sheet aluminium. This comes in different gauges or thicknesses. Gauge 3–4 is good quality, gauge 12–16 average, and cheaper pans may even be thinner.

From the health point of view there is no evidence that the small quantities of metal likely to be ingested by people who regularly cook in aluminium pans are harmful in any way.

ALUMINIUM FOIL

This is an important labour-saving aid in the modern home, being useful both for wrapping food for storage and for cooking in. The following are some of the things for which it is most useful:

1. For making lids. A piece of foil pressed over the top of a bowl or any other container makes a very effective lid for storage in the refrigerator, in the larder, for casserole cooking, for containers in the pressure cooker, or for a lid to a fry pan when poaching eggs or doing slow frying.

2. For wrapping food. Use it for wrapping and sealing food for storage in the refrigerator; for food for picnic meals; and for cooking meat, fish, and vegetables to retain all the juices. Cooked food which has been stored in foil can be reheated in the oven in its wrapper. Wrap tightly for food storage, to exclude air; wrap loosely for cooking. A heavy duty foil 40 per cent thicker than the standard one is useful for wrapping food for the freezer and for other jobs, such as lining tins and wrapping large objects for storage in the refrigerator.

3. Lining tins, cake tins, grill pans, Yorkshire pudding tins. Greasing is no longer necessary, the food is easily removed, and the pan requires little if any washing.

4. Bread, rolls, and sandwiches keep fresh in foil, though do not keep sandwiches more than a few hours, unless they are in the refrigerator. Rolls can be reheated in foil wrappings in a moderate oven for about 15 mins.

5. When baking several trays of biscuits, put the biscuits on sheets of aluminium foil as they are prepared, then slide the sheets onto baking trays as required. No greasing is necessary.

APPLE CORER

A metal cylinder with a handle attached. The metal part is pushed through the centre of an apple and removes the core, useful when baking apples. The hole in the apple can be filled with sugar, honey, syrup or jam with spices, fruit or nuts for extra flavouring.

AUTOMATIC COOKER

This is a cooker which can be pre-set to turn on at the required time and off at the end of the cooking period. It is usually for oven cooking, but with some cookers it can be used to control a warming cupboard as well. This device is available on gas as well as electric cookers.

An automatic cooker is the greatest help to those who cannot be in the kitchen when it is time to put the meal on. It is, however, necessary to spend time earlier in the day, or the night before, to prepare the food and arrange it in the oven. With many things, the preparation can be done the night before and the food stored in the refrigerator until it is time to put it in the oven.

Food which is to be put in the oven in the morning to wait until late afternoon or early evening before cooking, needs to be something which will not spoil during the long storage period. It is also important that the oven should be quite cold before the food is put in.

Manufacturers of automatic cookers provide instructions for using them, and these should be followed carefully while you are learning the new cooking technique. I think it is important to use the automatic setting frequently if you are going to become an expert and make the most of the advantages of it. Apart from the obvious benefits to the woman who is away from home during the day, who wants a hot meal at night which will be ready to serve as soon as she gets home, I think the automatic timer is very useful to the gardener who doesn't want to interrupt her work to come in and start the dinner; to the housewife who wants to go shopping or visiting in the afternoon but has to have a hot meal ready for the family in the evening – each has a use for this type of cooking.

Once you have learnt the rudiments of using it, work out menus which suit your requirements, and make notes of how to do each one so that you can prepare the things quickly and easily next time. All of which means that, if you are going to make full use of an automatic cooker, you have to learn the technique and organise yourself to use it.

BAIN-MARIE

In English this is a 'water-bath', but it is customary to use 'water-bath' when referring to laboratory experiments or technological processes, and '*bain-marie*' in connection with cooking.

A *bain-marie* is used for keeping food hot by standing the pan containing the food in another vessel (the water-bath), containing hot water. By this means sauces and other similar foods are kept hot without spoiling. The water is kept near to boiling point, either on top of the stove or in the oven. A double boiler serves a similar purpose, provided that the water in the lower half is not actually boiling.

When food is cooked in the oven in a water-bath, this is also called a *bain-marie*, e.g. when a custard is being baked with food requiring higher temperature, and the custard stands in an outer container of water which should be kept just below boiling. Many people always make a custard this way, but it isn't essential if the oven has a thermostatic control.

BAKING TRAYS, see *Cake Tins*, page 23

BASINS

A basin usually has fairly straight sides, wider at the top than at the base, and is the traditional shape for steamed puddings. A bowl, or mixing bowl, usually has more rounded sides. It is useful to have some of each, ranging from ½ pt. (250 ml.) upwards, depending on the numbers you are cooking for. Both basins and bowls are available in earthenware, oven-proof glass, or stainless steel. Plastic bowls are also used, but they are not as generally useful as those made of more durable materials.

BEATERS

Many utensils can be used for beating. The most useful are simple wooden spoons and an egg whisk or beater. The latter may be hand-held or electric. The best egg whisks are either the balloon-shaped whisks made of many strands of wire, or the flatter whisks which are basically a coil of wire. It is useful

21

to have a small one, even if you use an electric beater for larger mixtures. For beating just one egg white, use a fork or a palette knife, and beat the egg on a plate.

When you are using the rotary or electric type of beater, choose a bowl small enough to allow the mixture to come well up the blades of the beater, otherwise it takes ages to beat the mixture satisfactorily.

BLENDER, also called a Liquidiser or Liquefier, or a Blending Attachment

This device is also known by various brand names coined by the manufacturers. It is an electric machine consisting of a motor, to which is fitted a goblet containing blades which revolve at high speed, and blend and pulverise a great variety of foods. Most frequently purchased as an attachment for a general-purpose electric mixer, it may be bought as a separate unit.

Blenders take a lot of hard work out of many cooking operations and also make it possible to serve some entirely new types of dishes. They are, perhaps, the most useful power-driven cooking aid yet devised. The manufacturers provide booklets of instructions and recipes.

Some of the uses to which they may be put are as follows:

Beating For making batters for pancakes, Yorkshire pudding, and waffles. For beating the fat, sugar, and eggs when making cakes by the creaming method. The mixture is tipped into a bowl, and the other ingredients added.

Blending Mixing drinks of all kinds, and blending ingredients for smooth sauces and soups.

Chopping Parsley and herbs – either dry or to add to sauces and soups – and chopping onions for soups and sauces, chopping peel for cakes, and chopping nuts.

Grating They do not really grate, but chop finely and serve the same purpose. They can be used for dry bread, dry cheese, nuts.

Grinding Some manufacturers recommend using blenders for grinding coffee, but it is usually more satisfactory to use a separate coffee-grinding attachment.

22

Preserving To speed up the making of jams and marmalades. See *Marmalade*, page 191.

Sieving When sieving is required for the purpose of making a *purée*, the blender does it much faster and more efficiently than any other method. It is more economical too for there is no waste as there is with ordinary sieving. Particularly useful with fruit and vegetables. Also used to make meat, fish, and poultry *purées* for such things as Sandwich Spread, *Soufflés*, Cream Soups, *Pâtés*, Mousses – and a host of other uses.

BOWLS, see *Basins*, page 21

CAKE RACKS OR COOLING TRAYS
These are usually made of criss-cross strands of tinned wire mounted on a stout frame, and have small feet to raise them off the table top. There are also some made from plastic. They are designed to allow air to circulate round the cooling cake, and prevent the condensation and dampness which would result if the warm cake was turned out on a flat surface. They are also used for holding cakes during icing, or savouries when adding aspic. Put a plastic tray or large dish under the rack to catch drippings.

CAKE TINS AND BAKING TRAYS
Many different sizes and shapes are available, either in tinned steel or aluminium. And there are several non-stick types that require no lining with paper or greasing – which saves a lot of preparation time. Alternatively, there are non-stick silicone-impregnated papers available for lining, and there is also foil which is used for the same purposes.

CAN OPENERS
The most satisfactory type is the hand-operated rotary one, where a toothed wheel cuts the tin. Similar types are available for permanent fixing to the wall.

CASSEROLES
These are dishes with a lid, used for cooking in the oven. Some are suitable for cooking on top of the stove as well as in the oven, and most are attractive enough to serve the food in. The latest casseroles for use both on top and in the oven, are made

23

of glass/ceramic. Some metal stewpans have short handles and they can double as casseroles. Other casseroles are made of earthenware or oven-proof glass, but neither of these can be used on the top. When buying casseroles, make sure that they are a suitable size for the sort of food you want to cook, and that they do not waste space in the oven. Some are very tall and deep (hotpots), and in addition have quite big knobs on top so that they need practically the whole of a small oven to themselves. More practical are the flatter lids and shallower bases without any knobs on top. Modern casseroles have 'ears' at the sides to lift the lid up with, but do not buy ones with very large ears as these too are wasteful of oven space. The slow temperature used for casserole cooking is ideal for many other foods, and you want to be able to put some of these in the oven at the same time.

CELLOPHANE

Special kinds are made for use in the freezer, and are especially useful for separating layers of food. Other similar-looking materials are made to use as moisture-proof food wraps for the refrigerator and for storing food. Some are also suitable for cooking meat in to retain moisture. Keep a supply handy among other kitchen paper, in a drawer, or in a wall-holder.

CHINA

The name of tableware made from china clay and distinguished from earthenware by its finer construction and by the firing at a very high temperature which gives it the characteristic translucent and vitreous appearance. English bone china is made from china clay mixed with Cornish stone and bone ash. It is first fired at a temperature of 1,200–1,300°C.

CHOPPERS

A meat chopper or cleaver is like a large, long-headed axe with a short handle, and can be seen in use in any butcher's shop. It is not generally required in a domestic kitchen unless in the country, or when the home cook buys large pieces of meat which she prefers to cut up for herself.

A good chopping knife, on the other hand, is an essential tool in a well-equipped kitchen, see *Knives*, page 33.

There are also many gadgets designed to make chopping things like onions and parsley easier jobs. The simple French wooden bowl with a curved chopping knife, or *hachoir*, is one of the most useful and durable of these, but there are many others on sale.

A good mincer or electric blender (see page 22) can more quickly do many of the chopping jobs and is especially time-saving when large quantities are required.

CHOPPING BOARD

Modern boards of laminated plastic are more hygienic than the old wooden boards, and they are available in attractive colours and shapes and in many sizes. But a wooden board is less slippery to use and kinder to knife blades. A wooden board should be smooth and close-grained, and should be kept well scrubbed.

I use two smallish boards, one plastic and one wood. I use the plastic one for things which are smelly – like crushing garlic, cutting fish in pieces and such jobs. Any fine chopping I prefer to do with the *hachoir* (see *Choppers*) or on a wooden board, unless the quantity is enough for the blender to deal with.

CLEAVER, see *Choppers*, page 24

COCOTTES

These are individual oven-proof dishes with a small handle or with ears on each side. The food is usually cooked and served in the *cocotte*. Any food cooked in an oven-proof dish can be done in individual portions this way. They are also useful for melting small amounts of butter to serve as a sauce with vegetables, fish, etc.

COFFEE GRINDERS

Essential for those who want coffee at its freshest. Grinders can be hand- or electrically-operated. Some hand grinders are wall-mounted with an upper compartment for storing a supply of beans. These are usually very efficient and the best hand grinders.

COFFEE MAKERS

There are many different kinds, using a variety of brewing methods. I still think the glass Cona coffee maker is the best.

The most economical for those who like really strong coffee are the domestic versions of the Espresso coffee maker. They are available in many sizes.

COLANDERS, STRAINERS, AND SIEVES

Stainless-steel or aluminium colanders are more durable than polythene ones – which tend to stain and become scratched. Strainers are generally made of metal gauze, and round ones with hooks to fit over the sides of basins are the most useful. If only one is to be purchased, have a fairly large one.

Strainers can do duty as sieves. For sieving acid fruits use a plastic one, as some metals tend to discolour and taint fruit. Some sieves have hand-operated paddles attached, and this makes the job of rubbing to a *purée* much easier. These are usually suitable for acid fruits as well as vegetables. Sieving attachments are available with some electric mixers and the blender or liquidiser can also be used for *purées*, but you may need to strain afterwards to remove pips.

Strainers and sieves can also be used for sifting flour, although special ones are made for this purpose, and they are much quicker and neater to use (but it is difficult to find really strong ones).

COOKERS

Although solid-fuel cookers are still in use in many homes, most people prefer to use either gas or electricity if they are available. Today there is not much difference in performance and cost of running either a gas or electric cooker, but it naturally depends on the local charges for these fuels. Modern design and finishes make both types easy to clean, and self-cleaning ovens are becoming more common. They are the alternative of catalytic liners, which make cleaning easier.

The control of temperature with boiling plates or rings still tends to be easier with electric cookers, although many people prefer to see a naked flame, even though it has disadvantages, such as making food stick to the pan unless the cook is careful. And some electric hotplates have sensers and thermostats which are an advance on the ordinary hotplate thermostat.

Grills vary perhaps more than any other part of both types of cooker. If you are fond of grilling this is a point to go into when buying a new cooker. Some have rotary grills or spits, but if you want this on a gas cooker, you will also need to have it connected to the electricity supply for the motor to drive the spit.

Auto-timers for automatic cooking (see page 20) are available on both gas and electric cookers. On gas cookers this is a clockwork device.

Warming cupboards, which were often missing on older cookers, have become more common and are usually also suitable for low-temperature cooking; it is a great convenience to have two ovens.

Split-level cookers are made for both gas and electricity and in a variety of sizes so that, if you do a lot of hotplate cooking but don't use an oven much, you can choose a large hotplate unit and a small oven.

Other extras that are worth looking for – if they seem important to your needs – are having the cooker on rollers so that it is easy to move; having a griddle for girdle cooking; having an inner glass door to the oven; having automatic ignition on a gas cooker; having gas taps which adjust for simmering; and having dual electric hotplates where the centre can be used on its own for small pans.

Research and development are going on continually, so that when you want to buy a new cooker it is wise to have a good look around to see what the latest developments have been, and to decide whether they are important to you.

COOLING TRAYS, see *Cake Racks*, page 23

COPPER UTENSILS

Copper used to be considered the best metal for all cooking pans because it heats up quickly and, provided it is of good quality, it distributes the heat evenly, thus giving good results. It is doubtful today whether the average copper pan is any better than a good aluminium or stainless-steel pan. Copper is more expensive and needs more care to keep it in good condition. It has to be lined with a layer of tin or steel to protect it from the action of many foods which produce poisons when they react with copper.

CORKSCREWS

Many different kinds are available, some very expensive, but they are not necessarily better than some of the cheaper ones. I favour the double wooden-topped corkscrew which fits over the top of the bottle and helps to ensure that the screwing part will go straight into the cork.

CUTLET BAT
A heavy metal utensil used for flattening and enlarging boned cutlets or escalopes. The flat side of a cleaver may be used instead, or a wooden rolling pin. Moisten the rolling pin and meat with water before beginning operations.

CUTTERS
Metal shapes used for stamping out biscuits, pastry, sandwiches, etc. They are sold in a wide variety of shapes and in sets of different sizes. Choose ones with a good sharp edge and no rough joins. Usually called 'pastry' cutters. When using them, cut with a sharp tap to make a clean edge. Keep a little flour nearby and dip the cutter in this occasionally if there is any tendency for it to stick.

DARIOLES
Small bucket-shaped metal moulds used for making individual portions of steamed puddings, baked sponge puddings, jellies, and other moulded foods.

DISH-WASHING MACHINES
These are a boon to those who hate washing dishes, for saving time when there is a large family and many dishes to be done, or for those who entertain frequently. For a small family it can take as long to load and unload the machine as it would to do the dishes by hand so in these conditions a dish washer is only useful if washing-up is a distasteful task, or if you save up dishes until the machine is full. But even with a machine there are always some things which have to be done by hand.

It pays to buy the biggest and best you can afford, as these machines are usually more versatile than smaller and cheaper ones, and it is advisable to have them permanently fixed to a cold-water supply and waste pipe, and let the machine heat the water. Most work better this way.

DOUBLE BOILER AND DOUBLE SAUCEPAN
One saucepan which fits into the top of a second, in which water is kept boiling or just below boiling, so that the food in the upper saucepan cooks by heat from the steam. Useful for

keeping sauces hot and for cooking mixtures which tend to burn readily, e.g. milk puddings. An improvised double boiler can be made by putting a basin over a pan of water but this is not as convenient as a proper double boiler because the food cannot be brought to the boil in a basin as it can in the saucepan, a process which speeds up the cooking.

DREDGERS

These are containers like large pepper pots, often with a handle at the side. They are used in the kitchen for holding things like icing and caster sugar for dusting over fruit and puddings or cakes, or to hold seasoned flour used for sprinkling on food during preparation. They are made of metal or ceramics and are often in pretty colours and attractive designs.

EARTHENWARE UTENSILS

Many kitchen utensils such as mixing bowls, pudding basins, storage crocks, baking and entrée dishes, casseroles, and hot-pots are made of earthenware. It is often misnamed 'china' but there are important differences (see *China*). Earthenware has four main ingredients, Ball clay, flint, china clay, and Cornish stone. It is given its first firing at a temperature between 1,050 and 1,150°C. and the finished article is opaque with varying degrees of porosity under the glaze.

Although many earthenware utensils are made heat-resisting for oven cooking, treat them kindly and do not plunge a hot dish straight into cold water.

EGG BEATERS, see *Beaters*, page 21

EGG SLICE

Is a flat perforated or slotted metal device on a long handle used for lifting eggs from the pan when frying or poaching. The perforations or slots allow the liquid to fall away from the egg as it is lifted. The slice also has many other uses in the kitchen.

EGG SLICER

Is a device for slicing a hard-boiled egg in one quick operation and is a real time saver.

EGG TIMER

The traditional type is a glass container holding sand. It has two compartments with a narrow constriction in the middle. When it is stood upright with the sand in the top compartment it takes approximately 4 mins. for the sand to run from top to bottom. These are now largely out-dated by modern timer-clocks which can be set to ring a bell after any number of minutes required.

EGG WEDGER

A device for cutting hard-boiled eggs into 8 equal segments, useful for preparing eggs for garnishing.

EGG WHISKS, see *Beaters*, page 21

ENAMEL UTENSILS

Enamel consists of silica, minium, and potash which are fused on the surface of a metal (usually steel) at a very high temperature. The higher the temperature the harder the enamel. It is used on cooking stoves and other large items of kitchen equipment. Some small items like jugs and saucepans are also made of enamelled steel, though the tendency today is for these to be replaced by other materials. Enamel has the great disadvantage that it chips easily if handled roughly and once damaged in this way nothing can be done to repair it and the exposed metal soon begins to rust.

Do not use chipped enamel as small bits are liable to come off in the food. Never put an empty pan on a hot stove as this is liable to chip the enamel.

Good-quality enamel pans will last a long time if they are carefully handled but they are not for the careless cook.

FIRE-PROOF DISHES

Baking dishes and casseroles which will withstand oven temperatures. They may be earthenware, enamelled iron, heat-resistant glass, aluminium, copper, or stainless steel.

FISH SLICE, see *Egg Slice*, page 29

FLAN RING

A metal (usually tinned steel) band used for shaping pastry for flans. The ring is placed on a baking tray for shaping and cooking. Flan rings are sold in many sizes, the most useful being 6–7 in. (15–18 cm.) for 4–6 portions, or 8–9 in. (20–24 cm.) for larger ones. Tart tins with a loose base can be used instead.

To bake a flan 'blind' or unfilled, prick the bottom of the pastry with a fork and put in a piece of crumpled foil. Remove this when the pastry is almost cooked and return the flan to the oven to finish drying the bottom.

FORCING BAG

A conical bag with a small hole at one end to take forcing nozzles and a larger opening at the other end. The mixture to be piped is put in to three-parts fill the bag, the top gathered up in the right hand, and given a twist to begin forcing the mixture down to the end. The left hand is used to guide and steady the nozzle while the right hand squeezes the mixture down from the top. Forcing bags can be improvised from cones of stout paper, but a nylon bag is better and is easily washed and used again. These bags are available in most kitchen-equipment departments.

The most useful nozzles are a large rosette for piping whipped cream, meringues, or mashed potato, and a plain $\frac{1}{2}$ in. (1 cm.) nozzle for éclairs and plain meringues.

FORKS

The most useful size of cooking fork is one about 11–12 in. overall (28–30 cm.). Cooking forks usually have two strong prongs, and are preferably made of stainless steel, with a wooden handle.

FREEZER, see *Food Storage*, page 103, and *Food Preservation*, page 207

FRY PANS

The most useful size is 7–8 in. diameter (18–20 cm.), measured across the base. The pan should be of a thick, heavy metal such as enamelled cast iron, heavy-gauge aluminium, or stainless steel. With lighter pans the non-stick variety are the most satisfactory but you need to take care in washing and using them so as not to damage the special surface. Newer types have a specially hard non-stick lining which is more durable than the earlier types; but no non-stick pan will last for very long and they need replacing fairly frequently.

FUNNELS

One or two small plastic funnels are useful to have when you want to pour liquids into a bottle; for example, oil after it has been used for frying.

GIRDLE

Also known as griddle, plank, or stone. It is a very heavy flat cast-iron circular plate with a handle over the top. It can be hung on a chain over an open fire or put on top of a stove. Scones, flat bread, drop scones, and pikelets are cooked on the hot metal. Earlier models of electric cookers had solid cast-iron hotplates which made excellent girdles. With modern high-speed hotplates a separate girdle is needed (sometimes an optional extra with a cooker), or, better still, an independent electrically-heated girdle, with automatic control. This is a great help in getting consistently good results, otherwise the heat of the girdle fluctuates and much experience is needed.

Modern electric girdles are designed to cook additional items like bacon and eggs, meat, and other savoury dishes, a form of dry frying. The manufacturers supply instructions for their use.

GLASS UTENSILS

Heat-resistant glass is an important material for basins, casseroles and other baking dishes as well as for serving dishes. A specially tough type of glass is made into pans which can also be used on a hotplate.

GRAPEFRUIT KNIFE

A small saw-edged curved knife, shaped to make it easy to cut round the fruit and remove flesh from pith without peeling.

GRATERS

Simple round or square metal graters held in the hand are very satisfactory, and durable. Other types are known as 'food mills' and may be either hand models or ones which clamp to the table. There are also electrically driven mills, either as separate machines or attachments to food mixers.

JUICE EXTRACTORS

Probably most frequently required for lemon and orange juice. The simplest, the traditional lemon squeezer, can be part of an electric mixer, useful if a lot of juice is required. A juice press is a more powerful tool, now largely being replaced by the electric juice extractor. This appliance makes juice from any fruit or vegetable and extracts more of the juice than is possible by any of the other methods. It can be a separate machine or an attachment for an electric mixing machine. Manufacturers supply instruction booklets and suggestions for its use.

KETTLES

An electric kettle is quicker and more convenient than boiling on a hotplate, and has the added advantage of being useful in any room which has a suitable plug socket. Choose one with a safety device to switch off if the kettle boils dry or one which has a device for switching off when the water boils.

If you don't want an electric kettle use a good-quality aluminium one and, if you are a forgetful person, buy a whistling kettle.

KNIVES

Stainless-steel knives are easier to look after than the old carbon-steel ones, and can be kept sharp by using a modern knife sharpener. Electric ones are very good.

Vegetable or paring knives are made in different shapes and the sizes vary from 3 in. (8 cm.) to 6 in. (15 cm.) in the blade. The larger ones can be used as a substitute for a cook's knife for chopping small quantities of food.

A cook's knife has a sharp point and broadens to a wide base near the handle. It is really triangular in shape with the sharp edge sloping and the unsharpened edge straight. Its main use is for chopping and slicing. For chopping, the point of the knife is held on the chopping board with one hand and the knife pivots about this point as chopping proceeds.

Boning and filleting knives have thin, flexible blades, the blade of a boning knife being shorter than that of a filleting knife.

A palette knife or spatula is a flexible knife with both edges unsharpened, and is used for lifting and turning food during cooking and for spreading purposes, for example, icing a cake.

A bread knife should have a saw edge. Don't use other kitchen knives for cutting bread as this blunts them quickly.

For carving, a small sharp cook's knife is one of the best to use, especially when carving is done in the kitchen. Alternatives are either a conventional carving knife or an electric carving knife.

LADLE

A utensil for serving liquids, consisting of a small bowl or deep spoon to which is attached a long handle. Kitchen ladles usually have a hook at the end of the handle to hang them up by. Ladles for use at table are often of silver, plate, or stainless steel, and there are pretty, light, modern plastic ones as well. At table they are used for serving soup from a tureen or for serving punch from a punch-bowl. Small ladles are used for serving sauces from a sauce-boat.

LIQUIDISER, see *Blender*, page 22

MASHER

This is a metal utensil with a wooden handle, used for breaking up cooked vegetables such as potatoes, swedes, carrots, turnips, parsnips, when they are to be served mashed. If a finer texture is required, the vegetables must be put through a ricer, rubbed through a sieve, or put in an electric blender.

MEASURES

These are available marked with pints and fluid ounces and also with the metric litres and millilitres.

Standard British measuring spoons have been used to a limited extent in the past, most people preferring to use ordinary tablespoons and teaspoons. To prepare for a change-over to the metric system the British Standards Institution has published a specification for Kitchen Measuring Spoons, Measures, and Jugs (British Standard 1348, 1970) in which the recommended sizes for spoons are 20 ml.; 15 ml.; 10 ml.; 5 ml.; 2·5 ml.; and 1·25 ml. Of these, the 15 ml. spoon corresponds to the medicinal tablespoon and the 5 ml. measure to the medicinal teaspoon, both already in use in Britain. Small medicine measures one buys at the chemist's are usually marked in both millilitres and tablespoons.

It is useful to know that tablespoons and teaspoons in most countries where the metric system is used, are 15 ml. and 5 ml. respectively. They also use decilitre measures (1 dl. = 100 ml.).

For a table of comparative measures, see page 9.

MINCERS

These may be hand-operated and clamped to the table, or free-standing, or they may be electrically operated, either as separate machines or as attachments for electric mixers. Be sure to follow the maker's instructions regarding the choice of blade for the food to be minced, as using the wrong size can choke the mincer and stop operations. If this happens with meat it takes a long and messy time to right things.

MIXERS

A good strong electric mixer can save a great deal of time and effort either by doing a job faster than is possible by hand, or because it can free the cook to get on with other jobs. Many people also find they can make better cakes with the aid of a mixer than when they mix by hand.

The best kind of mixer to choose depends on the kind of cooking you do. If you are not likely to want to make many cakes and puddings, then a cake-mixing machine of the larger type is probably not going to be very useful. Instead you might find it better to buy a portable mixer. Some of these also have a stand and a small mixing bowl, but the mixer can be used in any bowl according to need. A good portable mixer will mix cakes and puddings and do all jobs except mixing heavy things like bread doughs and large, rich fruit cakes.

The chief advantage of buying a large mixer is the range of attachments that can be bought with it, mincer, juice extractor, blender, and so on. These are not usually avilable with portable mixers, though a few are.

The most useful thing to have is a basic motor unit for which you can buy the particular attachments you personally will find useful and can add to as required. Such convenience is hard to come by and one usually has to buy the cake-mixing apparatus whether one wants it or not.

NEEDLES

Used in cookery for trussing and larding. Trussing needles are very large long steel needles used for trussing poultry and in preparing boned and rolled joints of meat. They are threaded with fine white string. Large steel sewing needles threaded with coarse white cotton may be used for sewing up stuffed meat and similar foods.

OMELET PAN

This is a small fry pan with slightly rounded sides, traditionally made of black steel but also made in other materials. Many people keep such a pan just for making omelets but a good-quality general purpose aluminium pan is satisfactory provided the surface is kept smooth by cleaning with soap pads when washing the pan.

PASTRY BRUSH

Used for brushing baking tins with oil or melted fat; for brushing a glaze on pastry before baking; for moistening the edges of pies and pastry; and many other purposes. Special brushes are sold for this, but a small, new paint brush is equally effective.

PATTY PANS OR TINS

Plain or fancy tins for making small cakes such as Queen cakes and small tarts. Not very much used today as the sets of bun tins and paper cases are quicker and more convenient to use.

PIE DISH

An oval or rectangular baking dish with a rim, necessary for holding the pastry in position. They are made of earthenware, oven-proof glass, enamel, or metal. Glass ones are the best as it is easy to see if the fruit is cooked.

POTATO PEELER

A special knife for paring fruit and vegetables. A good, sharp one is easier to use than a vegetable knife though some people don't agree about this. Potato peelers are made for right- or left-handed users.

PRESS

A utensil used for squeezing and pressing food. A fruit press is a device for squeezing out the juice. A meat press is for pressing cold meat into a compact shape as it cools, e.g. pressed beef, pressed tongue. Presses are also used to extract fruit juices for wine and cider making.

PRESSURE COOKER

This reduces cooking time to about a quarter of the normal.

Pressure cookers are sold in a variety of sizes, but a fairly large one is more useful than the smaller sizes. The cooker is a hermetically sealed pan which prevents steam from escaping until it builds up a pressure equal to 5–10–15 lb., according to the design of the pressure gauge. When water boils under increased pressure the temperature is raised and cooking takes place more quickly.

Cooking at 15-lb. pressure is the most common; 5-lb. pressure is used for bottling fruit and vegetables and cooking light sponge puddings; 10-lb. pressure for softening fruit when making jams and marmalades.

Because steam cannot escape freely from the pressure cooker once it has reached the pressure point, less water is required than for ordinary boiling. The amount of liquid depends on the cooking time rather than on the amount of food being cooked, e.g. $\frac{1}{2}$ pt. water (250 ml.) for the first $\frac{1}{4}$ hr. of cooking and another $\frac{1}{4}$ pt. for every extra $\frac{1}{2}$ hr. Never use less than $\frac{1}{2}$ pt. of water (250 ml.).

The maker's instructions should always be followed carefully for, while all modern cookers have a safety valve to prevent accidents, it is possible to get a nasty fright if the apparatus is carelessly handled. The most important instructions to observe are those relating to the amount that the cooker will safely hold, cooling instructions after cooking is completed, and the use of the pressure gauge.

A pressure cooker is of greatest benefit when used for speeding up the long cooking processes such as making stocks and soups, softening tough meat, cooking vegetables like beetroot or dried beans (be careful with lentils because they froth), cooking the Christmas pudding, dried fruits, and in preserving fruits and vegetables.

37

RICER

A perforated metal press for sieving potatoes prior to creaming them with milk and butter.

ROLLING PIN

The traditional type is made of wood, about 16 in. long (40 cm.), and 1½ in. in diameter (4 cm.), sometimes more. Modern ones may be of heat-resistant glass, earthenware or polythene, and sometimes have a tank in the middle to hold iced water. The latter is useful for people trying to make pastry in a very hot climate.

The important thing when using a rolling pin is to try and exert even pressure over the whole surface, so that the pastry is rolled to an even thickness.

RÔTISSERIE

Rôtisseries or spit-roasters are available as separate appliances, or as extras on gas or electric cookers, either for use in the oven or under the grill. This is a revival of the ancient method of cooking meat on a rotating spit in front of an open fire.

A *rôtisserie* can be used for cooking any good-quality meat which is a suitable shape for fixing on the rotating spit. Boned and rolled joints are the easiest to handle, but more difficult shapes can be satisfactorily spit-roasted provided that care is taken in fixing them in position. Boned meat and poultry can be stuffed before cooking.

One of the advantages of spit-roasting is that the meat is self-basting, though very lean meats need some assistance, best provided by basting with oil or melted butter several times during cooking.

When buying a *rôtisserie* make sure that you get an instruction booklet, and follow the maker's recommendations until you have enough experience to experiment for yourself.

SALAD BASKET

This is usually made of either polythene or wire, and consists of two bowl-shaped pieces hinged at one side and with handles at the other. The washed salad vegetables are hung to drain, or alternatively, the basket is twisted and shaken gently to get rid of the moisture as rapidly as possible, without bruising the contents.

SAUCEPANS AND STEWPANS

A saucepan has a lip on one or two sides for pouring, and usually has no lid. A stewpan does not have a lip but has a fitting lid. A stewpan can be used for sauces but a saucepan is not suitable for all the cooking that is normally done in a stewpan. The word 'saucepan' is often used for both types. If you are frequently going to cook scrambled eggs, heat milk, and make porridge, it is worth while investing in one of the non-stick pans. For other pans always buy as heavy a quality as possible because this helps to produce good cooking and reduce the tendency for food to stick. Copper looks marvellous and is quick heating, but remember that someone is going to have to keep it polished. More practical are stainless steel or heavy aluminium. Good-quality enamel pans are useful if you are a careful cook, but if you are liable to let things burn or bang the pans around, then it is wiser to choose something else, because enamel is fairly easily damaged by careless use. Some people like to use coloured enamel pans because they are attractive enough to go to the table, and so do duty for serving dishes as well as cooking. Glass/ceramic and enamelled cast-iron pans are also suitable for table use.

Whatever material is chosen, make sure that the pans have insulated handles and lid knobs, rounded corners for easy cleaning, and no crevices for dirt to stick in and make cleaning difficult. Wide shallow pans heat up more quickly than deep ones, and give more even cooking.

SAUTÉ PAN

A deep fry pan with sloping sides and a lid.

SAW

A meat saw is a very useful tool in any kitchen for sawing through bones when preparing meat, or for dividing a joint into smaller pieces.

SCALES

There are three main types of these, spring balances, sliding-weights scales, and counter scales with separate weights. As a general rule the dearer the scales the more accurate they are likely to be. This applies within one type but it is possible to have an expensive one in one type which is not as good as another type costing less. The wisest thing is to buy scales made by well-known manufacturers and buy the most expensive you can afford.

Scales marked with metric weights are now available, some combining both the British system of pounds and ounces with the metric grammes and kilogrammes, in a double scale.

If you have scales with separate weights it is now possible to buy sets of gramme weights, so that you can use the scales for either system of weighing. For table of comparative weights, see page 9.

SCISSORS

An important tool in any kitchen for cutting paper, string, trimming fish, meat, and bacon, and for jobs such as cutting parsley and other herbs. For coarse chopping, hold the herbs in a bunch and snip them with the scissors. For fine chopping put the herbs in a glass far and snip them in the jar. They can also be used for snipping nuts coarsely and dried fruit like dates.

Special scissors for dissecting poultry are also made, as well as ornamental scissors for cutting bunches of grapes at table.

SIEVES, see *Colanders*, page 26

SKEWERS

A set of fine steel skewers is useful for all sorts of jobs such as fastening meat together when it has been boned and rolled; or for testing cakes to see if they are cooked in the middle. Skewers are essential for kebabs, but special brochette or kebab skewers are made for this, and are the best to use because they have square shafts instead of round. This prevents the food from slipping about during cooking.

SOUFFLÉ DISH

This is a round, straight-sided, fireproof dish made of china, earthenware, or heat-resistant glass. It is made in many sizes from individual ones upwards. They are useful for other purposes than cooking *soufflés*, e.g. setting cold sweets of all kinds, serving fruit salad or compote, and for serving baked savoury dishes.

SPOONS, see *Measures*, page 34, and *Wooden Spoons*, page 43

STAINLESS STEEL

Is an alloy of steel with chromium, which gives rust-resistance to the steel. Some stainless steels also contain nickel and others molybdenum as well, and vanadium is used to give hardness to cutlery steels. Stainless steel is very hard and strong, harder than either copper or aluminium, but it does not conduct heat as rapidly as these metals. Its hard, smooth surface is easy to clean and very hygienic.

STEEL, see *Knives*, page 33

STEWPANS, see *Saucepans*, page 39

STRAINERS, see *Colanders*, page 26

THERMOMETERS AND THERMOSTATS

Thermostats are devices for controlling temperatures automatically and, where temperature is important, most modern appliances have thermostatic control, for example, ovens, dishwashing machines, hotplates, automatic fry pans, and deep fat fryers.

If you don't have thermostatic control available for things like deep fat frying and sugar boiling, then a separate thermometer is the answer. One thermometer will do for both frying and sugar work, provided its top register is over 400°F. (200°C.).

Thermometers are also useful for registering low temperatures, as with yeast work and making junket and yogurt. Here, a cheap photographic thermometer is suitable.

TIMER

A clock for timing cooking operations. It can be pre-set to cover the estimated cooking time and rings a bell to announce when time is up. Many modern cookers have timers fitted, but small portable ones are useful specially those which cover 3 hrs. or more.

TIN

This is used for coating iron and non-stainless-steel cooking utensils, and for coating tins for use in canning foods. The utensils most frequently tinned are cake tins, kettles, and small items like strainers, biscuit cutters, etc. Copper cooking pans are lined with tin to protect the food from contact with the copper. Today, many of the utensils which used to be of tin are either aluminium or stainless steel and much more durable.

Good-quality tinned goods are coated after shaping so that the joints are well covered with tin. Cheaper goods are made from steel sheets coated before cutting and shaping and the joints are very liable to rust.

TOASTERS

These can be automatic toasters to use on the table, or grills. Small horizontal toaster/grills are available for table use and are more versatile than the vertical toasters.

TOWELS

Paper towels are the most hygienic to use in the kitchen. Keep a roll by the sink or some other convenient place, and use for wiping hands, drying food, and mopping up spills. If you hand-wash utensils use paper towels or a clean linen towel for polishing glasses and silver. It is better to leave other equipment to drain dry, certainly much better than drying them with a damp, soiled towel.

TRAYS

Metal trays are used in the oven for baking things like scones and biscuits, for holding paper cake cups, flan rings, and so on. If trays have not been supplied with your cooker, buy the aluminium trays with a turned-up edge. They should be a little smaller than the wire racks in the oven so that heat can circulate freely round them.

Apart from ornamental trays for serving drinks, the most useful to have are the easy-to-clean plastic trays or the specially treated light and washable wooden trays. Two or three of different sizes are invaluable in the kitchen.

VEGETABLE PRESSER

This is a flat wooden object with a handle, used for pressing vegetables in a colander to squeeze out water. A great help when straining spinach and other watery vegetables.

WOODEN SPOONS

A selection of different sizes is needed for stirring and mixing foods. A metal spoon is not as satisfactory for most of these jobs, the handle gets too hot and the metal scratches the saucepan.

Wooden stirrers, which are flat instead of spoon-shaped, are in some ways even better, but a mixture of stirrers and spoons is the best.

When stirring in a saucepan, use the spoon to scrape the bottom of the pan, thus helping to prevent food from sticking and keeping it evenly mixed.

Chapter Three

BUYING AND STORING FOOD

One learns about these from personal experience, but much can be learnt from others. How good you are at these two jobs will be important in conserving your own time and energy, in budget economy both in buying, and in storing food properly to prevent waste. The health of the family also depends on what you buy, see page 146.

PLANNING THE SHOPPING

If you are the sort of person who looks on shopping as a pleasant occupation to be indulged in as often as possible skip this bit. It's not meant for you, but for those who, for various reasons, want to visit the shops as infrequently as possible.

Shopping for food can be broadly divided into two kinds, the dry stores with a long-keeping life, such as flour, sugar, and so on; and the perishables, meat, fish, milk, eggs, fruit, and vegetables. How often you need to shop for each of these depends partly on how well organised you are, and partly on the storage facilities you have. Obviously if you have plenty of the right kind of storage space, including a freezer, you need to shop much less frequently than a person with only a larder for storage.

If you're really well organised, shopping for non-perishable or dry stores can be cut down to once a month. To be able to do this you need your own car or a delivery service, enough space to store enough food; and a system.

The system I have found to work best for us is to have a list of the foods we use regularly, together with a note of the amounts I've found by experience will last us about a month. When the time comes to make up a shopping list I take the list to my store cupboard and check to see that we do in fact need to replenish the lot. We don't, usually. Sometimes I use more than anticipated and stocks have to be replenished before the month is up.

44

Because I have a freezer I include some perishables in this list, for example, butter and other fats. A month in the freezer makes no appreciable difference to their quality. And, even if you are less ambitious and aim at shopping once a week or fortnight, the same system is worth trying.

For perishables I rely on a weekly menu plan, different each week, and a weekly shopping plus the use of a small supply of perishables in the freezer. I think the use of a menu plan is essential to good kitchen management. It's so much easier to do all one's thinking about the meals at once; write it down, buy the necessary food for the week, and there you are. This is the time to get out your recipe books to give you ideas for varying the menu from week to week. I juggle the menus about from day to day, and I don't think any week's menu is followed exactly as planned, but at least the basis is there and the food has been purchased.

BUDGETING AND ECONOMY

I hesitate to offer advice on this subject because it is such an individual and personal matter. What is an economy to one person is extravagance to another. Food is the first thing some people cut down on when they have to watch the spending, the last for others.

There are the people whose ideas on economising are satisfied if they buy rump steak instead of fillet, Canadian salmon instead of best Scotch salmon, and so on.

Then there is the attitude of the person who considers any recipe expensive to make if she hasn't got the necessary ingredients in her store cupboard, even if such ingredients are not expensive items. She obviously works to a very tight food budget and buys a limited number of often-used foods. How much easier it is to provide interesting food at low cost if one has a well-stocked store cupboard, not of expensive foods, but a variety.

I think the best advice one can offer to those who have to look closely at the cost of food is to use your eyes and brains to see what is an inexpensive buy at the time. If you don't know how to cook the food, look it up in a cookery book; if you have only luxury cookery books, go buy yourself a basic paperback that tells you how to cook all the cuts of meat, and the different kinds of fruit and vegetables.

Be cautious when buying meat, and count the cost of fat and bone. True, the fat can be rendered down for cooking and the bones used for stock, but this is often a pretty expensive way of getting these two commodities.

When you compare prices of meat, compare like with like. For example, compare the cuts without bone to decide which gives you most for your money. If you compare the price of a cheap, bony, and fatty piece of meat with some lean stewing steak you get quite a wrong idea of values unless you make allowance for the fat and bone. Remember that chops and cutlets are usually about 50 per cent bone and fat, and are one of the most expensive meats to buy.

What is an economical buy to the owner of a freezer or refrigerator is an extravagance to someone without the storage needed to keep the food in good condition until it is all used up.

I don't agree with those who generalise about the high cost of convenience foods when compared with fresh foods. It is by no means true all the time. For example, the price of canned milk per diluted pint is often less than fresh milk; it's a handy food, easier to store than fresh milk, and excellent for cooking. To take just one more example, there aren't many times when peas in the pod as purchased from the average shop are better and cheaper than frozen peas. Each food needs to be judged on its own merits, with the application of commonsense and intelligence.

BUYING DIFFERENT KINDS OF FOOD

MEAT

Before setting out for the butcher's shop or supermarket it is important to have some idea what you would like to buy, even if it's as vague as wanting a roast, or meat for a casserole; this means having done your home-work on a menu plan. Quite frequently you will have to change your ideas when you arrive at the shop, but that's better than having no idea what you want.

I think the most useful thing to know about buying meat is what cut is suitable for what kind of cooking, particularly if you are economising. You could, of course, just buy the most expensive cuts for everything, and some people do that as the easy but expensive way out. This works because the expensive cuts are usually the most tender, and you have to be a pretty awful cook to spoil them.

I prefer the shops which label meat properly, telling me what the cut is, or one where a butcher will give me what I ask for by name. Provided you don't set out to be awkward and a know-all, most butchers like to serve someone who knows what they want. If you shop for meat at a supermarket, use a large one with a big range of well-labelled meat.

Below is a table showing which cuts are suitable for which methods of cooking. Names of cuts vary slightly in some parts of the country but these I have used will be known to all butchers, so ask for what you want and explain what you want to do with it.

When you are new to a shopping area, or new to shopping, look around until you find a butcher or supermarket which consistently gives you good-quality meat.

Apart from looking at the colour of meat to see if it is fresh-looking, and at the amount of fat, bone, and gristle, it is very difficult to tell with the eye whether the meat is good of its kind. Thus the reliability of your butcher is very important.

If you are working on the once-a-week shopping plan, meat for the end of the week will need to go in the freezer or be purchased frozen. On page 110 you will find the approximate safe storage times for different kinds of meat.

WHAT GOOD MEAT LOOKS LIKE
BEEF

The best quality has a 'marbling' of fat throughout the muscle. It is then likely to be tender and of good flavour. If there is a lot of gristle the meat will be tough unless it has long, slow stewing, at least 3–4 hrs., to make it tender. If a joint of beef has a layer of gristle under the outer layer of fat, this shows it is from an old animal, and it, too, will need long, slow cooking, and is quite unsuitable for roasting.

LAMB

There is little in the look of lamb to show the quality. All good-quality lamb has a fair amount of fat with it. A very light-coloured meat usually indicates young lamb. The difference between mutton and lamb is that mutton joints are larger and the meat darker in colour.

47

PORK

A pink colour, fine texture, and 'marbling' with fat show the meat is from a young animal of good quality. A darker pink, sometimes with a brownish tinge, and coarse flesh comes from an older animal, and will be coarse and tough.

VEAL

Colour is a good indication of quality. The flesh should be either very pale (a milk-fed calf), or a light pink (grass fed). A brownish colour shows that it is stale.

POULTRY

Oven-ready birds with a well-known brand name are usually a safe buy. If they are frozen, make sure there is no sign of freezer burn which shows in patches of discoloured skin. With other kinds of poultry it is wisest to buy from a shop which you know sells good-quality food.

WHAT TO BUY FOR GRILLING OR FRYING

BEEF   Fillet; rump; sirloin.

LAMB OR MUTTON   Loin chops; best end of neck cutlets; slices from the fillet end of leg.

PORK   Sliced or cubed fillet; loin chops; spare rib cutlets.

VEAL   Escalopes; loin chops; cutlets.

CHICKEN   Halves of *poussin* or spring chicken; joints of a frying or broiling chicken, or a small roaster.

OFFAL   Lamb's kidneys; calf's, lamb's, or pig's liver.

GAME   Young blackcock, guinea fowl, teal or quail, all skewered flat; venison steaks.

WHAT TO BUY FOR ROASTING

BEEF   Sirloin; wing rib; top rib; fore rib.

LAMB OR MUTTON   Loin; leg (whole or fillet end); shoulder; best end of neck; saddle.

PORK   Loin; leg; spare rib.

VEAL   Loin; leg; fillet; shoulder (boned and rolled); neck; breast (rolled).

POULTRY   Any except boiling fowls and older ducks. Capons are the finest roasting chickens.

GAME   All except old and tough birds or hares.

WHAT TO BUY FOR SLOW ROASTING, POT ROASTING, AND BRAISING

BEEF Top, fore, and back ribs; topside; silverside; brisket; thick flank.

LAMB OR MUTTON Shoulder; stuffed breast; shank end of leg; best end of neck.

PORK Spare ribs; blade; hand and spring.

VEAL Shoulder (boned and rolled); neck; breast (stuffed and rolled); hock or knuckle (boned and stuffed).

POULTRY Any.

OFFAL Stuffed hearts.

GAME Old birds; joints of venison.

WHAT TO BUY FOR STEWS AND CASSEROLES

BEEF Flank; shoulder; blade; chuck; skirt; leg and shin (needs long slow cooking); clod and sticking (neck).

LAMB OR MUTTON Shoulder; neck; shank end of leg; breast.

PORK Spare ribs; hand and spring; belly; leg (for pies).

VEAL Shoulder; neck; breast; hock or knuckle.

POULTRY Boiling fowl and any other may be used.

OFFAL Kidney; liver; tripe; heart; sweetbreads; brains; feet or trotters.

GAME Pigeons; any of the game birds except the very young ones; capercailzie; hare; rabbit; venison.

QUANTITIES GUIDE FOR MEAT, POULTRY, AND GAME

With bone	½–¾ lb. per portion (250–375 g.)
Without bone	4–6 oz. per portion (125–175 g.)
Chicken: spring, broiler or *poussin*	1 bird for 2 portions
roaster or boiler	½ lb. per portion drawn weight (250 g.)
Duck and duckling	¾ lb. drawn weight for small birds (375 g.); ½ lb. per portion (250 g.) for birds over 3½ lb. (2–3 kg.)
Goose	½ lb. per portion drawn weight (250 g.)
Turkey	½ lb. per portion drawn weight (250 g.)

Ortolan, plover, ptarmigan, quail, snipe, teal, woodcock	1 bird per portion
Grouse, partridge, pigeon, widgeon	1 bird for 2 portions
Blackcock, guinea fowl	3 lb. bird (1½ kg.) for 3–4 portions
Capercailzie	½ lb. per portion drawn weight (250 g.)
Pheasant	1 bird for 2–4 portions; brace for 5–6
Hare	1 for 5–6 portions
Leveret	1 for 3 portions
Rabbit	1 for 4–5 portions

FROZEN MEAT

Carcase meat is frozen soon after killing and has not had the usual hanging which makes fresh meat tender. Cuts of this kind of meat need to be purchased either already thawed by the butcher, when a day or so in the refrigerator will improve them; or, if you buy the meat frozen, thaw it slowly in the refrigerator allowing time for it to mature for a day or so after thawing. For thawing times, see page 213.

You can also buy supplies of well-hung meat from a butcher and freeze them yourself. These will be ready for cooking as soon as thawed, or cook frozen. Many butchers will cut up a carcase for you to freeze in this way but you can just buy the occasional joint or pieces of meat in the usual way and freeze them yourself. I do this with all meat I buy at the beginning of the week to use at the end, including offal.

Steaks, chops, and other small cuts have usually been matured before they are frozen commercially, and they can be used as soon as thawed, or while still frozen.

BACON AND HAM

There is such a wide variety of types and grades of bacon and no clear system of labelling that the best thing to do is to find a shop that keeps the kind of bacon you like.

In general, cuts from the back leg (gammon) provide the choicest meat; the front leg and shoulder (hock, butt, fore slipper, collar) are saltier and coarser. The middle of the animal provides most of the rashers (back and streaky). It is not possible to tell the degree of saltiness by the look of bacon, which is another reason for buying it from the same source once you have found a kind that you like.

Smoked bacon has a dark rind; green or unsmoked a pale rind. Some brands are stamped on the rind, e.g. Danish and Polish.

After cutting, bacon dries quickly and becomes hard, so buy your bacon from a shop which has a quick turnover, or one which cuts the bacon to order, and do not buy cut rashers if they look dark and dry.

Bacon sold in transparent sealed packets is a better buy than bacon cut and exposed to warm, dry air. Freshly cut bacon has a deep pink or good bright red colour, and looks freshly cut. The fat should be white and firm. Poor-quality bacon fat may have yellow and green stains and be soft and oily.

For Boiling, the best joints are prime collar or middle gammon; also suitable are end of collar, corner gammon, gammon slipper, top back, back and ribs, top streaky, prime streaky, butt end of fore hock, fore slipper, or whole fore hock.

For Rashers, the best cuts are long back, short back, and middle gammon; also suitable are top streaky, prime streaky, and thin streaky.

For Grilling, thick rashers are best, from $\frac{1}{4}$–$\frac{1}{2}$ in. ($\frac{1}{2}$–1 cm.); use corner gammon, middle gammon, or top back.

HAM

Ham is the hind leg of the pig cut off and cured separately, very much more slowly than gammon or bacon. The cut end is usually rounded, but may be squared off when the ham is known as a 'short cut'. A well-cured ham develops a bluish-green mould on the cut end. The fat may be white or have a pinkish tinge, e.g. York ham. Hams are cured in a variety of ways, but all methods include salting and some are smoked as well. A whole ham weighs between 10 and 20 lb. (5–10 kg.).

COOKED MEAT

Ready-sliced meat should only be purchased from a refrigerated cabinet and used within 24 hrs. This is because if it is kept too long it can become a source of food poisoning. Never buy cooked meat from a butcher who handles raw meat as well as slicing the cooked joints; infection from the raw meat can be transferred to the cooked.

51

The safest way of buying cooked meat is in vacuum packs stored in a refrigerated cabinet.

FISH

Modern methods of storing and marketing fish have resulted in a big improvement in the quality when compared with a few years ago. But fish is a very perishable food, and it is still important to know what to look for when choosing it.

When buying fillets or steaks the two best tests for freshness are to examine the quality of the flesh and to smell it. The flesh should be firm and elastic, not collapsed and flabby-looking, and the smell should be pleasant, of salt water and the sea.

With whole fish, look for bright red gills, and eyes that are full and bright with black pupils. The eyes of a stale fish are sunken and dull with grey pupils. The walls of the stomach should be firm.

Most fishmongers will draw, scale, and fillet fish for you and prepare shellfish if you ask them to.

If you are working on the weekly shopping plan and want to serve fish at the end of the week, it can be frozen quite satisfactorily; or buy it frozen and keep a store in the freezer. Be careful when buying already frozen fish to see that the packs are not misshapen or damaged in any way. This is important, because fish quality is lost by poor methods of storing and handling frozen fish. Poor-quality frozen fish will have a stringy, dry texture when cooked.

Smoked fish which is sold on the bone or filleted keeps longer than fresh fish. Some is sold vacuum-packed, which gives a longer life, and some is frozen. It is difficult to tell by looking at it whether or not it is fresh, so buy from a reliable shop and complain if it is stale. It will smell and taste unpleasant.

QUANTITIES GUIDE FOR FISH AND SHELLFISH

Large whole fish, as caught	8–10 oz. per portion (250–300 g.)
Large whole fish, gutted but with head on	7–8 oz. per portion (225–250 g.)
Small whole fish (herrings, mackerel, etc.)	1 fish per portion
Fish steaks	1 × 5–6 oz. per portion (150–175 g.)

Fish fillets	4–5 oz. per portion (125–150 g.)
Crabs	1 small per portion
Lobster (in shell)	½–¾ lb. per portion (250–375 g.)
Mussels (in shells)	1 pt. per portion (½ l.)
Prawns (in shells)	½ pt. per portion (250 ml.)
Frozen or shelled fish such as prawns, scampi, etc.	Allow 3–6 oz. per portion (75–175 g.) according to the way it will be used.

Yields

½ pt. prawns or shrimps in the shell gives 5 oz. shelled (150 g.)
½ pt. shelled prawns or shrimps weighs about 6 oz. (175 g.)
2 lb. lobster in the shell gives about ¾ lb. meat (375 g.)

COOKING FISH

While it is traditional to cook some fish in special ways, most fish can be cooked by any of the usual methods of frying, grilling, poaching, baking, sousing and so on.

VEGETABLES

The appearance of fresh vegetables gives a very good idea of their quality. Quality varies a great deal because the time lapse between gathering and selling, and the methods of handling make an enormous difference. Some sturdy vegetables keep well, especially root vegetables, but most green vegetables deteriorate very rapidly, cabbage being one of the best greens for keeping, while the soft leaves, like spinach and lettuce, wilt rapidly.

If you are shopping for vegetables just once a week, keep green vegetables in good condition by washing them gently, draining thoroughly and then placing them in polythene boxes or bags in the refrigerator. Keep a store of frozen vegetables as a reserve for the end of the week.

Frozen vegetables are a better buy than tired and stale vegetables, and are not always more expensive when the question of waste has been taken into account. The following notes are a guide to tell you what to look for when buying different kinds of vegetables.

AUBERGINES

Should be firm and have a full, shining skin which is un-wrinkled.

BEANS

With broad beans you should be able to see the shape of the bean clearly in the pods, but the pods should be fresh green in colour and not too large. If the pods are losing their fresh look and becoming grey-green the beans are probably over-mature and will be mealy with tough skins. On the other hand, tiny bright green pods, which don't show the shape of the beans, probably have none inside.

French and similar beans should be firm-looking, and the shape of the bean inside should not be very pronounced, the flatter the better, provided they are not undersized.

New kinds of runner beans in the shops are less inclined to be stringy than the older varieties, but even so, don't buy runner beans which are showing the shape of the bean inside. They'll almost always be too mature for pleasant eating.

BEETROOT

These should be firm and free from blemishes. The roots should be intact and at least 2 in. (5 cm.) of the tops still on. Cooked beetroot should be sweet-smelling; if stale they are slimy to the touch.

BROCCOLI

Calabrese and green sprouting broccoli should be young. Avoid those with thick coarse stalks and wilted or discoloured leaves. See also *Cauliflower* below.

BRUSSELS SPROUTS

Small, tight heads are the best. Look at the outside leaves. If these are yellowing, the sprouts are stale.

CABBAGE

Look at the outside leaves. If these are yellowing and the green leaves have become soft, the cabbage is stale. A stale red cabbage will feel soft instead of firm and the outside leaves will be blackish. A stale white cabbage will be flabby instead of firm and crisp.

CARROTS

Should be firm and free from blemishes. Examine them carefully to see that they are not beginning to soften in patches, which can happen as a result of damage while they are being washed. Young carrots are the best to buy, but they are usually more expensive than old ones.

CAULIFLOWER

Outside leaves go yellow on a stale one, but these may have been removed. In that case look at the flower, and if it appears to be loose and soft it is probably stale. A good fresh cauliflower has a firm compact head surrounded by fresh green leaves.

CELERY

Look at the colour of the small leaves. If these are yellow and browning the celery is probably stale. The sticks should be firm and crisp, and there should be a good proportion of small inner ones, showing a good heart. If all the top leaves have been cut off and some of the outside stalks trimmed off as well, this shows poor quality.

CHICORY

The tips should be pale yellow. Stale chicory has greenish or even browning tips, and the edges of the outer leaves may be beginning to brown.

CUCUMBERS

These should look firm with the skins taut and shiny. Stale ones look dull and are flabby when touched.

ENDIVE

The green part should be fresh and not wilted; the bleached centre, crisp.

LEEKS

Go by the colour of the green tops. If these are yellowing the leeks are stale. The shopkeeper may have trimmed them off to disguise this. Small leeks are usually better quality than very large ones.

LETTUCE AND OTHER SALAD GREENS

Poor condition is very obvious here with wilting and discoloured leaves. Sometimes the shopkeeper removes the outer
leaves and sells just the heart, but it won't be really fresh either.

MUSHROOMS

Fresh cultivated mushrooms are firm with pale pink gills. The
whole mushroom darkens with keeping, especially the cut ends
of the stalks.

ONIONS

These should look dry and bright and be firm. Damp-looking,
soft onions are usually rotten in the centre.

PARSNIPS

Buy small to medium ones, as large ones can have woody
centres. Avoid any which look shrivelled.

PEAS

The pods should be rounded and full and a good fresh green.
Lots of very flat pods among them means you are buying pods
and not peas, while light-coloured, dryish-looking pods show
the peas inside will probably be too old.

PEPPERS, SWEET, GREEN, OR RED

It is easy to spot stale ones. Fresh ones have a taut, shiny skin,
stale ones have begun to wrinkle and may show soft patches of
discoloration.

POTATOES

If potatoes still have the earth on them it is difficult to tell the
quality; best to buy them from a reliable shop. Examine
washed potatoes to see they are not badly blemished nor are
showing green patches. These will have to be discarded as it is
not advisable to eat green potatoes. They develop a substance
which acts as a poison to some people.

SPINACH

It is obvious when this is stale, the leaves look limp and wilted.
Avoid spinach which is beginning to go to seed as it has lots
of coarse stalks which make a large amount of waste.

SWEDES

These usually keep very well. Avoid any which have become withered.

TOMATOES

Firmness is the important thing. Such a tomato has a shiny full skin and is light red in colour. As they become over-ripe the colour darkens and the skin loses its shine. Only buy this sort if they are very cheap and if you are going to cook them right away.

TURNIPS

Young ones are the best. Avoid very large ones and any which are beginning to wither.

QUANTITIES GUIDE FOR VEGETABLES

Amounts per portion

Artichokes, globe	1
Artichokes, Jerusalem	½ lb. (250 g.)
Asparagus	6–8 pieces
Aubergines	1
Beans, broad	¾–1 lb. (375–500 g.)
Beans, French or runner	6–8 oz. (175–250 g.)
Beetroot	6–8 oz. (175–250 g.)
Brussels sprouts, cabbage savoy	6–8 oz. (175–250 g.)
Carrots	6–8 oz. (175–250 g.)
Chicory	4 oz. (125 g.)
Leeks	½–¾ lb. (250–375 g.)
Mushrooms	2–4 oz. (50–125 g.)
Parsnips	6–8 oz. (175–250 g.)
Peas	½ lb. in pod (250 g.), 3–4 oz. shelled (75–125 g.)
Potatoes	½ lb. (250 g.)
Spinach	½ lb. (250 g.)
Swedes and turnips	6–8 oz. (175–250 g.)
Tomatoes	4 oz. (125 g.)

With other vegetables the amount you need depends on how they are being used, and on the size of the vegetables.

With some fruit the appearance is a good guide to quality, while with others it is difficult to tell from the outside what the inside will be like. It is wise to buy from a reliable shop and pay an average price for the fruit. Fruit which is very much below the current price is often, though not always, of poor quality.

Sometimes in the soft-fruit season a lower price simply means that the fruit is fully ripe and must be used at once, then it's a good buy for immediate use, especially for cooking. In the case of apples and oranges it may be that the fruit is unusually small, or not graded, which means a mixture of small and large fruit. Small fruit are often excellent value, ideal for small children. Small, thin-skinned oranges are usually very juicy and good for making drinks.

When any fruit is scarce it is usually expensive, and thus prices fluctuate from season to season. This holds good for both home-grown and imported fruit. Some imported fruits are purchased for their novelty value, but can be disappointing and not worth the high prices charged for them.

It is true, of course, that fruit generally tastes best when it is locally grown, but we can't all travel to far-away parts to eat the fruit freshly gathered. Air-freighting of fresh fruit overcomes this difficulty for those who are prepared to pay the price. But it's a nice thought that some people can enjoy top-quality fresh strawberries in London in January which only a couple of days before were growing in the sunshine of New Zealand.

Frozen fruits are usually more expensive than the fresh in season, but out of season are a welcome luxury. Some of the fruits which are disappointing when canned or bottled are much better frozen, for example, raspberries and strawberries. In general, freezing preserves the natural flavour better than canning, though modern developments in canning are overcoming this defect.

When buying fruit the following are points to look for:

APPLES

Those with wrinkled skins aren't worth buying. Those sold as cooking apples (usually Bramleys) are sometimes more expensive than the cheaper dessert apples, which can equally well be used for cooking and provide variety of flavour. It is always worth experimenting with these. Avoid very cheap imported apples or very cheap home-grown ones which have been in store for many months. They are quite likely poor quality inside and there will be a lot of waste.

APRICOTS
Fresh apricots are not worth buying unless they are fully ripe. If picked too soon, they don't ripen off the tree and have little flavour. Canned are better.

BANANAS
For immediate use buy ripe bananas, shown by small black-brown flecks in the skin. For later use buy them all yellow or with the ends still green, and keep them cool but not in the refrigerator.

CITRUS FRUIT
Skins should be taut and firm. Smooth skins usually mean juicy fruit, rough skins are usually thick, although the flesh may be very good and juicy; but you pay for the greater amount of skin. Thin-skinned lemons are a much better buy than thick-skinned ones, even if you want to use the skin for flavouring purposes.

GRAPES
If many on the bunch look soft, especially at the stalk end which goes brown on over-ripe green grapes, the bunch will need to be used right away.

MELONS
Fully-ripe ones are soft when pressed at the ends and these needs to be used at once. For later use buy firm ones and keep them at room temperature. Unripe melons are tasteless and can cause indigestion.

NECTARINES
See *Apricots*; the same remarks apply.

PEACHES
Fully-ripe ones need eating at once. Firm ones can be kept at room temperature until ripe and then put in a polythene box

or bag in the refrigerator. Green ones won't ripen off the tree and have no flavour.

PEARS
Fully-ripe ones, specially Williams, will have to be eaten right away and are a dodgy buy anyway, as they are liable to be 'sleepy' in the middle already. For keeping a few days, buy pears not fully ripe and keep them at room temperature. Hard, green pears won't ripen off the tree and have little flavour.

PINEAPPLE
Very small ones are not a good buy as there is so much skin in relation to the flesh. Moderate-sized ones are a reasonable price at certain times of the year. The skin of a ripe pineapple is brown. Avoid those with a large amount of green skin.

PLUMS
Appearance will tell you if there are too many fully-ripe or under-ripe ones in the sample. Under-ripe ones can be cooked. They look very hard compared with the others, while over-ripe ones are usually darker in colour than the average and sometimes the skins look loose and dull.

SOFT FRUIT
Ask to see the fruit at the bottom of a punnet; it can be going mouldy. Squashy soft fruit sold by the pound, loose, is only fit for immediate use, preferably cooking or making a fresh fruit *purée*. Examine cherries to see there are not too many over-ripe or unripe among them. With currants, avoid those which have lots of very small fruit; they will be all skin and very tedious to de-stalk.

QUANTITIES GUIDE FOR FRUIT

Apples, apricots, plums	Allow 1 lb. for 4 portions (500 g.)
Bananas	1 average size weighs about 5 oz. (150 g.)
Citrus fruit	½ medium or large grapefruit per portion
	1 medium orange
	1 lemon of average size yields about 2 Tbs. of juice
Grapes	Allow 3–4 oz. per portion (75–125 g.)

| Pears | 1 per portion or 1 lb. for 4 (500 g.) |
| Soft fruit | Allow 3–4 oz. per portion (75–125 g.) whether for cooking or dessert |

BUYING DAIRY FOODS, EGGS, AND FATS

MILK DESIGNATIONS OR GRADES

Grades and descriptions of milk sold in Britain are controlled by Government regulations. The Ministry of Agriculture, Fisheries, and Food inspects all dairy farms and tests all herds for bovine tuberculosis. Milk which is not labelled either 'pasteurised' or 'sterilised' has not been heat treated ('untreated') and it can be a source of brucellosis (undulant fever), food poisoning, and dysentery. It is unwise to drink raw milk. It should be scalded first or else used in cookery.

In order to see what type of milk you are buying read the designation on the bottle top. The colour of the top depends on the dairy's system of labelling and the same colour from a different dairy may have quite a different milk in the bottle.

Channel Islands and South Devon Milk

This milk comes from Jersey, Guernsey, or South Devon cows. It must contain at least 4 per cent butter fat which means that it has more cream than some other milks. Whether this is an advantage depends on the kind of milk you like.

Homogenised Milk

This is processed to distribute the cream evenly and prevent it from rising to the top in a layer; it saves having to shake up the bottle if you want an even mixture. You can buy it either untreated or pasteurised.

Pasteurised Milk

This is milk which has been heated to 71°C., held there for 15 seconds, and then cooled rapidly to 10°C. This treatment reduces the number of bacteria in the milk, makes it safe to drink, and ensures better keeping qualities. The treatment destroys the lactic acid bacteria which cause normal souring, and the milk will not sour and clot in the same way as untreated milk.

61

Skimmed Milk

Skimmed or skim milk has had the cream removed. It still contains the most valuable nutrients of milk, the protein, calcium, and water-soluble vitamins, and is a very good food. Today it is more readily available as dried milk powder.

Sterilised Milk

This is milk which is first homogenised and then sterilised in the bottle by heating to 104–110°C. and held at that temperature for 20–30 mins. This destroys all bacteria and, provided the bottle is not opened, the milk will keep for a week or more without refrigeration. It has the characteristic taste of boiled milk.

Ultra Heat Treated Milk

This is also known as long-keeping or long-life milk. It is homogenised and then heated to 132°C. for 1 second. It will keep for 2–3 weeks without refrigeration as long as it is left in the unbroken sealed and sterilised containers in which it is purchased.

Untreated Milk

This milk is bottled under licence by farmer or dairy and has had no heat treatment; sometimes known as raw milk.

OTHER TYPES OF MILK

Buttermilk

Is the milk left after cream has been churned to make butter. It contains some fat and may have a sharp taste if the butter has been made from ripened cream. Buttermilk is drunk plain, preferably chilled, and is used in cooking chiefly for mixing scones, quick breads, and soda bread.

Cultured buttermilk has been inoculated with bacteria, which produce some thickening and a taste like yogurt. Some is made from ordinary milk with dried milk and a 'buttermilk culture' added.

Condensed Milk

This is canned milk from which about one-third of the water has been evaporated. There are three main types:

Sweetened condensed, which is whole milk condensed and sweetened with sugar.

Sweetened skimmed condensed milk, which is milk with the cream removed.

Unsweetened condensed milk, which is usually whole milk condensed, but may also be skimmed milk condensed. These two have no sugar added and are known as evaporated milks. See *Evaporated Milk*.

The sugar added to preserved milk helps to keep it after the tin has been opened but does not keep it indefinitely and it should still be treated with the same care as other milk once the tin has been opened.

Some people like to use sweetened condensed milk in tea and coffee, others eat it neat and prefer it to drinking plain milk. It can also be diluted and used to make sweet sauces and sweetened milk drinks of all kinds. It makes good fruit fools if a sour fruit *purée* is being used.

Dried Milk

This is milk which has been preserved by evaporating the water, the result being a fine white powder which stores well and can easily be mixed with water.

Dried milk may be made from full cream milk or from skimmed milk. The former is the one used for infant foods, and it is also used widely in the catering industry as a substitute for fresh milk. It has the advantage of easy storage and a cheaper price than liquid milk, and when used in cooking it is impossible to tell the difference. Dried skimmed milk is used as a cheap source of protein and calcium, particularly in hospital feeding and in school meals. It is the cheapest source of good-quality protein available, and the missing fat and vitamins are cheaply supplied by the use of margarine in cooking. Dried skimmed milk is also important in feeding people who need a low fat diet.

Both the dried milks can be used in the dry state, e.g. mixed with flour, as well as reconstituted with water. And they can also be added to liquid milk to increase its nutritive value. The proportions used are $2\frac{1}{2}$ oz. dried milk powder (60 g.) to 1 pt. water (or liquid milk) (500 ml.)

Evaporated Milk

Is milk which has been concentrated to about a third of its original volume by evaporating some of the water. It is then canned. Sometimes also known as 'condensed unsweetened milk'. It is usually made from full cream milk or even milk enriched with extra cream (see the labels), but it may also be made from skimmed milk. It is used as a substitute for fresh milk, or cream in coffee, in cooking, or on fruit and puddings. Its nutritive value is different from cream and for children certainly, evaporated milk is better. Most sauces, soups, and puddings which have cream as an ingredient can have evaporated milk added instead. It will also whip up like cream, but to a greater volume.

It is used undiluted for making custards, and other milk puddings, or diluted in the proportions of 1 part of milk to 2 parts of water.

Yogurt, Yoghurt, or Yoghourt

This is a cultured milk made by adding organisms such as *Lactobacillus bulgaricus*, *L. acidophilus*, and *Streptococcus thermophilus* to the whole milk. Fermentation takes place; the sugar in the milk (lactose) is converted to lactic acid, and the milk forms a soft clot, as in souring. It continues to mature even in cold storage and becomes thicker and sharper in flavour the longer it is kept. It can be purchased plain or 'natural', and also flavoured with fruit, nuts, coffee, and chocolate.

The process of making yogurt was introduced to Britain from the Balkan States and Turkey, and it has been used for a very long time in most of Europe and Asia.

Many claims have been made regarding the therapeutic value of yogurt, but there is no reliable evidence that it is any more beneficial than an equivalent amount of milk or cheese. It is made from skimmed milk for those on a low-fat diet, and it has a lower calorific value than milk because most or all of the milk sugar has been used up by the culture. This applies to plain yogurts but not necessarily to the flavoured ones.

CREAM

Creams vary in quality according to the amount of butter-fat they contain. There are legal minimums for fat content in most of the different kinds of cream sold. No product may be called 'cream' unless it has a minimum of 18 per cent fat, and many kinds have to have more than this.

Single Cream

Usually has 18 per cent fat, but may have more, though not enough to make it suitable for whipping.

Double Cream

This must be not less than 48 per cent fat. It is thick and rich, rather too thick for whipping, but excellent for thickening sauces and on fruit. For whipping, mix it with either equal parts of single cream, or 1 part of single to 2 parts of double.

Cultured or Soured Cream

Usually about 18 per cent fat, and produced by the action of bacteria in a similar manner to yogurt (see page 64). When used for thickening sauces, it can replace fresh double cream, and it gives a pleasant sharp taste to the sauce. It can replace fresh cream in any recipe, and can be mixed with double fresh cream for whipping.

Canned Cream

It contains between 18 and 23 per cent fat.

Sterilised Cream

It must contain a minimum of 23 per cent fat, and is sold in cans and bottles. It keeps indefinitely.

Whipping Cream

This is 38 per cent fat.

Clotted Cream

Clotted cream comes from Devon and Cornwall, and is produced by heating the milk and skimming off the cream. This gives it a special flavour and texture. The legal minimum for fat is 48 per cent, but clotted cream is often much richer than this, as much as 50–60 per cent fat.

Ultra-Heat-Treated Cream

This is available either as single or double cream, and is produced in a similar way to *U.H.T. milk*, see page 62.

Cheese varies in texture and flavour according to the way it is made. All cheese begins by the milk being set in a curd or clot with the aid of a starter, which contains rennet and lactic acid bacteria. The curd is then strained to remove the liquid part (whey) from the solid curd. Finally the curd is moulded, pressed to remove more whey, and stored to allow it to mature. The following are the main types of cheese:

Hard Pressed Cheese, which is firm in texture. For example, Cheddar.

Lightly Pressed Cheese, which is a little softer and more moist. For example, Caerphilly.

Blue Vein Cheese, which is inoculated with special moulds to produce the blue veining, and a special flavour (such as in Stilton).

Soft Cheeses, which include cottage cheese, curd cheese, cream cheese and many named varieties. With these, the curd is not pressed, and they contain much more whey than the pressed cheeses. They are mostly mild in flavour. They may be made from skimmed milk, whole milk, milk with extra cream added, or cream — some of the cream cheeses being more like butter than cheese.

Processed Cheese, which is made from various hard cheeses by heating them with flavourings and other ingredients.

CHEESE FLAVOURS

Some people like a very mild-flavoured cheese, others prefer something with plenty of flavour. A strong flavour is produced during maturing, and thus, with some cheeses such as Cheddar, we get a fairly new cheese which is mild or a well-matured one which is strong.

To help you when shopping for cheese I give below a rough classification of some of the best-known cheeses. Naturally what some people consider a medium cheese others would consider either mild or strong according to personal taste.

MILD CHEESES

Bel Paese; Caerphilly; Cheshire; Edam; Gouda; New Zealand Cheddar; Port du Salut; Provalone; Wensleydale.

SOFT MILD CHEESES

Cottage cheese; Cream cheese; Curd cheese; Demi-sel; Double-Crème; Fontainebleau; Fromage à la Crème; Petit Gervais; Petite Suisse; Philadelphia; Pommel; Ricotta (Italian cottage cheese)

MEDIUM CHEESES

Brie; Bresse Bleu; Cheddar, English and some New Zealand; Danish Blue; Derby; Dolce-latte; Emmental; Gruyère; Lancashire; La Tomme au Raisin; Leicester; Pecorino; White Stilton.

STRONG CHEESES

Blue Dorset; Blue Stilton; Blue Vinney; Camembert; Canadian Cheddar; Danish Blue; Double Gloucester; English Cheddar; Gorgonzola; Limburger; La Tomme de Savoie; Pont l'Évêque; Provalone dulce; Roquefort; Samsoe; Smoked cheese.

BUYING CHEESE FOR COOKING

While all cheeses can be used for cooking, the most useful are those which are firm enough to grate easily, and have a flavour that is distinct but not too strong. Cheddar and Cheshire cheese are good ones for this, while Lancashire is an excellent one for toasting.

Parmesan, an Italian cheese, is considered the finest cooking cheese because it is hard and dry, can be very finely grated, and has a good flavour. It is better to buy this in a piece and grate it yourself as the drums of ready-grated Parmesan often taste very stale.

The Swiss cheeses, Emmental and Gruyère, are both good too, although the former is inclined to become stringy when heated. Other good ones are Dutch Gouda and Italian Mozzarella.

EGGS

Some people hold very strong views about the sort of eggs they think are good to buy. There are those who are not happy unless the eggs are labelled 'free range', while others think that the colour of the shell is important, and are willing to pay a higher price to get brown eggs. My main concern is whether or not the eggs are fresh, and this depends on where you buy them. A shop with a good, fast turnover of stock is more likely to sell fresh eggs than one where the eggs are in the store for several days – and, perhaps, are not kept in cold storage. If eggs are kept warm they very quickly deteriorate.

The prices of eggs vary with the size and in Great Britain eggs are graded within legal limits, as follows:

LARGE eggs are not less than $2\frac{3}{16}$ oz. (62 g.) per egg.
STANDARD eggs are between $1\frac{7}{8}$ oz. (53 g.) and $2\frac{3}{16}$ oz. (62 g.).
MEDIUM eggs are $1\frac{5}{8}$ oz. (46 g.) to $1\frac{7}{8}$ oz. (53 g.).
SMALL eggs are $1\frac{1}{2}$ oz. (43 g.) to $1\frac{5}{8}$ oz. (46 g.).

Most recipes are based on the standard egg, but you can often economise by buying small eggs, for example, 4 small eggs can cost less than 3 standard and give about the same amount of egg.

FATS AND OILS

Fat includes butter, margarine, lard, dripping, and cooking fats. Personal taste, price, and the way you want to use it will determine which you buy.

For Spreading

These are usually butter or margarine, though many people like a good beef dripping, and some use pork dripping. The soft margarines are excellent for spreading. Lactic butters (made from soured cream) are the softest, and spread more readily than sweet butter and there is also a special soft butter that is being developed to compete with the soft margarines.

For Making Cakes

Butter is the first choice whenever the flavour of the fat is important – as in cakes such as Madeira, Victoria sandwich, rich fruit cakes, Genoese sponge, shortbread, and so on. For ones such as gingerbread, chocolate, spice, and similar strongly-flavoured cakes, margarine and cooking fats are suitable. Lard or good beef dripping can be used for plain cakes such as rock buns and plain fruit cakes where the flavour of these fats is often an asset. The soft margarines and cooking fats are very easy to cream, and are ideal for the 'Quick Mix' type of cake, where all the ingredients are mixed together in one operation.

For Making Pastry

Butter gives the best flavour, and lard, cooking fat, and soft margarine the shortest pastry. A good mixture is half butter and half soft margarine or lard; or use all margarine. Soft margarines and cooking fats can be mixed in with a fork instead of the usual rubbing in.

Suet pastry is best made with freshly-prepared butcher's suet, but packet suet is a good substitute. For puff pastry use a firm butter or margarine, and for flaky pastry use a mixture of either butter or margarine, and cooking fat or lard.

For Frying

In shallow fat use butter (clarified, if it is salted butter), cooking fats, lard or clean dripping. No fat is as good as an oil for deep fat frying, the best oils being peanut or ground-nut oil, or corn oil. If oil is not available use one of the cooking fats specially made for frying.

BREAD

All breads must be sold by net weight if the amount sold exceeds 10 oz. (283·5 g.); above this weight it must be sold in multiples of 14 oz. (396·9 g.). One doesn't normally ask for so many ounces of bread but buys it by name. Thus what is commonly called a 'small' loaf weighs 14 oz. (396·9 g.) and a 'large' loaf 28 oz. (793·8 g.). Bun loaves, fruit loaves, and malt loaves are not included in this weight rule.

If you want crusty bread you need to buy an unwrapped loaf as the wrapping makes the crust soft. Sliced bread costs more than the same size unsliced, and you can usually buy it either finely sliced or thicker, according to your taste.

WHITE BREAD

The most common shape of loaf is known as a 'tin' loaf, with straight sides and bottom and a domed top. Other shapes are sandwich loaves (4 flat sides), cottage loaves (double-decker), plaits, French loaves, Vienna rolls, coburgs, bloomers, farmhouse or Dutch, bannocks or baps, and batons. Some shops label the loaves and others have a display card with pictures and names. If your baker does neither you have to start by pointing to what you want, then ask the name. In that way you will learn. A good baker has such a variety of bread that it is a pity not to try the whole range.

White bread is made from white flour with various additions which are compulsory by law, and others which are permitted in controlled amounts.

BROWN BREAD

This is made from various mixtures of white and wholemeal flour. It is most commonly baked as a tin loaf but sometimes in other shapes.

WHOLE WHEATMEAL

Also known as 100 per cent wholemeal stone-ground, it is the only loaf which does not contain added vitamins and minerals, but it may contain other substances permitted by law. It is sold under various trade names and in several shapes, sometimes with whole wheat grains on the outside. Some are made from finely-ground wheat and others are quite coarse. The latter type seems to keep fresh longer.

MILK LOAVES

White loaves with milk or dried milk added and with a soft crumb and crust. They must contain not less than 8 per cent milk solids.

GERM-MEAL LOAVES

White loaves with wheat germ added which makes them a light brown colour. They are sold under a variety of trade names and cost more than an ordinary brown loaf. For the money you get more B vitamins and iron, and a distinctive flavour.

MALT BREAD

Made from white or brown flour plus some malted flour or malt extract, they also often contain some lard, milk, and golden syrup, and are always sweet.

RYE BREADS

These may be very dark brown and solid in texture, being made from the whole rye grain. Paler ones are usually a mixture of white wheat flour and rye flour. Many contain caraway seeds. Some of the dark ones are sold sliced and packaged.

CARAWAY BREAD
May be white or rye bread containing caraway seeds throughout the loaf.

POPPY-SEED BREAD
White bread with poppy seeds sprinkled on top.

FARLS
Bread made with baking powder instead of yeast.

SODA BREAD
Bread raised with bicarbonate of soda instead of yeast; may be brown or white.

FRUIT BREAD
White bread with currants and sultanas worked into the dough; may also be malted.

CRISP BREADS
Like dry thick biscuits and made from wheat or rye; either white or brown.

PROTEIN BREAD
Must contain not less than 22 per cent protein. If it is called gluten bread it must contain not less than 16 per cent protein. The additional protein makes a bigger and lighter loaf.

STARCH-REDUCED BREAD
Must have less than 50 per cent carbohydrate based on the dry weight (ordinary bread has 83 per cent).

BREAD FROM COMPOST-GROWN WHEAT
The wheat is grown without the use of artificial fertilisers. It is generally sold in health-food shops, and those who eat it generally believe that they will be more healthy as a result.

Today most groceries are standardised or graded, and packaged so that buying is largely a question of personal taste for a specific brand at a price the customer is prepared to pay.

It is a help to the beginner to know a few facts about groceries, and the following notes are meant for this.

BREAKFAST CEREALS

The cereals used to make breakfast foods are chiefly wheat, rice, and maize or sweet corn. Some, most of the wheat ones, are made from whole-grain cereals while the other two are usually refined, i.e. they have the germ and the husk removed. Until recently the wheat cereals were the best value nutritionally, but today many of the rice and corn cereals are having vitamins, iron, and protein added to them. This is a good thing, especially for those who usually breakfast on cereal and nothing else. Bran breakfast cereals are made from the branny layer or outside layers of a grain and are chiefly important for their high cellulose content, which helps to prevent constipation in those whose basic diet is normally rather lacking in cellulose-rich foods.

Wheat germ, sold under various trade names at chemists, health-food stores, and some grocers, is of high nutritive value and is a good cereal to sprinkle on stewed fruit, or to add to other cereals to enrich them.

CANNED FOODS

Avoid buying cans which are bulging at the ends or which look pushed in at the ends. The contents are not necessarily bad, but it isn't worth risking. Cans which have been knocked about and have received dents on the sides are safe to use unless they are leaking, but don't buy them unless you intend to use them fairly soon. They should be sold at a lower price than perfect cans, but many shops try to avoid doing this.

If you buy larger cans than are required for one meal, remember that once the can is opened the food will not keep any longer than other cooked food. If you have a freezer, surplus food can be frozen and this is useful for remains of things like canned consommé for stock, canned sweet peppers, and other items where you sometimes only need a little for a recipe.

The weight shown on cans is the net weight – which includes the weight of the solid food and any liquid. The best varieties give you plenty of solid in relation to the liquid, and are worth paying a little extra for.

COLOURINGS

Some naturally-occurring food colourings have been in use for hundreds of years. Among these are cochineal or carmine, which comes from an insect, *Coccus cacti*; annatto, a yellow colouring from the seeds of the tree *Bixa orellana*; and saffron, a yellow colour from the stigma of the saffron crocus, *Crocus sativus*.

Other natural colourings used domestically are the finely-grated rind of lemons and oranges, the liquid from spinach and beetroot. One of the disadvantages of using such colours is that there is an accompanying flavour which may not be appropriate for the dish. Synthetic colourings are used instead. In Britain there is a list of permitted colourings, and no others may be legally sold, or used in food for sale. This list is, however, a controversial matter, as many other artificial colourings have been shown to be cancer-producing in animals. The list is constantly under review but many people think that lack of proof that the colourings are harmful does not necessarily mean that the long-term effects may not be bad. Those who believe this can, of course, avoid artificial colourings if they do most of their cooking themselves, and only buy foods which have not been coloured.

DRIED FRUIT

Most dried fruit for cakes is sold in packets and is already washed and ready for use. Dried fruits such as apricots, pears and so on are often sold loose, and these need to be washed in cold water. If you buy loose dried fruit for cakes, this needs to be washed too, and then spread out on kitchen paper on a rack to dry.

Raisins are sold as small seedless, large juicy seeded, and large juicy with the pips still in; removing the seeds is tedious, but you often get the best-flavoured raisins this way.

Dates come in two grades, for dessert where the individual whole dates are packed in small boxes, and solid packs of stoned dates ready for cooking.

Most candied peel today is sold ready cut and mixed but if

73

you want just one kind of peel you can still buy the uncut pieces in some shops, either lemon, orange, or citron peel.

Glacé and crystallised fruits are always expensive. The glacé ones have a moist sticky outside and the crystallised have a sugary outside, e.g. crystallised ginger; but sometimes they are all called by one or other of these two names. Some shops sell this fruit loose and this is a more economical way of buying them than when they are packed in gift boxes.

FLAVOURING ESSENCES

These are sold in small bottles at chemists and food shops. They include natural, artificial, and compound (a mixture of natural and artificial) essences. Their composition is controlled by law, and which you like to buy is a matter of personal taste and experiment. Natural essences are the most expensive.

FLOUR

Many different kinds of flour are sold under many brand names but the chief ones are:

Plain White Flour

A general-purpose flour used for making pastry, thickening sauces and for many different kinds of cakes. For cake making it is generally necessary to add baking powder or some other raising agent, and most people prefer to use self-raising flour, but it is not suitable for all cooking purposes so you really need some of each kind.

Plain Strong White Flour

Is specially for making bread, and you may not need this one at all.

Self-raising White Flour

Has baking powder mixed with it, and is probably the most widely-used of all flours.

100 per cent Whole Wheatmeal Flour

Sometimes called stone-ground flour. This is the brown flour made from the whole wheat grain, and is sold as plain or self-raising flour.

74

Brown Flour

Sometimes called whole meal. It is not as brown as the 100 per cent whole wheatmeal flour and is usually more finely ground, sometimes called 80 per cent flour (white flour is 70 per cent or less).

Cornflour

Is made from maize or sweet corn, and is a white flour used for thickening sauces, making blancmanges and other cold puddings.

Potato Flour

Also called fécule, it is a white flour made from the starch in potatoes. It is used for thickening sauces, specially sweet ones, and in many continental recipes.

MUSTARD

This is sold as dry mustard powder or as ready-mixed English or French mustard, the latter under many trade names. The differences are largely due to flavourings added. French mustard is mixed with oil and vinegar and has a milder flavour than English mustard.

NUTS

It is best to buy these ready-shelled unless you want them on the table for dessert.

When comparing the relative prices of shelled and unshelled, reckon that a pound of nuts ($\frac{1}{2}$ kg.) will yield about half a pound shelled ($\frac{1}{4}$ kg.), less if there are many bad ones among them.

Almonds for cooking are sold ready-blanched (skinned), or halved (split), or coarsely-chopped (nibs), and salted. Ground almonds are sold by the pound or already made into marzipan, which is often cheaper than making it for yourself.

OATS AND OATMEAL

Oatmeal is sold in various grades: fine, like flour (used in baking and for thickening soups); medium and coarse, used for porridge and oatcakes. Patent groats consist of fine outmeal with the less digestible branny parts removed.

Rolled oats are made by flattening and crushing the grain

between rollers and partly cooking it. This means it takes less time to cook than oatmeal.

PEPPER

Black and white peppercorns are sold for use whole in flavouring such things as stocks and marinades, or are ground in peppermills for cooking or table use. Freshly-ground pepper always tastes better than the fine ready-ground powder. Cayenne (chilli) pepper is sold ground and is exceedingly hot. Paprika pepper is a mild red pepper with the flavour of sweet peppers or pimentos; also used for decorating dishes.

PICKLES

These vary a great deal in quality, chiefly due to the type of vinegar used in their manufacture. Some have a very sharp crude flavour, but there are good ones worth paying extra money for.

RICE

There are a number of different varieties of rice suited for different types of cooking. The most commonly used in Britain are:

Rounded Grain

Short or medium length, which is used for puddings. The grains have a tendency to stick together when cooked. This type is also used for risotto, paella, and pilaff, though in the countries where these dishes originated a special variety of round rice is used.

Long Grain

Of which Patna is the best-known variety. The long thin grains will stay separated if the rice is not over-cooked, and it is the variety preferred for boiled rice and also for savoury dishes; some people prefer this to the round rice for risottos, etc.

Parboiled Rice

This is partly cooked under steam pressure before milling. After milling, this type of rice contains more minerals and vitamins than the ordinary white rice. It also absorbs more water during cooking, and remains separate and fluffy.

Pre-cooked or Quick-cooking Rice

This is now sold in most stores, and only requires heating before serving.

Brown Rice

Has only part of the branny layers removed, and contains more minerals and vitamins than the milled white rice. It takes longer to cook and absorbs more water, has more flavour, but the appearance spoils the traditional look of many rice dishes.

Ground Rice

Coarsely-ground white rice, and similar to semolina in texture. It is used in the same way.

Rice Flour

Used for thickening purposes and also for making starch for stiffening clothes.

Rice Breakfast Cereals

These are made from the white rice, the most common being puffed rice.

Canned and Packet Rice Products

There are many of these available today and they form a useful emergency supply. Canned rice pudding is very good, and is a useful basis for many puddings. Paella, risottos, and other savoury rice preparations are available, either dried or canned, and are of variable quality.

SALT

Unrefined or crude salt is sold in coarse crystals as either rock or sea salt. Both contain, among their impurities, some minerals useful in human nutrition – for example, iodine. Many people prefer the flavour of this sort of salt and its coarse grittiness when it is ground in a salt mill. It is suitable for cooking or table use. Other cooking salts are block (becoming scarce), which needs to be crushed before use, and free-running cooking salt treated to keep it dry.

Table salt, too, is treated to keep it dry and free-running. It may also be iodised, useful for those who live in districts where there is a deficiency of iodine in the salt and water.

SUGARS

Granulated Sugar

The cheapest white sugar and suitable for most cooking purposes.

Caster Sugar

Fine white sugar which dissolves more readily than granulated, and is preferred in cake-making using the creaming method.

Cube or Loaf Sugar

Made from sugar formed into slabs and then cut up into cubes.

Icing Sugar

A powdered white sugar which has a substance added to keep it from lumping.

Pieces or Moist Sugar

Fine brown sugar (often called 'soft') which may be very pale or dark like treacle. It is less refined than white sugar and has more flavour. There is no medical or scientific evidence that brown sugar is better for you than white sugar.

Demerara Sugar

A brown crystalline sugar which tastes of sugar cane. It comes from the cane fields of Demerara in Guyana.

Golden Syrup

A by-product from the early stages of refining of white sugar.

Black Treacle

Similar to syrup, but darker in colour, it has a sharp taste. Both syrup and treacle can be used as a spread on bread, for sweetening porridge and breakfast cereals, and in baking. The molasses of American cookery is similar to black treacle.

Honey

More expensive than other sugars, but has a quite different flavour, varying with the source of the nectar that the bees have collected. It is mainly used as a spread, but can also be used in cooking. There is an extensive mythology about the supposed health-giving properties of honey. The cheapest honey is a blend from several sources, and is quite adequate for general use. Special honey with a distinctive flavour of one flower, for example, heather or clover, is usually more expensive, as is honey in the comb. With keeping, and in cold weather, clear honey naturally goes thick, but some is treated to make it remain clear. Thick honey will go clear when warmed.

VINEGAR

This is a weak solution of acetic acid. 'Brewed' vinegar is produced by the action of acetic acid bacteria on the alcohol in wine, cider, or beer. Malt vinegar is made from beer and has the strongest flavour. Wine or cider vinegars are more pleasant for most cooking purposes. 'Non-brewed' vinegar is made from pure acetic acid, is cheaper than brewed, and lacks the flavour. White vinegar is produced by distilling other vinegars and is useful when a colourless vinegar is needed.

Herb-flavoured vinegars such as tarragon, chilli, onion, and so on, are used mainly for making salad dressings and can easily be made at home from fresh herbs and wine or cider vinegar. The herbs are left to infuse in the vinegar until you get the flavour you like.

HERBS AND SPICES

HERBS

The best results come from using fresh herbs, so if possible either grow your own or try to find a shop or market stall where you can buy at least some of them fresh. Most fresh herbs keep their flavour well when frozen, and this is the best way of preserving them, see page 212.

Depending on the locality, the following are available fresh for most of the year, though the flavour is not usually as strong in the cold months: bay leaves, chervil, fennel, horseradish, parsley, rosemary, sage, and thyme.

Dried herbs are usually sold finely-powdered, in small drums. Keep the drums tightly closed and dry. Replenish the herbs frequently as they very quickly lose flavour and begin to taste like hay. The herbs which retain most flavour when dried are bay leaves, caraway seeds, dill and fennel seeds, garlic, horseradish, rosemary, sage, and thyme.

SPICES

Some are sold whole, for example, nutmeg, blades of mace, sticks of cinnamon bark, allspice, cloves, coriander, and ginger (fresh or dried). It is often more convenient to buy some of these ground to a powder and sold loose or in small drums. Spices keep their flavour longer than dried herbs do, but should be kept dry and in tightly-closed containers.

Mixed spice is a mixture of ground spices, sometimes confused with allspice, which has a quite different flavour and is used mainly for savoury dishes, whereas mixed spice is mainly used for cakes and sweet dishes. Other mixtures are sold as 'seasonings', and may be a mixture of salt, pepper and spices, or herbs.

ALPHABETICAL LIST OF HERBS AND SPICES

ALLSPICE (*Pimenta dioica*) or Jamaica pepper

It comes from a plant grown in the West Indies, Mexico, and South America. It tastes like a blend of nutmeg, cloves, and cinnamon, hence its name. It is also called 'pimento'.

Whole allspice are about the size of small peas, and are a light cinnamon colour. They are used to flavour stock, especially when boiling beef or ham (about 6 to a 3 lb. (1½ kg.) joint), and in making spiced vinegar for pickles, and for flavouring sauces.

ANISEED or Sweet Cumin

Seeds of the *Anise* plant and used as a flavouring in confectionery and to flavour liqueurs, e.g. Anisette.

BALM (*Melissa officinalis*), also known as Lemon Balm or Sweet Balm.

A plant native to southern Europe, the flowers being favourites of the honey bee. *Melissa* is the Greek word for bee. It is used for flavouring savoury dishes, for salads, in fruit salads, and in wine and fruit cups. A herbal tea is made from the fresh leaves using 1 oz. balm to 1 pt. of boiling water (30 g. to ½ l.) infused for 15 mins., cooled, and strained.

The herb has a mild flavour and is used in fairly large amounts, e.g. about 2 Tbs. chopped balm for 4 people.

BASIL (*Ocimum basilicum*) or Sweet Basil

It is difficult to grow in Britain and is most frequently used dry. It has a very strong flavour and needs to be used with discretion. Dried leaves are best used in soups, stews, meat dishes, on lamb chops, and the fresh leaves added to salads, especially tomato salad.

BAY LEAVES

Leaves of the sweet bay or *Laurus nobilis*. Used for flavouring any savoury dish, and also as part of a *bouquet garni*, see page 222. It has a fairly strong flavour, a piece of a leaf usually being enough to flavour a dish for 4 people. It is used either fresh or dried. The trees are often seen growing in tubs outside restaurants.

BORAGE (*Borago officinalis*)

A herb with hairy leaves and a bright blue flower. The young leaves are used in salads and for flavouring claret cups and Pimm's No. 1. The leaves have a faint flavour of cucumber. The flowers are sometimes used to decorate salads.

CAPERS

The flower heads of *Capparis spinosa*, which grows wild in Mediterranean countries. The buds are pickled in vinegar and then sold in small jars. Some people pickle small nasturtium seeds in the same way and use them as a substitute. Capers are used chiefly for caper sauce and for garnishing purposes. There is an English plant which has buds like a caper, *Euphorbia lathyus* or caper spurge, which is poisonous and is said to be heartily disliked by moles who will not come anywhere near its roots.

CARAWAY

The fruits of a plant, *Carum carvi*. In cookery, the fruits are usually referred to as 'seeds'. An essential oil is extracted from them and used in flavouring liqueurs, especially Kümmel. The seeds are used in both sweet and savoury cooking, e.g. in bread, in goulash, in biscuits and buns, and in cake.

81

CHERVIL (*Anthriscus cerefolium*)

A herb belonging to the family of *Umbelliferae*. It has a sweet aromatic flavour, is used for flavouring savoury dishes and forms part of '*fines herbes*', see page 235. It is also used for garnishing in the same way as parsley, but is more delicate in appearance.

CHILLI POWDER

A blend of chilli pepper with other spices, much used in Mexican cooking.

CHIVES (*Allium schoenoprasum*)

A member of the onion family, with small bulbs and grasslike leaves which are cut and used in salads, sauces, and garnishing to give a mild onion flavour. Are seldom sold in shops but are easy to grow in garden or window-box. They are in season from spring to autumn but the tops die down in the winter.

CINNAMON

A spice from the bark of an evergreen tree, *Cinnamomum zeylanicum*, which grows in Ceylon, India, and the East Indies. Curled strips of the bark are called cinnamon sticks, and these are used whole for flavouring. Ground cinnamon is also used for flavouring both sweet and savoury dishes.

CLOVES

The dried unopened flower buds of an evergreen tree, *Eugenia aromatica*. It is cultivated in a number of tropical countries including Zanzibar, Sumatra, Java, and the West Indies. Cloves are used whole for flavouring apple puddings, baked hams, sauces, and pickles. Ground cloves are used for flavouring many sweet and savoury dishes, either alone or with other spices.

CORIANDER (*Coriandrum sativum*)

The dried fruit of this plant is used as a flavouring in pickles, cheese and rice dishes, sweets, gingerbreads, biscuits, and in the making of liqueurs. Coriander grows in Europe, India, Iran, Morocco, and Egypt.

CUMIN (*Cuminum cyminum*)

A spice which gives a pungent tang to bread, stews, meat, cheese, and egg dishes. It is used extensively in oriental and Mexican cooking, and as an ingredient in curry powder. Also used in liqueurs such as Kümmel and Anisette. It is a native of the Mediterranean, and also grows in India, China, and Mexico.

CURRY

The general name for dishes flavoured with curry powder, a mixture of pepper and spices which varies widely in composition. In countries where curry is a national dish, people grind and blend their own curry powder to produce different mixtures for different dishes. Sometimes they are very hot with a lot of chilli peppers included, others are mildly hot and very spicy. Ready-made curry powders and pastes sold in Britain vary too, and it is a matter of finding one you like and using it in quantities to suit yourself.

DILL (*Anethum graveolens*)

A herb which is a native of the Mediterranean, but grows throughout Europe, India, North America, and in England. It is similar in flavour to fennel and caraway, and is used in cucumber pickles and to flavour vinegar. It is very good with fish, egg dishes, and salads. Serve it with cucumbers and yogurt dressing; with new potatoes and lemon butter; in fish salads and potato salad. Both the leaves and the seeds are used.

FENNEL

There are two varieties of this plant used for food. *Foeniculum vulgare*, *F. officinale*, or common fennel, leaves and seeds being used as a flavouring herb. *Finnochio* or Florence fennel (*F. dulce*) is grown in Italy and used as a vegetable. Fennel leaves are used for cooking with fish or boiled mutton and for the accompanying sauces.

FENUGREEK (*Trigonella foenum-graecum*)

A spice used in India and Europe. It has a bitter flavour similar to burnt sugar and is used in chutneys and curry powders and other flavourings.

GARLIC (*Allium sativum*)

It belongs to the same family as the onion. Each garlic bulb consists of a number of segments or 'cloves'. The flavour is very pungent and, unless used very lightly, is disagreeable to many people, both the 'after-taste' in their own mouths and the smell of it on the breath of others.

The flavour is most subtle when a cut clove is used for rubbing on food before cooking, e.g. a slice of meat or a chop, or for rubbing round a bowl before mixing a salad in it. Otherwise garlic should be used in minute amounts and very finely chopped. Alternatively, a garlic press can be used to give juice for flavouring; garlic salt (salt plus dried garlic), dried garlic, and garlic vinegar are available for condiments. ⅛ tsp. dried garlic = 1 clove of fresh.

Garlic goes particularly well with lamb or mutton, as well as with tomatoes and many vegetables which grow in warm countries, such as aubergine. A piece of a clove of garlic is often inserted by the bone of the cut end of leg of lamb, and this flavours the gravy and the meat.

GINGER

The tuberous root of the plant *Zingiber officinale*, which grows in damp moist tropical parts, chiefly in Jamaica, but also in South America, West Africa, China, and Australia. The root is used both fresh and dried, and it is crystallised and used as a sweetmeat or in baking in the same way as dried fruit. It is also preserved in syrup (stem ginger) and eaten as a dessert with cream or ice-cream. The root is dried and ground to give powdered or ground ginger, a widely-used spice. Ginger is also used for making non-alcoholic beverages like ginger ale or ginger beer, and also for making ginger wine.

HORSERADISH (*Cochlearia armoracia*)

A plant which grows wild throughout Britain, and in many gardens becomes a troublesome weed. The leaves look rather like dock leaves. The root is the part eaten as a condiment. It is very hot and pungent and makes the traditional accompaniment to roast beef, either fresh (raw grated) or made into a sauce. It is also used with oily fish, with grilled steak, and with beetroot and other salads.

To prepare horseradish, scrub the root well and grate it

moderately finely. Grated horseradish may be preserved, if packed loosely in small jars and covered with vinegar.

LOVAGE (*Levisticum officinale*)

A herb related to angelica. It used to be a popular herb for flavouring savoury foods, but today is chiefly used like angelica, the stem being candied. It grows chiefly in Mediterranean countries.

MACE

A spice which comes from the outer covering of the nutmeg. This is used as thin flakes (blade mace), or ground. It is a lighter colour and has a milder flavour than nutmeg. Used in flavouring cakes, sauces, soups, mashed potatoes, stuffings, veal, rabbit, and chicken dishes.

MARIGOLD (*Calendula officinalis*)

The flowers of the common marigold are sometimes used for garnishing and flavouring. They are also used for home-made wine.

MARJORAM

There are a number of varieties of this herb all belonging to the family of *Origanum*. Some authorities list those cultivated for use as herbs under the name *Marjorana*.

The two varieties most commonly grown are the 'sweet marjoram' or *M. hortensis* or *Origanum marjorana* (this is also the Italian *Oregano*); and the variety called 'common' or pot 'marjoram' or *M. onites*. They are both perennials, but the latter is more robust and is the one most commonly grown in gardens in Britain. Others have to be treated as biennials. Wild marjoram (*O. vulgare*) is a common perennial wild plant found on chalky hills in south-eastern England. It is easily recognised by its foot-high stems with a violet cluster of flowers in July and August and its characteristic perfume. Fresh and dried marjoram are used for flavouring foods such as stuffings, sauces, stews, soups, minced meat, roast pork, veal dishes, some fish, and many other savoury dishes. Leaves of fresh marjoram are used in salads.

MINT (*Mentha*)

An aromatic plant of which there are many varieties including culinary, medicinal, and decorative ones. Culinary varieties are used for making mint sauce, mint-flavoured stuffings, meat pasties, dried fruit tarts, in beverages, in fruit cocktails and fruit cups, and for flavouring apple jelly to serve with cold meats. Sprigs of mint are also added to new potatoes and green peas during boiling.

NUTMEG

The kernel of the fruit of a very large tree belonging to the *Myristica* species, natives of the East and West Indies and grown in many warm climates.

The outer envelope of the kernel is used as mace (*see* Mace). Nutmeg is sold whole or ground. Whole nutmegs are easily ground as required, using a small mill or a nutmeg grater which is a very fine grater, also useful for grating lemon rind and onions (to produce onion juice).

In traditional English cookery, nutmeg is used to sprinkle on the top of baked rice puddings, custards, junkets, and in Christmas cooking for mincemeat, cake, and pudding. In other countries it is widely used in cooking meat and other savoury foods and can be used with practically any food.

OREGANO

A herb used extensively in Italian cookery. It is a wild marjoram, but cultivated marjoram can be used in the same way (*see* Marjoram). Oregano is used in sauces to serve with *pasta*, tomato dishes, fish, chicken, and lamb.

PARSLEY (*Petroselinum crispum*)

This is the parsley commonly used for flavouring and garnishing. Some varieties have broad flat leaves while others are tightly curled. Hamburg parsley, *var. radicosum*, has roots which are cooked like a parsnip and leaves which are used in the same way as the other variety of parsley.

PEPPERMINT (*Mentha piperita*)

A variety of mint grown for its volatile oil which is used for flavouring medicines, sweets, cordials, liqueurs and, as essence of peppermint, it is used as a flavouring in cooking. It is one of the strong flavours which some like and some dislike.

ROSEMARY (*Rosmarinus officinalis*)

An evergreen shrub with needle-like dark green leaves, and a pale blue flower. It is a fairly pungent herb but an excellent flavouring for meat and poultry. A sprig put in the pan when roasting lamb, chicken, or veal gives a pleasant flavour; or sprinkle chopped leaves over the meat; or use a little in the stuffing. Use in small amounts in soups, stews, sauces, and salads.

SAFFRON

A yellow powder made from the dried stigmas of the saffron crocus or *Crocus sativus*. It flowers in the autumn, but must not be confused with the autumn crocus, *Colchicum autumnale*, which is poisonous. Saffron is very expensive (4,000 flowers make 1 oz. [28·35 g.]), but a little goes a very long way. It is used to colour and flavour rice dishes, fish soups like *bouilla-baisse*, and Spanish *paella*. It is also used in Indian cookery.

SAGE (*Salvia*)

There are many varieties of this herb but the one chiefly grown for culinary use is *S. officinalis*. There is a red variety, *var. purpurea*, which is considered by some to be better for flavouring than the more common green-grey type. It is always a strong herb, used traditionally for flavouring duck, goose, and pork.

It is also used to flavour marinades, and sometimes peas and beans, especially dried beans.

SAVORY (*Satureja*)

A herb from the Mediterranean coast. There are two varieties, Winter Savory or *S. montana*, a perennial shrub, and Summer Savory or *S. hortensis*, an annual. Either fresh or dried leaves are used for flavouring and go particularly well with broad beans, but are also used to flavour stuffings for veal, pork, duck, goose, and chicken, and as a flavouring for sausages and meat rissoles. It is used for lentil soup and goes well with any dish using pulses. Summer Savory is usually more fragrant than the winter variety.

87

SWEET CICELY (*Myrrhis odorata*)

A pretty herb with a faint anise flavour, good with most things except poultry. The flavour is mild and the herb can be used generously. Is sometimes used in salad dressings.

TARRAGON

Two varieties of this herb are grown, *Artemesia dracunculus* or French tarragon and *A. dracunculoides* or Russian tarragon. French tarragon is a native of southern Europe and has a much stronger flavour than the Russian variety which can be pretty tasteless.

Vinegar flavoured with tarragon leaves is used in cooking, for making salad dressings, for sauces, in French mustard, and in marinades.

The fresh leaves are used for flavouring salads (especially tomato and egg salads), for stuffings and sauces (especially with fish and eggs), and in stews and pickles. The leaves can be dried for winter use but lose much of their flavour and to freeze them is a better way of preserving the flavour.

THYME (*Thymus*)

One of the most widely used herbs. The common thyme is used in making a *bouquet garni* (see page 222) and to flavour savoury dishes of all kinds. It is used fresh or dried. Lemon thyme can be used in the same way and is especially good with veal and fish and in salads. All thymes have a strong flavour and need to be used sparingly.

TURMERIC (*Curcuma longa*)

A plant native to Ceylon, but also growing in India and the East and West Indies. The rhizome (root) is dried and ground to give a bright yellow powder with a slightly bitter aromatic flavour. It is used in making curries and other savoury dishes, and also in pickles such as piccalilli.

BUYING DRINKS

COCOA

You can buy this as cocoa powder for mixing the kind of brew you want or, provided you like it very sweet, one of the chocolate drinks which are basically cocoa and sugar. A mixture of cocoa powder and instant coffee makes a very good drink.

COFFEE

Coffee is sold as roasted beans to grind yourself, ready ground, and instant. Each variety of coffee has its own name, usually that of the country of origin, while ground beans are sold under various trade names and are usually a blend of different coffees. Some coffee is roasted to a very light colour (cinnamon roast), while others are burnt nearly black (Italian roasts), to give a strong bitter flavour. Sometimes a small amount of molasses is used to coat the beans and delay evaporation of the aroma. This gives the beans a shine and a better colour. If you buy ground beans, get only small amounts as they soon lose their aroma, which is why coffee lovers prefer to buy beans and grind them as required.

Instant or soluble coffee is made from ordinary coffee, ground and percolated, using water at high pressure. The coffee liquid may then be either spray dried or, more recently, freeze dried. Once the container has been opened the coffee very quickly loses its aroma, so it isn't wise to buy larger amounts than you can use up fairly quickly.

TEA

Tea varies in price and quality depending on where it is grown, the part of the tea plant from which the leaves are picked, and the method of preparing and blending. The finest teas come from the small, growing tips, while the next three or four leaves produce a poorer quality.

Black tea comes from leaves which are allowed to ferment before being toasted and dried. Green tea comes from leaves which are dried without fermenting. In Britain this is usually called China tea. When brewed it gives a pale, scented tea which is usually drunk without milk but with slices of lemon in it and sugar.

Some people like a tea with a very fine leaf which brews quickly and gives a strong cup; others prefer the larger leaves which take longer to brew, and to get strong tea you need more spoonsful than with a small leaf.

Teas sold under different brand names are blends, and so is the tea in tea bags.

ALCOHOLIC DRINKS

Wine is the fermented juice of grapes, though many other fermented juices are called wines, e.g. fruit and vegetable wines. Today wines at fair prices are available in Britain from all over the world. The wines that most people drink at home are those they know and like, or those which have been recommended to them. When drinking out, the choice is limited to the wine list presented, and the 'best' is not necessarily the most expensive. A lot depends on the policy of the management and the clientele. Most wine waiters in this country tend to treat you fairly, and there is no disgrace in asking for advice. No one can know the contents of all the cellars available. You might have acquired a comparative chart showing the best years for various wines. Do not consult it at table – this enhances nobody's reputation, and such a list cannot give anything but a general indication. Even in generally 'bad' years there are some good wines.

A wine gives pleasure via three senses, taste, smell, and sight. Assuming the wine is good, the first two qualities are governed by the state of your palate. Smoking, and eating highly-seasoned foods will radically alter your sense of taste and appreciation of delicate flavours. It is necessary to find from experience something that suits your own palate.

The shape of the glass is important for getting the best flavour from a wine. It is not easy in Britain to buy retail the standard clear wineglass found on every good European table. The shape should be such as to enhance the aroma when drinking, or, in the case of sparkling wines, to show and preserve the play of bubbles. Many modern glass designers are spoiling wine drinking by exaggerating their own phantasy for colour and form. It is noteworthy that many of them come from non-wine countries.

The 'best'? Certainly not necessarily that with the highest alcoholic content (which rarely exceeds 10 per cent). Some wines, notably champagne, are more expensive to produce than others. Within any one type, commercial competition largely takes care of price levels against quality.

Broadly, the very best white wines come from Germany and reds from France. 'Appellation controlée' on a French wine label is a real guarantee that the label describes the contents. The best vintages, i.e. wines from grapes of a specific year's harvest, can be checked from a number of reliable sources and when the product is really noble it has to be paid for. Non-vintage wines, which are quite pleasant, are a matter of experiment and advice.

Should you want to buy wine to 'lay down' you must get advice from a good wine merchant or shipper. Quality of wine varies with age. Only the professional can tell you which young wines, uninteresting to drink now, will improve in so many years if kept properly. To store wines it is important to have a cool, dark place free from vibration, and it is essential to have proper racks in which to store the bottles so that the corks are always kept moist and evaporation prevented. The ideal temperature is between 50° and 55°F. (10–13°C.). When serving wines, red table varieties are served at room temperature, white and sparkling wines are cooled. Port may be served either way, sherry is sometimes cooled.

Certain traditions of wine drinking exist but if you like it a different way, drink what you like when you like it. Red wine is generally best with meat or poultry. Champagne, hock, or Moselle go with any course in the meal. A sweet white wine is best kept for the sweet course or dessert though many women like it throughout the meal. Dry white wines are best with fish and *hors-d'œuvre*. Any wine can be served with cheese, though many people prefer a red wine, or Madeira.

WINES AND SPIRITS FOR COOKING

The wines most frequently used in cooking are red and white table wines, sherry, Madeira, Marsala, port wine, cider, rum, brandy, and liqueurs. Dry cider is used in the same way as white wine, and can be substituted for it in any recipe.

In Soups

Add just before serving; to clear or cream soups, add Italian vermouth, Madeira, Marsala, or sherry; to turtle soup add sherry or Madeira; to oxtail soup add Madeira or port wine; to game soups, port wine.

In Fish Dishes

Dry white wine or cider is the best to use, either for cooking the fish in, or to add to the sauce. For fish to be eaten cold, sprinkle the wine over it about 30 mins. before serving.

With Meat and Game

Red wine or port wine are the chief ones, though sherry is used with chicken, kidney, and veal dishes. Add the wine to sauces and gravies, use as part of the liquid in stews and casseroles, and to mix the stuffing for poultry.

In Fruit Salads

Use a liqueur, brandy, rum, or cider. Do not use too much syrup with the fruit or it will take a lot of liqueur to have any effect on the flavour. Kirsch, Cointreau, or Grand Marnier are the best liqueurs.

With Cold Sweets

For jellies, trifles, mousse, sauces and ice-cream, use liqueurs, rum, brandy. Crème de cacao goes well in cold coffee and chocolate sweets. Maraschino and apricot and cherry brandy are other good ones.

Flambé

Or flaming, i.e. setting light to alcohol on food. Spirits are used for this because of the high alcohol content necessary for a good flame. Those most often used are brandy and rum, used with pancakes, fruit, Christmas Pudding, meat, and fish dishes. The spirit is either poured round the food and then lighted and spooned over it, or else a metal ladle is heated, the spirit put in, set alight, and then poured over the food.

BEER OR ALE

Beer is made from a mixture of barley, water, and sugar with yeast added to produce fermentation. Hops are added for flavour and for the resins they contain. These have preservative and antiseptic properties and help the beer to keep well.

Varieties of beer include:

Mild

This usually has the lowest alcohol content of all beers, about 3 per cent.

Bitter

Draught pale ale (beer) usually contains more alcohol.

Best Bitter

A stronger bitter (more alcohol), the strength varying with the brewery.

Light Ale

Filtered and chilled bitter.

Stout

Flavoured and coloured with toasted malt, and has about 4 per cent alcohol, though stouts vary widely in content and name.

Lager

Has a higher alcoholic content than most other beers.

Porter

A draught stout.

Lager is the only beer which is not spoilt by being served chilled. Most British beers are made to be served between 55–58°F. (13–14°C.).

In addition to alcohol, most beers contain some carbohydrate, protein, calcium, and vitamins of the B complex. A pint of beer will provide about two-thirds of the requirements of nicotinic acid for a moderately active man. Beer and bread and cheese make a good meal nutritionally provided that some source of vitamin C is added, e.g. tomatoes, watercress, spring onions.

BEER AND STOUT FOR COOKING

The best to use for this are sweetish draught strong ales, barley wine, or stout. Very light beers and bitter beers are not so good. Beer and stout can be used in most recipes to replace wine or cider, the flavour naturally being different, though pleasant, especially with the more robust dishes, e.g. beef and game.

Suitable ways of using beer are:

Soups

To thick brown meat or game soups add 4 Tbs. per pt. ($\frac{1}{2}$ l.) of soup, just before serving.

Fish

Poach in beer or stout and thicken the liquid for a sauce. Especially good with herring or mackerel.

Meat

In stews and casseroles substitute up to half the normal liquid with ale or stout, for basting roast gammon or ham. Also use ale or stout for basting lamb during roasting.

Cakes

Use stout for mixing fruit cake and gingerbread.

Puddings

Use stout for mixing steamed fruit puddings, especially Christmas Puddings.

GLOSSARY OF ALCOHOLIC BEVERAGES

ACQUAVIT or Akvavit or Aquavit   These are spirits of a fairly high proof, colourless, and flavoured with aniseed or other herbs.

AMONTILLADO   Is a pale dry sherry with a little more alcohol than the average sherry.

AMOROSO   A pale sweet sherry.

ANGOSTURA BITTERS   A spirit made from rum with a mixture of herbs used for flavouring including angostura bark and sandalwood. It is used to make the pink in 'pink gin'.

ANISETTE   A liqueur, coming mainly from France and Holland. A colourless spirit sweetened and flavoured with aniseed.

APPLE JACK   An American brandy made from cider.

APRICOT BRANDY   A liqueur tasting of apricots and brandy. 'Abricotine' has a special flavour derived from small apricots grown in the valleys of the Isle de France.

ARMAGNAC   A brandy distilled from grapes grown in Armagnac in the south-west of France. Its characteristics are derived from the soil in which the grapes are grown, a sub-soil of limestone. It is stored in casks made from black oak from which it gets its colour.

AROMATIC GENEVA   A liqueur made from very old Geneva or gin flavoured with aromatic herbs. It should be served ice-cold from the refrigerator but should not have ice put in it. It is taken as an aperitif with bitters and olives, salted almonds, or potato crisps. Also taken as a 'nightcap'.

ARRACK   Originally made from fermented and distilled juice of the coconut palm but now made from many different materials.

ATHOLL BROSE   A Scottish drink made of honey, oatmeal, and whisky.

BARLEY WINE   The original English name for beer, now used for a brand of very strong beer.

BAROLO   A red Italian wine from Piedmont and one of the best Italian wines.

BARSAC   A sweet white French wine, a Sauterne.

BEAUNE   A red wine from certain vineyards in Burgundy.

BENEDICTINE   A liqueur made by the Benedictine monks in 1510 and to a secret formula, using herbs for flavouring.

BITTERS   Spirits flavoured with herbs and used to give a tang to cocktails.

BLACK VELVET   A mixture of equal quantities of stout and champagne.

BORDEAUX   White and red wines from the district of Bordeaux in France and including many of the best-known French wines.

BOURBON WHISKY   An American whisky made from wheat, barley, or maize.

BRANDY   A spirit distilled from wine.

BURGUNDY   White or red wines from the district of Burgundy in France. White varieties include Chablis, Mersault, and Pouilly-Fuissée. Red ones include Beaujolais.

CALVADOS   A French brandy made from apples in the Calvados district of Normandy, the main cider district of France.

CASSIS   A French aperitif made from brandy, sugar, and blackcurrant juice, often served with vermouth. It is also the name of a wine drunk in Marseilles with the fish soup *bouillabaisse*.

CHABLIS   A white Burgundy.

CHAMPAGNE   An effervescent (contains carbon dioxide) white wine made in the Champagne district in France.

CHARTREUSE   A liqueur originally made by the Carthusian monks at La Grande Chartreuse monastery, Grenoble, France. Green Chartreuse is 96° proof and yellow 75° proof.

CHERRY BRANDY   An infusion of cherries and brandy. Morello cherries are the usual variety. Two of the most famous are the Danish Cherry Heering and the Dutch one made by Weduive Avarden Eelaart.

CHIANTI   The most well-known Italian wine, the red chianti being considered better than the white.

CIDER   A wine made from apples, special tart cider apples. Made in many countries including Britain.

CLARET   A red wine of the Bordeaux district.

COCKTAILS   Mixtures of alcoholic beverages drunk as aperitifs before a meal. They usually have a high alcoholic content.

COGNAC   A brandy distilled from grapes grown in Cognac. The presence of much chalk in the soil is responsible for the fine flavour. The soil varies in different parts of the district and produces different qualities and flavours of brandy. It is matured in casks made of a special oak which contributes to the colour and taste. The longer it is kept in the cask the finer the colour and aroma.

COINTREAU   A colourless liqueur with an orange flavour.

CRÈME DE CACAO   A cocoa-flavoured and coloured liqueur produced in France and Holland.

CRÈME DE MENTHE   A liqueur with a peppermint flavour. It may be colourless, green, or pink. It is good served 'frappé' with crushed ice, and drunk through a straw.

CRÈME DE NOYAUX   A colourless or pale pink liqueur with a strong almond flavour produced by using cherry stones.

CURAÇAO   A liqueur flavoured with orange and either colourless or orange-coloured. It came originally from the island of Curaçao in the West Indies. Now many similar liqueurs are made: Cointreau, Grand Marnier, Triple Sec, and Van der Hum.

DRAMBUIE   A Scottish liqueur made from Scotch whisky which is more than ten years old.

EAU-DE-VIE   A variety of brandy. In Italy known as *grappa*.

FENDANT   A white Swiss wine.

FINO   A dry sherry.

FLIPS   A mixture of beaten eggs, wines, or spirit with sugar.

FRAMBOISE   A liqueur flavoured with raspberries and made in Alsace.

GIN   Diluted alcohol flavoured with juniper berries and sometimes other flavourings.

GRAND ARMAGNAC   The best of Armagnacs.

GRAND MARNIER   An orange-flavoured liqueur made from brandy.

GRAPPA   See *Eau-de-vie*.

GRAVES   Bordeaux wines, red and white, from the district of Graves, the most usual one in Britain being white Graves.

GROG   See page 100.

HOCK   A generic term used in Britain for German white wines.

HOLLANDS GENEVA   Dutch gin.

IZARRA   A Basque liqueur, being a distillation of flowers of the Pyrenees with Armagnac. There are both yellow and green varieties.

JOHN COLLINS   A long drink made with gin, the juice of 2 oranges, and 1 lemon with soda water.

KIRSCH   A colourless liqueur with a bitter almond flavour got from the kernels of cherries.

KÜMMEL   A liqueur flavoured with caraway seeds and made chiefly in Holland.

LA VIELLE CURE   A liqueur from Bordeaux, dark gold in colour and made by infusing herbs in Armagnac and cognac. It has been made by monks since the Middle Ages.

LIQUEURS   Sweetened, flavoured, and sometimes coloured spirits. They are usually drunk at the end of a meal with the coffee.

MADEIRA   A fortified wine from the island of Madeira. Used as a dessert wine.

MÁLAGA   A very dark Spanish dessert wine.

MALMSEY   A dark, sweet, strong Madeira wine.

MANZANILLA   A dry sherry.

MARASCHINO   A liqueur made in Italy and Yugoslavia, from the kernel of the Marasca cherry. Cherries preserved in maraschino are used for cocktails and for garnishing. The liqueur is used for flavouring ices, icings, fruit cocktails, and jellies.

MARSALA   A sweet brown dessert wine made in Italy from grapes grown in Sicily. The flavour of the wine is fairly strong and this is made use of in cookery. It is the wine used in the Italian sweet, *zabaglione*, and the Italians also use it for flavouring other sweet dishes, including ice-cream, and for cooking meat and making sauces. It can be used in the same way as sherry, in trifles, sauces, etc.

MARTINI   A cocktail made of gin and French vermouth, and chilled.

MEAD   A wine made from honey.

MÉDOC   A district in Bordeaux famous for clarets.

MIRABELLE   A liqueur made from wild cherries.

97

MOSELLE or Mosel   White German wines from the district round the Mosel river.

MUSCADEL   Portuguese wine made from muscat grapes which have a characteristic flavour.

OLOROSO SHERRY   A sweet, dark sherry.

ORVIETO   An Italian white wine which may be sweet or dry.

OUZO   A Greek spirit flavoured with aniseed.

PERNOD   A proprietary brand of Absinthe, a spirit flavoured with wormwood which has toxic properties when taken in too large amounts.

PERRY   A wine made from pears.

POMMARD   A red wine from Burgundy.

PORT   A red wine made in Portugal and very popular in Britain.

PROOF SPIRIT   The term used to denote the amount of alcohol in a spirit. Those sold in Britain are 70° Proof meaning they contain 40 per cent alcohol by volume.

PUNCH   A drink made usually with alcohol, water, and flavourings, served hot or cold. Special punch bowls and ladles are made for serving it.

Swedish punch is served ice cold from the bottle and is very potent. It is served in small glasses.

Punches are also made from non-alcoholic ingredients.

QUETSCH   A liqueur made from plums.

RATAFIA   A liqueur, flavoured with the kernels of the nuts of fruit such as apricots, peaches, or cherries. It has an almond-like flavour.

RED WINES are made from black grapes.

RETSINA   A Greek wine flavoured with resin.

RHINE WINE   German wine from vineyards on the banks of the river Rhine.

RIESLING   A German white wine made from the Riesling grape, now also grown in other countries.

ROSÉ   Pink wine usually made by light pressing of red grapes and then quick fermentation.

RUDESHEIM   See *Rhine Wine*.

RUM   A spirit made from molasses from sugar cane.

RYE WHISKY   American whisky made by malting rye or barley.

SAKÉ   A Japanese alcoholic drink made from rice.

SAUTERNE   A sweet white Bordeaux wine.

SHERRY   Wine fortified with brandy. True sherry is made only in a small area of Spain near Cadiz. The name of sherry is derived from the town of Jerez.

SPIRITS Beverages containing 40 per cent or more of alcohol by volume, and include whisky, rum, brandy, gin, vodka, and liqueurs.

TIA MARIA A liqueur from Jamaica made of rum, spices, and coffee.

TODDY A drink made by fermenting the sap of a number of palms.

TOKAY A sweet Hungarian wine made by fermenting over-ripe grapes.

TRAPPESTINE A French liqueur made by the monks of the Abbaye de Grâce de Dieu. It is made on a base of Armagnac with fresh-gathered herbs from the mountains near Doubs.

VALDEPEÑAS Dry red and white Spanish wines.

VAN DER HUM An orange-coloured and flavoured liqueur made in South Africa.

VERMOUTH A herb wine, fortified with spirit and containing added sugar and colouring.

VODKA A spirit made from rye or potato, chiefly in Russia and Poland.

WHISKY A spirit made from barley.

WHITE WINE Made by fermenting either white grapes or skinned black grapes.

WINE-BASED DRINKS

WINE CUPS

These are cold long drinks with a wine basis and there are many possible combinations.

Claret Cup

 2 *tsp. mixed spice*   1 *oz. caster sugar (2 Tbs. or 25 g.)*
 1 *bottle claret*   ½ *pt. cold water (¼ l.)*

Mix these together until the sugar is dissolved.

     ½ *small lemon*

Peel the rind very thinly and add to the cup. Chill before serving.

Hock Cup

  1 *oz. sugar (2 Tbs. or 25 g.)* ½ *lemon*
   ¼ *pt. boiling water (150 ml.)*

Peel the lemon rind thinly and put in a jug with the sugar and water. Allow to infuse for 15 mins.

1 *small glass sherry*   ½ *pt. water* (¼ *l.*)
1 *bottle hock or chablis*

Add to the first mixture and stand for 30 mins. Strain and chill well before serving.

MULLED WINE
Temperature E.375° (190°C.), G.5.

1 *dessert apple*

Bake the apple for 10 mins.

A pinch of mixed spice   2 *Tbs. honey*
2 *Tbs. sweet sherry*   1 *bottle red wine*

Put in a pan and heat until almost boiling. Serve with the apple floating on top. It should be served in a large bowl with a ladle to use for filling the glasses.

GROG
Quantities for 1.

1 *slice of lemon*   1 *tsp. brown sugar*

Put these in a heat-resistant tumbler.

Boiling water   2 *Tbs. rum*

Fill the tumbler three-quarters full with boiling water. Stir well, and add the rum. Serve at once.

CHERRY GIN
1 *lb. Morello cherries* (½ *kg.*)   8 *oz. caster sugar* (250 *g.*)

Wash cherries and remove stalks. Put fruit in layers with the sugar in screw-top jars. Screw down and leave to stand for 3 days, shaking occasionally.

12 *blanched almonds*   1 *bottle gin* (1¼ *pt. or* ¾ *l.*)

Add the almonds and gin and leave for at least 3 months before decanting.

SLOE GIN
½ *pt. sloes* (¼ *l.*)

Wash and prick each with a darning needle putting them into an empty gin bottle.

6 *oz. sugar* (¾ *c. or* 150 *g.*)   3 *drops almond essence*
Add to the sloes.

¾ *pt. gin* (5 *dl.*)

Add the gin and cork well. Leave for at least 3 months before decanting.

STORING FOOD

Three different types of food storage are required. You need a dry cupboard, drawers, or storage jars in which to keep such foods as flour, sugar, and cereals; for the second type you need cool storage for things like vegetables and fruit; and the third need is for cold storage for perishable foods like milk, cream, butter, meat, fish, left-overs, and foods prepared in advance of cooking time.

While most things requiring cool storage can go in cold storage, the usual cool storage, which is a larder, is seldom cold enough all the year round to make an adequate substitute for cold or refrigerated storage.

In any kitchen, steam and condensation are the main obstacles to having really dry store cupboards. The solution is never to let the kitchen become really cold. If you don't have a boiler in the kitchen for hot water and heating, keep a small amount of background heating of some other type. Also essential is good ventilation to carry steam away, best done by an extractor fan.

In the following pages I have given approximate storage times for different kinds of foods, but these will vary depending on how fresh the food is when you buy it. Try and buy all food, but particularly perishable foods, from shops which date-stamp these foods to show when they should be eaten.

STORAGE TEMPERATURES
Cool storage or cold larder 54°F. (12°C.)
Refrigerator   36–46°F. (2–8°C.)
Freezer   0°F. (−18°C.)

FOODS FOR STORING IN COOL, DRY CUPBOARDS OR IN CONTAINERS

For more than 6 months	Up to 6 months	2–3 months	Less than 2 months
Anchovy essence	Cake mixes	Baking powder	Breakfast cereals
Canned foods (except ham)	Canned hams	Bicarbonate of soda	Cocoa
Chutneys	Condensed milk	Candied peel	Coffee
Colourings	Flour	Chocolate	Instant beverages
Essences	Gelatine	Cornflour	Milk, dried whole
Evaporated milk	Herbs, dried	Cream of tartar	Nuts, shelled
Extracts, meat and yeast	Jellies	Custard powder	Sugar, brown
Golden syrup	Spices	Fruits, dried or glacé	Sugar, icing
Gravy browning	Yeast, dried	Honey	Tea
Haricot beans		Meat cubes	
Jams and marmalade		Milk, dried, skimmed	
Lentils		Patent milk drinks	
Pasta		Sauces, bottled	
Peas, dried		Vinegar	
Pepper			
Pickles			
Rice			
Semolina			
Sugar (except brown and icing)			
Treacle			
Worcester sauce			

FOODS REQUIRING REFRIGERATED STORAGE

DAIRY FOODS

Fresh milk and cream
Yogurt, cultured creams, and butter milk

Opened canned, sterilised, or U.H.T. milk and cream
Eggs in the shell or separated
Cottage and cream cheeses
Butter and other fats

FISH

All raw, cooked, thawing, and thawed fish and shellfish
Open cans of fish and shellfish
Made-up fish dishes such as fish pie, fish cakes, and so on

FRUIT AND VEGETABLES

Soft fruits
Salad vegetables
Green vegetables and fresh herbs
Cooked vegetables

MEAT

All raw, cooked, thawing and thawed meat, game, poultry, and
    offal
Made-up dishes containing any of these, pies, casseroles,
    sandwiches, and so on

PUDDINGS

Any made with milk or cream
Any made with gelatine and jellies
Custards and other cold egg puddings

SAUCES AND SOUPS

All except unopened canned and packet ones, or bottled sauces

REFRIGERATED STORAGE

The simplest refrigerator consists of a storage cabinet which
is kept at 36–46°F. (2–8°C.). It usually has a drawer for
storing salad vegetables, and a compartment for making ice
cubes and ice-cream. This compartment is also suitable for
storing frozen foods for 24–36 hrs., but is not cold enough to
keep them longer. For this, a freezer compartment or a separate freezer is essential.

Most modern refrigerators have a freezer compartment.
Those marked with three stars are capable of freezing small
quantities of food and storing food purchased already frozen
for 3 months; two-star models will keep food for one month

but are not cold enough to freeze it yourself; one-star compartments will keep frozen food for a week.

The more sophisticated modern domestic refrigeration consists of a combination of three units in one: a cold store for fruit, vegetables, and drinks; a refrigerator; and a freezer. Cost, kitchen space, catering and shopping habits, are all important in deciding which kind of refrigerator storage is the best to have.

HOW TO USE THE REFRIGERATOR

Don't attempt to store any food which is not fresh and in good condition. A refrigerator won't make bad food good.

And never put warm food in a refrigerator in the mistaken belief that it will cool more quickly. Warm food will raise the temperature of other food in the cabinet, and cause steaming and dampness. It is much better to allow food to cool to room temperature first. This can be hastened by standing the food in a container surrounded by iced water, or by putting the food in a cold draught.

Cover all food to prevent evaporation. Uncovered food becomes dry, causes frost to form, and allows flavours to mix so that foods acquire a 'refrigerator' taste.

Suitable ways of storing foods are in covered casseroles, polythene bags and boxes, any container with a piece of foil as a lid, wrapped in foil, or in polyester film wrapping to use in the same way as foil. Foods which are sold in bottles and other containers can be stored in these, but if the seal is broken, cover with foil or other protection. Any glass, china, earthenware, enamel, or steel container with a lid is suitable.

Be careful not to pack the refrigerator so tight with food that cold air cannot circulate freely, and follow the maker's instructions for the best method of defrosting and cleaning.

Placing the Food

The coldest part is directly under the ice-making compartment, and the cold air moves downwards from here. In this part place meat, fish, casseroles of cooked meat, left-overs, and meat and fish dishes which have been prepared in advance. The less-cold parts are where the current of air rises after having moved down from the ice compartment. Racks on the door of the refrigerator are also less-cold parts. In these parts store milk, cream, drinks, fats, butter, eggs, cheese, jellies, other cold sweets, salads and vegetables, and fruit.

HOW TO STORE DIFFERENT KINDS OF FOOD

BACON

Store rashers in foil or polythene. They will keep 2–3 days in a larder, 7–10 days in the refrigerator. Store bacon joints in the same way.

Cooked bacon and ham should be cooled quickly and then closely wrapped. It will keep in the refrigerator for 5–6 days. If purchased sliced, it should be used up within 24 hrs., or according to the date stamp on vacuum packs.

BISCUITS

Store in airtight containers in a dry cupboard. A cupboard above a refrigerator is ideal, because warm air rises continually and keeps the cupboard dry.

BREAD

Wrapped bread or rolls should be left in the wrappers, as these are designed to prevent the bread from staling. Soft-crust bread and rolls purchased unwrapped can be stored in polythene bags. Crisp, crusty bread and rolls are best eaten while they are very fresh, and any method of storage leads to a softening of the crust.

No advantage is to be gained by storing bread in a refrigerator, except that it retards the growth of mould. It does not arrest staling, and may even hasten it.

Boxes and bins for storing bread should have some ventilation, and should be kept in a cool dry place. Stone crocks are amongst the oldest type used, and still one of the best.

Be sure that stale crusts are not allowed to accumulate in the bin, or they will become mouldy and infect the new bread. Turn out the contents weekly and wash, scald, and dry the bin thoroughly.

BUTTER

Sweet butter keeps longer than lactic butter, and salted keeps longer than unsalted. It keeps best in a cold dark place. Keep it in its wrapper and well away from strong-smelling foods. If possible, put the butter in a plastic bag or in a plastic or other container with a fitting lid. For table use, take out enough for one meal a short while beforehand, to allow it to come to room temperature.

Butter should keep 1–2 weeks in the refrigerator and in the larder for 3–4 days, or longer depending on the kind.

CAKES

If cakes are not going to be eaten the day they are made, it is essential to have an airtight container in which to store them. This might be a tin with a tight lid, or a polythene box if you have one, with a lid that really fits tightly. Cakes with a cream, egg, or gelatine filling should be stored in the refrigerator, in a polythene bag or box.

Some cakes are better not eaten for a few days after making as they improve with storage – especially cakes made with syrup, treacle, or honey. Storage softens them and makes the crumb more moist and pleasant to eat.

Most cakes will deep-freeze very satisfactorily, and this is the best way of keeping them for long periods. Some, such as sponges, are often improved by freezing (see page 214).

Very rich cakes, like a Christmas or wedding cake, are often stored for a month before using, again in an airtight tin. The idea is that the flavour has time to mellow.

It is not wise to try and store different varieties of cakes in the same container as flavours mix, and if crisp things are stored with soft ones the crisp ones will soon lose their crispness. This applies particularly to items like biscuits and meringues. If these are well baked until dry and stored in airtight tins, they will keep in good condition for weeks.

CANNED FOODS

They should be kept in a cool dry place, but do not need refrigeration. Canned fish, such as sardines, keep better if the tins are turned over occasionally to make sure the oil remains mixed with the contents. If you buy new stocks before the old are finished, make sure that the old come to the front of the cupboard to be used first.

The times that canned foods may be kept safely vary, the best keepers being meat and fish, which will remain in good condition up to five years, always provided they are properly stored and the tins are undamaged. Canned hams are an

106

exception, and their life is short. Those under 2lb. (1 kg.) in weight should be kept in a refrigerator for safety. Fish in tomato sauce is another exception and is best used up within a year.

Canned vegetables will keep for two years without losing flavour and appearance. Milk and fruit are best used within 12 months. After this milk is inclined to change colour, and acid fruit may react with the tin to produce hydrogen gas which is harmless but makes the contents smell.

CEREALS (rice, oats, etc.)
For long storage an airtight container is necessary. For short storage, leave in the packets but keep the tops closed.

CHEESE
Wrap it loosely in a polythene bag or in aluminium foil, and put it in a cool place or in the refrigerator. Remove from the refrigerator 1 hr. before using, and allow it to come back to room temperature. Grated cheese can be stored in a glass jar, covered loosely, and in a cool dry place or refrigerator. Shake the jar occasionally. If the cheese is purchased in a box or wrapper, store in this.

Keep soft cheese in the container in a cool larder for 24 hrs., or in the refrigerator for up to a week.

CONDIMENTS
Keep in covered containers in a cool place.

CREAM
Fresh cream in covered jars or containers will keep for 24 hrs. in a cool larder, 3–4 days in a refrigerator. For longer keeping, buy sterilised cream (keeps 2 years), U.H.T. (keeps 2–3 months), or canned. Cultured or soured cream will keep 1–2 days in the larder, 7–10 days in the refrigerator. Double 'extended life' cream will keep 2–3 weeks, and clotted cream 3–4 days, in a refrigerator.

DRINKS
Keep a few bottles of those to be served cold stored in the refrigerator. Coffee and tea should be stored in airtight containers. Cocoa, drinking chocolate, and other proprietary drinks sold in powder form should be stored in the original

containers with the lid on. Keep in a cool dry place, but not in the refrigerator.

EGGS

They need to be kept in a cool place, not too dry, or the moisture will tend to evaporate through the shell. A cold larder is suitable, or a refrigerator. Keep the eggs standing upright in their boxes with the broad end uppermost, as this helps to keep the yolk in the middle. Keep away from strong smells, because these can get through the porous shells and taint the egg. Under proper storage conditions the eggs should keep for 1–2 weeks.

Hard-boiled eggs can be kept for a day in a cool larder, or a week in the refrigerator; leave them in the shell.

A broken egg or separated eggs should only be stored if you have a refrigerator. They should be covered closely, and it helps to preserve yolks if a little cold water is put on top of them. Whole eggs and yolks will keep 1–2 days, but whites will keep a few days longer.

Stuffed eggs and egg salads should only be kept in a refrigerator, covered, and for not more than 2–4 hrs.

FATS

Keep away from foods which have a strong flavour, for fats readily absorb flavours. In a refrigerator, keep fat covered, either in its original wrapper, or in foil, or in a plastic box, or in other container with a lid. This is specially important with butter. Far too many catering establishments are careless about storing butter, and serve it up tasting of all the left-overs which have also been stored uncovered in their refrigerators. Fats all need to be kept cool and away from strong lights, as heat and light help to turn them rancid. If dripping is to be kept for any length of time it should be clarified.

The keeping times vary with the kind of fat but they should keep in good condition in a refrigerator for 2–3 weeks.

FISH

Freshly-caught fish will keep for 1–2 days in a cold larder, but fish from a shop (unless frozen) should be used the same day, or stored not more than 24 hrs. in a covered dish in the coldest part of the refrigerator. Freshly-caught fish will keep 3–4 days in the refrigerator. It can be wrapped closely in foil.

Don't store cooked fish in the larder, but put it in a covered dish in the refrigerator. Use within 2–3 days, or the same day if it has been mixed with mayonnaise or a sauce. If you haven't a freezer, frozen fish can be kept for 2 days in the refrigerator in its original wrapping.

Smoked fish, foil-wrapped, will keep 1 day in a larder, 2 days in the refrigerator.

Shellfish should be used up on the day of purchase.

FRUIT (dried)

Store unopened packets in a dry cupboard. Put fruit purchased loose, or an opened packet, in a covered container.

FRUIT (fresh)

Inspect all fruit frequently to see that none has started to go bad, for mould spreads very rapidly. Home-grown *apples and pears* can be kept for 3–4 months if they are wrapped individually in paper and stored in boxes in a single layer in a cool dark place. If you have a special refrigerator for fruit and vegetables, apples, pears, and other fruits can be stored there, but not for more than 1–2 weeks.

Bananas should be stored at ordinary room temperature. Never put them in the refrigerator unless they are peeled and mixed with other ingredients, such as in ice-cream or other cold sweets.

Oranges and grapefruit should keep for a week in a larder, and for two weeks in a polythene bag in the refrigerator.

Soft fruit should be picked over carefully and spread out on a flat dish. They will keep for a day in the larder, or 2–3 days in the refrigerator if in a covered box, or put the dish in a polythene bag.

Stone fruits should keep for 1–3 days in a larder, depending on how ripe they are, and 3–7 days in a box or polythene bag in the refrigerator.

Lemons can be stored at room temperature, but the skins will gradually become hard and dry even though the inside will remain juicy. A better way of keeping them is in a polythene bag in the refrigerator. They should keep 2–3 weeks, depending on quality.

Melons are best stored at room temperature. If cut, cover closely with foil and store in the refrigerator, but for not more than 2–3 days.

Whole fresh *pineapple* can be kept in a cool larder and cut pineapple in a covered container in the refrigerator for 3–6 days.

Stewed fruit and opened cans of fruit can be stored in a cold larder for 1–2 days; or 3–6 days in a covered dish in the refrigerator.

GAME

Fresh game is often hung for a week or so in a cool larder to develop the desired flavour. Game purchased ready for cooking will keep 3–4 days in the refrigerator. If it is smelly, it is best to wrap closely in foil to protect other foods in the cabinet.

HERBS

Keep dried herbs in airtight bottles in a dry cupboard, or on a kitchen shelf.

Wash fresh herbs, put the stems in water, and keep them in a cool place. Otherwise, drain well and put in polythene bags in the refrigerator where they will keep for at least a week.

MEAT

Always keep meat in the coolest possible place, preferably in a refrigerator, and only buy it from a shop where it is displayed in clean, cold conditions, away from flies and dust. The length of time that raw meat will keep depends on its freshness when purchased, and on the storage facilities available.

If only a larder is available for storage, wrap the meat in muslin and hang it from a hook, or put it on a plate and cover with a metal meat cover, or with muslin, but arrange the muslin so that it does not touch the meat or flies will be able to get at it through the muslin. In the refrigerator, put raw meat in the chiller tray immediately under the freezing unit, or on a plate under the unit. Put a loose piece of aluminium foil on top. It is unwise to shut meat up in a covered container except for very short periods, as this tends to encourage souring and 'off' flavours.

Cooked meat should be stored in a larder in the same way as recommended for raw meat. In the refrigerator, wrap it in polythene, or put it in a polythene box, or wrap it in foil.

APPROXIMATE SAFE STORAGE TIMES

Raw joints   2 days in cold larder; 4–5 days in refrigerator.

Steaks and chops   1 day in larder; 3–4 days in refrigerator.

Stewing meat   1 day in larder; 2–3 days in refrigerator.

Minced meat   use the same day, or keep 1 day in refrigerator.

Offal   use the same day, or keep 1–2 days in refrigerator.

Sausages   use the same day, or keep 3–4 days in refrigerator.

Sliced bacon   2–3 days in larder; 7–10 days in refrigerator.

Cooked joints   2–3 days in larder; 3–5 days in refrigerator.

Sliced cooked meat (from shop)   use the same day, or keep 1 day in refrigerator.

Sliced cooked meat (home-cooked)   2–3 days in refrigerator.

Cooked casseroles or left-overs   2–3 days in refrigerator.

Pâtés and Spreads   1 day to a week in the refrigerator depending on the kind; *pâtés* keep better than spreads containing sauces and salad dressing.

MILK

Milk should always be kept in as cool a place as possible. If no refrigerator or cold larder is available, stand the milk bottle in a bowl of cold water with a piece of wet muslin over it, with the ends in the water. Stand it in a cool draught, and the water will slowly evaporate from the muslin and cause cooling.

Special porous pots are made to fit over a bottle and stand in water to perform the same job.

If the milk comes in bottles or cartons it is best not to tip it out into jugs until it is to be used. Wipe the outside of the bottle before doing this. Replace the cap if there is still some milk in the bottle, or use one of the caps sold for this purpose. Any jug or container for milk must be very clean, and should be washed out in cold and then hot water, and finally rinsed with very hot water, then turned upside down to dry, and stored upside down. Milk should always be protected from dust and flies, including flies crawling over the bottles. And it should not be left in sun or strong light, because this reduces the riboflavin content, and can bring about a total loss. As milk is one of the most important sources of this vitamin in the average diet, such a loss is serious. If you have to leave milk on the doorstep for some time provide a covered box or other covered container for the milkman to put the bottles in,

Keeping Times

Pasteurised and Homogenised keeps for 1–2 days in a cool place, and 2–3 days in a refrigerator. Sterilised for 1 or more weeks, and U.H.T. for several months.

Untreated milk can be kept 1 day in a cool place, and 2–3 days in a refrigerator.

PASTRY AND PIES

Raw pastry ready for rolling can be stored for a day or two in the refrigerator. Ready-mixes in packets should be stored in a cool cupboard, and home-made ones in a polythene bag or box in the refrigerator. Pies with meat, fish, or egg filling should be stored in the refrigerator, and not for more than 2–3 days. Store fruit pies in a cool larder or in the refrigerator, where they should keep from 3–5 days.

POULTRY

Fresh poultry (preferably hung up, as with meat) will keep for 2–4 days in a cold larder; in the refrigerator in a polythene bag a chicken will keep 3–4 days and a goose or turkey for a week. Pre-prepared stuffing should be stored in the refrigerator separately, and only put in the bird just before cooking. Cooked poultry should have the stuffing removed, be cooled quickly, and then wrapped and stored in the refrigerator. It will keep for 2–3 days.

PRESERVES

Store in a cool dry cupboard. Unless it is to be used up in a day or so, canned jam is best turned out into another container.

PUDDINGS

Cold puddings made with milk, eggs, cream, or jelly should be stored in the refrigerator for not more than 2 days, Steamed and baked puddings can be kept for 24 hrs. in a cold larder, longer in the refrigerator (see *Pastry* and *Fruit*).

SAUCES AND SALAD DRESSINGS

Store bottled sauces in a cool, dry cupboard. Other sauces should be put in containers, cooled quickly, covered, and stored in the refrigerator for not more than 1–2 days for those made with stock. Mayonnaise will keep up to 2 weeks (home-made, or opened bottle).

SOUPS AND STOCK
Keep packet and canned ones in a cool dry cupboard. Put others in a container, cool quickly, cover, and store in the refrigerator for not more than 1–2 days for soups. Stocks can be kept for a week, but make sure they have a good boiling before they are used.

SPICES
Store in small, airtight containers in a dry cupboard, or on a kitchen shelf away from steam.

STEWS AND CASSEROLES
Cool quickly, cover, and store in the refrigerator. Use up within 2–3 days and, for safety, boil for a few minutes before serving.

SUGARS, HONEY, AND SYRUP
Store in a cool, dry place. Once a packet of sugar has been opened it is better to tip the remainder into a covered container and keep it in a dry place.

VEGETABLES
Green vegetables can be washed, drained very thoroughly, and stored in polythene bags or boxes in the refrigerator, where they will keep in good condition for a week. Otherwise keep them wrapped and cool in a dry place, where they will keep for 1–2 days.

Root vegetables and potatoes need cool, dry, and dark storage. Washed and dried root vegetables can be kept in polythene bags in the refrigerator for 7–14 days. Prepared and cut ones will keep like this for 24 hours, sometimes longer.

Cooked vegetables should be stored in covered containers in the refrigerator. If they are mixed with a sauce, use within 1–2 days. Dry, they will keep longer.

Celery for storage in a larder should be kept wrapped, cool, and dry. For storage in the refrigerator, wash, drain thoroughly, and store in a polythene box or bag, where it will keep in good condition for 3–4 days; longer if only required for cooking.

Cucumbers should be kept cool and, if cut, cover the cut end and stand the other end in a little water. In the refrigerator,

113

store in a polythene box or bag. Then, provided that they are kept dry, they will keep for a week.

Mushrooms should keep for 24 hrs. in a cold larder, spread out in a single layer. In a covered container in the refrigerator they should keep for 2–3 days; but don't wash them before storing.

Onions and garlic of good quality will keep many weeks in a cool, dry place. Some people like to hang them up as a kitchen decoration, but don't put them in a steamy corner.

Peas and beans (shelled) will keep in a covered container or polythene bag in the refrigerator for 24 hrs. In the larder, leave them in their shells, but use them as soon as possible for best flavour.

Salad vegetables should be stored as green vegetables (see above). A few hours in the refrigerator improves all salad greens and, even after a week, good-quality ones will be good enough for a salad. Be careful when washing not to bruise them and to drain them very well or they will quickly brown and rot.

Tomatoes, if they are firm, will keep for several days in a cool larder. Put them in a single layer and inspect regularly. In a polythene bag or box, washed and dried, they will keep for 1–2 weeks in the refrigerator.

In general, vegetables retain their nutritive value well if stored so as to keep them in good condition. It is when they wilt, rot, or become soft and wrinkled that their value deteriorates.

YOGURT

Leave in the original container. It will keep 1–2 days in a cold larder; 7–10 days in a refrigerator. If a cap has been broken, cover with a fresh lid of foil.

Chapter Four

MEAL PREPARATION AND MANAGEMENT

MEAL PLANNING

To make a good job of family catering, forethought and planning are needed. The hand-to-mouth existence of the meal-at-a-time plan is not likely to provide interesting and varied meals, and is still less likely to provide healthy ones. The weekly plan is the best unit for most people, and a week starting on Thursday or Friday the most easily worked. This allows for one big shopping day to cover the basic needs of the week, the amount of possible advance shopping obviously depending on circumstances such as storage facilities and transport of goods (see pages 44 and 101).

It is unlikely that the week's plan will be followed in all details, as unforeseen events such as visitors, meals out, food unavailable or too dear, all necessitate last-minute changes. But the plan helps to reduce the time and worry of daily planning. The busier a woman is, the more useful such a plan can be.

Not only can food be bought in advance, but it may also be prepared in advance. While one meal is cooking, food can be partly prepared for the next meal and, if adequate refrigerator or freezer space is available, for further ahead than this.

How does one make a start with what can seem a daunting task? The best thing to do is to get a piece of paper large enough to hold an outline of meals for the week and rule it thus:

Meals	Fri.	Sat.	Sun.	Mon.	Tue.	Wed.	Thur.
Breakfast							
Midday							
Evening							

The number of meals depends on family customs and convenience. Three meals are enough for most people, except those with very small appetites, and those with specially large needs.

If yours is a household where week-end cooking is the most important, start with planning the meals for Saturday and Sunday, and work sideways from there.

When the scheme for the week has been made out, check it for the following points:

1. Have you planned meals which you can easily cook in the available time, e.g. if there is a complicated dish, or you plan to try a new recipe, are all the other items familiar and easy ones to do?

2. Is there variety of texture, flavour, and colour to make the meals interesting, and is there something in each which requires chewing (especially important for children)?

3. Have you included the basic daily and weekly foods recommended for good nutrition (see page 147)?

WHAT IS AVAILABLE, WHEN

We are fortunate, in Britain, in having most foods available throughout the year, either fresh or preserved. Nevertheless, with fresh foods, there are times of the year when some foods are more plentiful than at others, and are usually in better condition, and cheaper. Some foods never are cheap for those on a low budget, and these are ones which are fairly scarce at any time of the year (for example, game, fresh salmon, asparagus, and shellfish).

As an aid to getting variety in your menu planning I have given some lists of fresh, home-grown, and imported, foods which are in our shops at some time during the year. Whether you see all these locally, depends on where you live and the kind of shop that you use, but I think lists of this sort are useful as memory-joggers to help to keep us out of too deep a menu-planning rut. I have listed the foods in each group in alphabetical order, and where they are seasonal, I have indicated this.

FRUIT

APPLES Imported all the year. Home-grown start in July, and continue from store until April.

116

APRICOTS   Imported from June to August, and then December to February.

BANANAS   Imported all the year, but inclined to be scarce in very cold months.

BILBERRIES   June to November.

BLACKBERRIES   July to October.

CHERRIES   June to August.

CHINESE GOOSEBERRIES   (Kiwi fruit)   Imported from September to February.

CLEMENTINES   November to mid-January.

CRANBERRIES   September to February.

CURRANTS (black, red and white)   June to August.

DAMSONS   August to October.

FIGS   June to December.

GOOSEBERRIES   May–July.

GRANADILLAS (Passion fruit)   Imported throughout the year, but mainly in the winter months.

GRAPEFRUIT   Imported all the year; best choice in winter and very early spring.

GRAPES   Imported all the year. English hot-house ready in June and July.

GREENGAGES   August.

KUMQUATS   Imported from time to time.

LEMONS   Imported all the year; at their best in the summer months.

LICHEES   Imported from January to September.

LIMES   Always scarce—imported from March to July.

LOGANBERRIES   June to August.

MANDARINS   Some available most of the year; plentiful from December to February.

MANGOES   Imported January to July, and September.

MEDLARS   October to December.

MELONS   One kind or another imported all the year; best in spring, summer, and autumn.

MULBERRIES   August and September.

NECTARINES   Imported most of the year, except October and November.

ORANGES   Imported all the year. Special seasons are: Navels November to May; Jaffas in the winter; Spanish October to July; Seville January to March.

PEACHES   Available most of the year, except October and November.

117

PEARS Imported most of the year. Home-grown August to February.

PINEAPPLES Imported all year. Large ones, October to December.

PLUMS Imported ones most of the year except November. Home-grown June to September.

POMEGRANATES Imported April, and again in September to December.

QUINCES Late autumn.

RASPBERRIES July to October.

RHUBARB December to July.

SATSUMAS October and November.

STRAWBERRIES Imported from January to July. Home-grown June to August.

TANGERINES Some available most of the year, plentiful from December to February.

VEGETABLES

ARTICHOKES, GLOBE Imported or home-grown all the year, best in the summer.

ARTICHOKES, JERUSALEM October to March.

ASPARAGUS February to May, and September to June.

AUBERGINES Imported all the year.

AVOCADO PEARS Imported most of the year; scarce from June to August.

BEANS, BROAD June to August.

BEANS, FRENCH Imported all the year; best in the summer.

BEANS, RUNNER July to October.

BEETROOT Available all the year.

BROCCOLI, SPROUTING February to May.

BROCCOLI, WHITE September to April.

BRUSSELS SPROUTS October to March.

BRUSSELS SPROUTS TOPS January to May.

CABBAGES Available all the year.

CARROTS Available all the year; young, home-grown in the spring.

CAULIFLOWERS Available all the year.

CELERIAC September to March.

CELERY Some imported most of the year; best in the autumn and winter.

CHICORY September to June.

CORN ON THE COB August to October.

118

COURGETTES   May to September.
CUCUMBERS   Available all the year; best in spring and summer.
ENDIVE   Available all the year; best in autumn and winter.
FLORENCE FENNEL   October to January, and June to March.
GARLIC   Available all the year.
KALE   November to March.
KOHL RABI   November to May.
LEEKS   September to May.
LETTUCE   Available all the year; best in spring and summer.
MUSHROOMS   Available all the year.
OKRA   Imported June to September.
ONIONS   Available all the year.
PARSNIPS   September to April.
PEAS   May to October.
POTATOES, NEW   Imported or home-grown available most of the year.
PUMPKINS   Late summer and autumn.
RADISHES   Available all the year.
SALSIFY   October to June.
SEAKALE   December to March.
SHALLOTS   October to January.
SPINACH   Available all the year.
SPRING GREENS   January to May.
SWEDES   September to May.
SWEET PEPPERS (*Capsicum*)   Available all the year; best in summer and autumn.
SWEET POTATOES   September to June.
TOMATOES   Imported all the year; home-grown April to October.
TURNIPS   Available all the year; best in spring and summer.
VEGETABLE MARROWS   June to October.
WATERCRESS   Available all the year.

FISH

The kind of fish available at any one time depends very much on weather conditions. Some fish are more seasonal than others.

BASS   May to August.
BLOATERS   Available all the year; best in summer.
BREAM   June to December.
BRILL   February to April.

119

BUCKLING   Available all the year.

COD   Available all the year; best in winter.

CONGER EEL   March to October.

CRAB   Available all the year; best in summer.

CRAWFISH   Available all the year; best in summer and autumn.

DAB   June to February

DOG FISH OR HUSS   October to June.

EELS (FRESH-WATER)   August to November.

ESCALLOPS OR SCALLOPS   October to March.

HADDOCK   July to February.

HAKE   June to February.

HALIBUT   January and February; May to September.

HERRING   Available all the year.

LEMON SOLE   July to March.

LOBSTER   Available all the year; best in summer.

MACKEREL   Available all the year; best in winter.

MULLET, GREY   Available all the year; best in summer.

MULLET, RED   May to September.

MUSSELS   March to August.

OYSTERS   September to April.

PLAICE   May to January.

PRAWNS   Available all the year; best in summer.

RED FISH   June to October.

SAITHE OR COLEY   Available all the year; best in autumn.

SALMON   May to August.

SHRIMPS   Available all the year; best in summer.

SKATE   Available all the year; best in winter.

SMELT   November to February.

SMOKED HADDOCK   Available all the year.

SMOKED SPRATS   Available all the year; best in autumn and winter.

SOLE, DOVER   Available all the year.

SPRATS   November to February.

TROUT, RIVER   Available all the year.

TROUT, SEA   June to August.

TURBOT   Available all the year; best in winter.

WHITEBAIT   February to July.

WHITING   November to February.

WITCH SOLE   August to April.

MEAT

Beef, veal, lamb, mutton, pork, offal, and poultry are available all the year round. The following have seasons when they are at their best:

ENGLISH BEEF   October to March.
ENGLISH LAMB   July to September.
NEW ZEALAND LAMB   January to June.
SCOTCH BEEF   September to December.
SCOTCH LAMB   July to October.
WELSH LAMB   July to September.

GAME

This is a group of foods which have very definite seasons, although frozen game is available most of the year, and there is some imported.

BLACKCOCK   September to December.
CAPERCAILZIE   October to January.
GROUSE   August to December.
GUINEA FOWL   January to June.
GULLS' EGGS   Available all the year.
HARE   September to February.
ORTOLAN   November to January.
PARTRIDGE   September to February.
PHEASANT   October to February.
PIGEON   Available all the year.
PLOVER   September to January.
PLOVERS' EGGS   April to May.
PTARMIGAN   August to December.
QUAIL   June to September.
RABBIT   September to February.
SNIPE   August to January.
TEAL   September to January.
VENISON   June to January.
WIDGEON   September to January.
WILD DUCK   September to January.
WOODCOCK   October to January.

THE SHOPPING LIST

Make this up from your menus, dividing it into appropriate groups such as:

Meat, game, and poultry
Fish and shellfish
Frozen foods
Cheese
Eggs
Butter and fats
Milk, cream, yogurt
Fruit and vegetables
Bread and cakes
Groceries

If you shop regularly in one supermarket, divide the list up according to the way the foods are usually stacked there, and thus save yourself many steps and much time.

PREPARING THE MEAL – HOW TO MAKE YOUR OWN STEP-BY-STEP WORKING PLAN

The beginner finds the most difficult thing about preparing a meal is to have everything ready at the right time. This is a question of planning, organisation, and experience. Provided that you are prepared to do a little planning on paper it is really very simple.

Take the menu you have planned, write down the names of the dishes with approximate cooking times, from the recipes, or from your own experience. Make a list of which ingredients will need some preparation before you can start the cooking. These you can often do the day before and store (see *Advance Cooking*, below). Some recipes give you a preparation time as well as a cooking time, but preparation times vary a lot with individual skills and on whether you can have an uninterrupted time. It is wise to do the preparation well ahead. This is often the part of a meal which takes more of the cook's time than the cooking itself.

Write down when you should start cooking each dish to have it ready by meal time, and this is really all the working plan you need if you have done the preparation of ingredients in advance. This is a much simpler way than the complicated interlocking of preparation and cooking. You will also be able to see from this sort of plan whether there are too many things to be started at the same time; you may then want to alter the menu slightly.

It is always a good idea to include something which can be

122

made completely the day before, longer for the freezer; for example, a cold sweet, a soup to be heated up, sauces, and so on, see below for suggestions.

ADVANCE COOKING

Things to Prepare in Advance and Store in Refrigerator or Larder (for advice on *Safe Storage Times*, see pages 105–14).

BATTERS
Ready-mixed pancake and other batters can be kept in a covered container. Cooked pancakes can be piled flat on a plate and covered with a polythene bag. They can be reheated in the oven, plain, or as stuffed pancakes. Make the stuffing and store it separately.

BISCUIT DOUGH
It can be wrapped in foil, later to be rolled and cut in shapes, or the block of dough simply cut in slices. Serve freshly-cooked biscuits with fruit salad and other cold sweets.

BREADCRUMBS
These can be stored in a polythene bag.

CASSEROLES
Can be completely cooked the day before and reheated to boiling before serving. The flavour of casseroles containing wine, or the flavour of a curry or goulash, seem to improve with keeping, and they are the best kinds for advance cooking.

CHEESE
Can be grated and kept in a polythene bag or box.

COLD SWEETS
All kinds can be kept either in individual dishes, covered with a lid of foil, or in a bowl with a foil cover or other lid.

CREAM
Whipped cream will stay whipped for several hours, but cover it closely.

DRINKS

Store any that you are going to serve chilled or iced; iced coffee or tea, fruit drinks.

EGGS

Hard-boiled ones should be stored in their shells.

FISH

When cooked to serve cold with salad, or to be mixed with a sauce and reheated, is best stored separately and combined just before heating.

FRUIT

All kinds prepared for serving can be prepared in advance, especially fruit salad, grapefruit, and other citrus fruits and fruit juices; also fruit for dessert which is nicest when chilled, for example, fresh peaches or fresh strawberries. Avoid advance peeling of fruits which discolour, for example, apples, pears, peaches, and bananas, unless they will be covered by syrup as with fruit salad. If breakfast grapefruit is prepared the night before, cover closely and store in the refrigerator to preserve the vitamins.

GARNISHES

For parsley and other herbs, washed and ready in sprigs, or chopped; herb butters for grills; tomatoes, cucumber, and other garnishes, see pages 127–30.

HORS-D'ŒUVRE

Most ingredients for these can be prepared in advance and stored in the refrigerator in polythene bags or boxes.

MEAT AND POULTRY

These can be cooked to be served cold or heated up in a sauce. Best to store the sauce separately and combine just before heating.

PASTRY

Ready-made for rolling, or rolled to make flans, and other shapes.

PIES

Ready-prepared raw fruit pies and tarts to bake and serve hot. Cooked meat or fish pies to serve cold, or fillings to put in the pastry, cooked and served hot.

ROUX

White or brown for thickening sauces, casseroles, and other savoury mixtures. Also *beurre manié* for the same purposes.

SALAD FOODS

Should be washed, drained, and stored in covered boxes. Cucumber can be sliced, sprinkled with salt, and left for several hours in a cool place (not refrigerated). Drain off any liquid before using. Sliced beetroot sprinkled with lemon juice or vinegar doesn't need refrigeration either. Make potato salad and store. Other dressed salads (not lettuce) can be stored for 2–4 hrs. with safety, if covered and in the refrigerator.

SAUCES

Most can be made in advance and reheated, or kept warm in a *bain-marie* for a short period. If the recipe contains egg or cream, add these after the sauce has been reheated, just before serving.

SOUPS AND STOCKS

These should be kept in covered containers. Those with egg and cream in the recipe can be cooked up to the stage before this, refrigerated, and the remaining ingredients added just before serving. Make sure the soups have been brought to the boil before you add the finishing touches. This ensures that they will be hot.

VEGETABLES

Apart from washing, peeling, drying, and storing in polythene bags in the refrigerator, avoid advance preparation. Don't cook in advance and reheat because flavour and vitamin content deteriorate too much. Rather than do this serve a salad instead, or use frozen vegetables.

YEAST DOUGH

For slow rising in the refrigerator if you want to serve freshly-cooked rolls.

GARNISHING AND SERVING

Garnishing has always been an important part of the art of cooking, and garnishes serve several purposes. They are used to add colour to foods which are basically colourless, e.g. white soups and fish dishes, or to enhance a dish by serving it with contrasting or harmonising colours e.g. a selection of different-coloured vegetables served with meat. Garnishes are also used to add flavour and interest to a dish, and a great deal of French cookery owes its diversity to the type of garnish used, the dish then being labelled with the name of the basic ingredient '*à la*' whatever the garnish may be. These garnishes are traditional; they form a large part of any French cookery book.

Foods with uninteresting shapes are also helped considerably by garnishes with plenty of form and character of their own, e.g. sprigs of parsley or watercress, the design and shape of slices of lemon or tomato, shaped pieces of toast, fried bread, or pastry. These last items also provide contrast in texture which is very welcome with soft foods, as is the crisp biscuit with sweet dishes which are soft in nature.

In Britain at the beginning of the century very ornate garnishing of food was popular and this was in sympathy with the style of decoration favoured in other directions. Illustrated cookery books of that period give plenty of examples, relics of which can be seen today in exhibitions and competitions in which professional cooks display their skill. This elaborate ornamentation is seen most frequently on the 'cold table' in hotels and restaurants, and on buffets at parties. Many of the items have taken hours to prepare and have required a great deal of handling, together adding up to a product that it is often wiser not to eat if one wants to avoid any risk of food poisoning. This applies particularly, of course, to items which include meat, fish, poultry, jelly, aspic, and cream amongst the ingredients.

Whether one's taste is for Victoriana in food decoration or for simplicity, one basic principle is the same, namely that the

126

food being garnished should live up to the promise of its appearance. Far too many of the cooks and chefs who have a taste for elaborate garnishing regard the flavour and quality of the dish as of secondary importance. Garnishing is easy, good cooking is more difficult, and to be able to say of a cook that the food produced both looks good *and* tastes good is high praise indeed.

Some Useful Garnishes

ANCHOVY FILLETS

These, or stuffed anchovies, purchased in small tins or jars, can be used on hot or cold meat (e.g. veal), fish, vegetables, and *hors-d'œuvre*.

CARROT STICKS and SHREDDED CARROT

Make good garnishes for grills, salads, hot or cold meat or fish dishes. To make sticks, peel carrots and cut in matchsticks; keep in iced water. Sprinkle grated carrot with lemon juice and keep in a covered dish until required.

CELERY

Use curled celery for garnishing salads and in *hors-d'œuvre*. With a sharp, thin vegetable knife, cut very thin slices of washed celery down the length of the stick. Then hold one end, and with the knife in the other hand, pull it firmly along the strip curling it as you go. Put in iced water where the curling process will continue. Drain well before using.

CHERRIES

Use Maraschino cherries for garnishing sweet or savoury; *glacé* for sweet; canned cherries for sweet or savoury dishes, especially duck, chicken, grills, and salads.

CHOCOLATE

Can be purchased as vermicelli, chips, or dots. Alternatively, grate it coarsely and use to garnish cold sweets. Cocoa powder mixed with sugar can also be used.

COCONUT

Can be desiccated or shredded, obtainable in packets or cans; useful on dark-coloured sweets or ices. It can also be coloured by putting a spoonful or two of the coconut in a jar, adding a drop of colouring, and shaking well. Then spread out on a piece of kitchen paper or foil to dry. Alternatively toast it under the grill or in a hot oven to make it brown, and shake frequently.

COFFEE
Sprinkle instant coffee on ices and cold sweets just before serving. It can also first be mixed with sugar.

CROÛTONS
These are small squares or cubes of toasted or fried bread used for garnishing soup or savoury dishes. They give a pleasant contrast of texture to liquid and soft foods, as well as supplying colour to pale foods.

CUCUMBER
Use thin slices of peeled or unpeeled, cut across to make circles, or at an angle to make ovals. Chunks of cucumber can be hollowed to make cups which are then filled with mayonnaise or a savoury filling and used to garnish cold and hot fish or meat.

EGGS
Can be hard-boiled, stuffed, or chopped. The yolks can be rubbed through a sieve to give a useful yellow garnish for soups, salads, and savoury dishes requiring a bit of colour to brighten them.

GLACÉ FRUITS
These are mostly for sweets; rinse in warm water and drain before using.

HERBS
Parsley and mint in small sprigs; leaves of chervil, tarragon, or mint. Finely-chopped parsley. Scissor-chopped parsley and other green herbs, one only, or a blend.

LEMONS
When the juice of lemon is meant to be used on the food as a dressing, lemon wedges should be the garnish. When the lemon is for decoration only, it is cut into a variety of shapes. Very

thin slices are cut across the lemon, pips removed, and a little chopped parsley put on each slice. Alternatively, cut through the slice almost to the middles on two opposite sides, then twist the pieces in opposite directions. Thin slices are also cut into halves or quarters to use for making patterns of lemon. If the lemon is peeled in strips before the slices are cut they will have serrated edges.

Cups make from large squeezed lemon halves are used to hold sauces such as hollandaise or mayonnaise and also for serving lemon water ices or sorbets.

MUSHROOMS

Use grilled or boiled. For boiling, use button mushrooms, wash carefully, put in a small pan with white stock or water and lemon juice to cover. Simmer for about 8 mins. Drain and keep hot. Use the liquid for stock.

NUTS

Use any kind, whole, halves, or chopped. Toasted almonds are useful for chicken, fried fish *à la meunière*, in rice dishes and for garnishing sweets and ices. To toast, blanch to remove the skins, or buy skinned, toast in a hot oven or under the grill, using a shallow tin to hold them and shaking frequently. Toasted hazel nuts make a good garnish for sweets and ices. Toast them in the oven until the skins will rub off easily. Chop before using or use whole.

OLIVES

Use plain black or green ones, stuffed ones purchased in jars, or plain ones, loose or in jars.

ORANGES

Use sections or slices free of all pith and pips on grills, meat and fish, salads, and so on. Drained mandarin oranges sold in small cans are excellent where a sweet fruit is suitable.

PAPRIKA PEPPER

For adding a dash of bright red to white and other pale foods, including soup. Use a pinch, a sprinkling from a perforated tub, or make patterns with it.

PICKLES

These are specially useful for garnishing cold meats and fish, or for *hors-d'œuvre*. Use cocktail onions, gherkins or sliced pickled cucumbers, pickled walnuts, and any others with a good shape.

RADISHES

Use whole, cut in fine rings or as 'roses'. To make the roses use a sharp-pointed knife and carve the petals from the root ends to within a $\frac{1}{4}$ in. ($\frac{1}{2}$ cm.) of the stem end. Lever up the red part from the white to free the petals. Put in ice water until required.

SHELLFISH

Use shelled shrimps or prawns as garnishes for any fish dish, hot or cold.

SPICES

Mix with sugar and sprinkle on milk and other pale puddings just before serving.

SWEET PEPPERS

Use fine slices of raw green or red peppers, or chopped. Canned red ones are very useful, and are best cut in strips.

TOMATOES

Use firm, ripe tomatoes of small or medium size. To remove the skins, nick them on the side, plunge them in boiling water for a minute, then in cold, and peel off the skins. Cut in slices or sections, quarters or smaller. Cut tomato lilies by using a pointed knife to cut an even zigzag round the middle of the unskinned tomato, separate the two halves. Small unskinned tomatoes may be stuffed, cut a slice off the stem end, scoop out the pulp with a teaspoon, drain cut side down. Fill with mayonnaise or savoury filling. These are usually easier to handle if the skins are left on. Baked, stuffed tomatoes also make a good garnish for hot meats and fish.

In many families this takes place in the kitchen, the cooked food being divided up into portions, put directly on the plates and taken straight to the diners. It is the ideal way of getting really hot freshly-cooked food as quickly as possible from kitchen to consumer. But for the food to be at its best the plates should be hot or cold as the food demands, and the food arranged neatly to make an attractive plate. This means not heaping masses of food roughly on the plate, a sure way of spoiling the look of it and an encouragement to the greedy to over-eat. Let the hungry come back for second helpings if they need them.

For entertaining guests and for special occasions, even the most simply-run home should have a little more ceremony and grace in serving the meal. For this, at least some of the food will be put on the plates at table, and some large serving dishes are needed. If a dinner service has been bought most of the essential serving dishes will have been included: big flat oval dishes for taking a joint or sliced meat; dishes with lids for vegetables; sauce-boats for gravy and sauces; and possibly a soup tureen and ladle. On these occasions roast joints usually come to the table uncarved and are carved in front of the guests but, unless there is an expert carver in the family, it is kinder to guests and food to do the carving in the kitchen and arrange the slices on a large meat dish, garnished with a few vegetables and moistened with a little thin gravy. It can then be put back in the oven for a few minutes to make sure it is really hot. Steamed puddings – and any which are turned out of a mould – can be put on a small oval meat dish, on a round cake plate or other ornamental plate, or on a round silver or stainless-steel dish.

Fruit salads and all soft puddings are usually served in bowls, glass, or china.

Many puddings look best served in individual dishes, and for this cereal bowls or sundae glasses are the best. Fruit salad sets are useful for serving many puddings. They usually consist of one large bowl and six or more small ones.

Not many people today use a soup tureen, and it is more usual for the soup to be portioned out in the kitchen and put on the table just before the guests sit down.

For *hors-d'œuvre* there are special sets of small dishes, but any small serving dishes will do. If the *hors-d'œuvre* is just one or two items, it is better to put a portion on each plate and have it in position when people sit down. If this is a colourful food it helps to decorate the table.

If you always use sliced bread, serve it in a bread basket with any rolls and biscuits as well, or serve it in any shallow dish which is easy to pass round.

Bread to be cut at table or on the sideboard is put on a bread board.

Cheese is served on a cheese board with a knife for cutting it, or it is kept in a cheese dish with its own cover. Celery to go with the cheese is served in any tall glass, and any other raw vegetables in small dishes.

Fresh fruit is served in any ornamental bowl or flat dish and if there is something messy like peaches or pears it is necessary to provide a fingerbowl of water. This can be one large one if all could reach it, or a small bowl each.

Nuts are served in a bowl, with the nutcrackers. Shelled nuts, sweets, and *petits fours* are served in any small dishes.

When the savoury course has been eaten, the table looks better if the salt and pepper and other condiments are removed before the sweet is served. If coffee is served at the table, all is cleared away except the sweets and *petits fours*.

TABLE SETTINGS

Most people today prefer a colourful table setting, but some still prefer to use white. If it is white, it must be beautifully laundered and of good quality, so for most families it is more practical to use colour. For general family use an easily-laundered cloth, or one only needing to be wiped down, is the best everyday table covering. For special occasions, if the table is of beautiful wood, table mats show it off to advantage; otherwise, a table cloth to harmonise with the dining-room colours is better. Consider, too, the design and colour of the china, so that the whole makes an attractive picture, including the flowers or other decoration. Flowers should be low arrangements so that people can see one another easily across the table. When setting the table, the cutlery is placed either side of the plate position, forks on the left and knives and spoons on the right. The cutlery needed first is placed on the outside, with the bread and butter knife on the extreme right.

The cutlery is placed with the ends of the handles a little in from the edge of the table.

Glasses are placed to the right and above the tips of the knives, bread and butter plates to the left. The table napkin either goes on the bread and butter plate or in the centre of the place setting. Other appointments are placed in convenient positions.

When there are to be several courses and a lot of cutlery, the dessert spoons and forks are often put at the top of the plate setting, one above the other, at right angles to the rest of the cutlery, with the fork handle to the left and the spoon handle to the right. Serving spoons, knives, and forks are placed where they will be required, usually in front of either host or hostess or on a side table. If you use a dinner wagon and serve from that, then this is the obvious place for them.

DIFFERENT KINDS OF MEALS

BARBECUES

The modern American name for cooking out of doors or camp cooking, but a barbecue usually means a party rather than day-to-day camp cooking, both more suited to a less moist climate than ours. The cooking apparatus for a barbecue can vary from a Boy-Scout contraption to an elaborate portable iron grill outfit, or even one built in as a permanent feature of the garden, some being complete with an electrically-driven spit roaster. Most shops supplying garden furniture show a selection of these.

Food that can be cooked in this way varies from a whole ox roasted on a spit to sausages impaled on a stick and held in front of an open fire, while the potatoes bake in the embers. Improving a little on this is an iron grid with legs which can be pushed into the ground over the fire. Meat is placed on the bars for grilling.

The simplest portable type of cooking apparatus is the bucket type, which can be a home-made one. In the days when one bought petrol in tins my father used to make wonderful ones from the empty tins with the aid of a tin opener. A hole was cut in the bottom of the container at one side, big enough to feed the fire through, and the top cut out completely and replaced by iron bars or a wire grid. On this grid the meat was grilled, or iron pots stood for boiling.

The container is stood on flat stones with the fire-hole facing the way the wind is coming. Modern versions of this use a charcoal fire instead of wood and may have a damper arrangement to regulate the draught. If you can get hold of an old-fashioned hand grill they are wonderful to use on top of a bucket fire. They are the wire contraptions used in Victorian times for grilling on a coal range. The top of the fire box was lifted up, and the hand grill with the meat clamped in was placed across the opening.

Permanent barbecues of brick or stone with iron grids on the top are not difficult for the handyman to make in the garden. The one essential to remember is to build it with the fire opening facing the direction of the prevailing wind.

SUITABLE FOODS FOR A BARBECUE

Anything that can be grilled:

Jointed young chickens or chicken halves

Fish steaks and small whole fish

Sausages

Gammon steaks

Kebabs

Lamb chops and cutlets

Ducklings jointed

Hamburgers and meat patties

Pork loin chops and spare-rib chops

Beef steaks

Thick pieces of liver

Rolled bacon rashers

Kidneys in their own fat

Toasted sandwiches

Vegetables

Any boiled in heavy iron pans on the grill grid

Grilled tomatoes and mushrooms

Grilled sweet peppers

Salads (as accompaniment)

Potatoes wrapped in aluminium foil and baked in the ashes or on the grid.

Fruits

Apples wrapped in aluminium foil and baked in the ashes or on the grid

Grilled apples or pears

Bananas grilled in an aluminium-foil nest

Raw fruit and fruit salads

BREAKFAST

People's ideas about breakfast vary greatly, ranging from the cup of tea or coffee, to the porridge, bacon-and-egg, toast-and-marmalade, traditional 'good' English breakfast.

Research made into this subject indicates that people are more likely to be healthy and able to work well if they have a good breakfast, though to be nutritionally good a breakfast does not have to be the traditional one, and not even a cooked one.

Some of the evidence which indicates the importance of breakfast comes from schools. It has been noted many times that children who come to school without an adequate breakfast cannot concentrate enough to learn well. Other evidence comes from surveys in factories, where it has been found that the non-breakfast eater generally has a lower output and a higher absentee rate than the person who regularly eats breakfast.

By breakfast-time, most people have been a minimum of 10 hrs. without food, some (including children) considerably longer, and if nothing is eaten until 'elevenses' this period of starvation then becomes 12 hrs. or even more. During this time stores of glucose are used up and the blood-sugar level falls, causing lack of energy, mental fatigue, and irritability, the effect being most noticeable from mid-morning to lunch-time.

Many people who start the day without breakfast have a tendency to be over-weight, and skip this meal as a slimming effort. This is not very sensible or effective, because they get so hungry that, when they do eat, they tend to eat more than they should. For slimming to be effective a person's eating habits have to be relearnt to a pattern of a more modest intake, and starving early in the morning is not usually much of a help.

A nutritionally good breakfast should contain more than just a cup of tea or coffee. Some bread or toast with it is better than nothing, but better still would be to turn the bread into a sandwich with a meat, cheese, fish, or egg filling, and add a glass of fruit juice or some fresh fruit or tomato.

A good plate of breakfast cereal or porridge with lots of milk or yogurt is an alternative to the sandwiches.

For suggestions for children's meals, see page 153.

BUFFET PARTY

This is a very practical method of entertaining a large number of people, whether for a wedding reception, a dance, or a birthday party, or any party at which you want to provide more food than just a few snacks to go with the drinks. In the home it is usual for guests to help themselves to the food from the table (buffet), and for the hosts or staff to see to the replenishment of drinks and hot or perishable food.

Before deciding to give this sort of party there are a few important things to bear in mind. You will need a large enough table or tables on which to put the food (usually all at once although sometimes in courses), and to put plates and cutlery; also needed are small tables for guests to put glasses and empty plates on, and enough chairs for people to sit down if they want to. The food must all be of a kind that can be eaten in the fingers or with either one fork or spoon. The table should be well lighted so that guests can see easily not only what is available but also to serve themselves without making a mess. Candles are a lovely decoration but candelabra, well above the food, are necessary, and floral decorations should also be tall and well away from the food. A basket of fruit is often a better decoration.

The table can be against a wall or in the centre of the room, the latter being the better method for a lot of guests if the room is big enough to take it.

It is better not to put all the food on the table at once but to replenish as necessary, this being particularly important for any perishable dishes such as those containing meat, fish, eggs, or cream, which should not stay more than about half an hour in a warm room. If hot dishes are to be served you really need a hotplate of some sort, either electrically heated or by a spirit lamp. Hot food, too, should be replenished when necessary, and no food should be kept just warm for long.

Be sure there are serving spoons beside each dish which needs them and a pile of plates, and the necessary cutlery. Other plates and cutlery are arranged at convenient intervals along the table. Large plates are better than small ones, so that guests can take small amounts of several foods at a time.

Table napkins are best either folded and put in large tumblers or decorative jars, or placed in overlapping rows near

136

the edge of the table, so arranged that it is easy to pick up one at a time.

The choice of menu depends on the number of guests, the time of day, the type of party, your taste in food, and the size of your purse. A successful buffet does not have to have an enormous range of food, and it does not need to be expensive food either.

The following are suggestions for suitable food. Sandwiches of all kinds, including sandwich cakes and loaves; rice dishes such as risotto, kedgeree, or pilaff; galantines and terrines; savoury flans and quiches; *vol-au-vents*; salads, stuffed eggs; cheese board.

For sweets: fruit salad; other prepared fruits; cold gelatine sweets like bavarois, trifles, cold *soufflés*; gâteaux.

For drinks: wines, beer, fruit juices, fruit punch; iced or hot tea or coffee.

CHILDREN'S PARTY

Children can, of course, eat anything that adults do, but their preferences tend to be different and it is not wise to give them too much cream and other fatty food, or indigestible items, as these plus the excitement may be disastrous. It does, however, add to the joy of a party if the children are allowed to have some of the foods which are more adult and sophisticated, especially the older children.

For very small children it does not matter much what they have as long as the portions are tiny and the food easy to handle, pretty, and gay. That makes it 'party', even though the basis is plain and what they have every day. To achieve this, serve drinks in coloured paper mugs and with a straw; stamp sandwiches out with tiny fancy cutters, or make pinwheels, ribbon sandwiches, or cornets. Cut plain biscuit mixtures into fancy shapes with animal or other cutters, and ice 'faces' on to them, or make small round biscuits with faces or initials on them. Make jellies and cold sweets in individual paper cases and decorate with cream.

For older children the sort of savoury snacks served at an adult buffet party will be popular, especially hot sausages on sticks, potato crisps and chips, cubes of cheese, small pastry savories (or hefty sausage rolls for hungry boys).

Above all, consult the child or children for whom the party is being given. You can draw up the menu between you with re-

137

servations for 'surprise' items you will provide. If they are old enough let them give a hand in the preparation. Simple things that they have helped to make are much better than an elaborate display mainly done to show your own skill as a cook. It is never too early to begin to teach them the mechanics of party giving.

CHRISTMAS DINNER

Christmas dinner is not a difficult one to cook, as much of the food is prepared in advance. The stuffing may be prepared and stored in the refrigerator. Ready-made Christmas puddings and mincemeat, or even mince pies, can be purchased and heated as required. There is thus no need for the traditional meal to be a burden to the housewife. After all, having the family gathering and the traditional food is more important to most than the small differences in quality between the home-made and factory-made articles.

If you use long, slow cooking for the poultry, it will need attention, and if the vegetables are got ready early in the morning they can be stored in a cool place ready for cooking. Making a sauce the day before is simpler than a custard at the last moment. If people like their puddings with liquid serve thin cream instead of custard. Get out all the plates and dishes you will want in good time, put them to heat, and get the table set as soon as convenient. Preparing a trouble-free dinner is really a matter of forethought and organisation rather than hard work.

DINNER PARTY

A menu for these occasions is more elaborate than the usual family dinner, but if you are not an experienced cook it is better to serve simple food that is good, rather than ambitious food that is poorly cooked. You can always help your simple cooking by having a beautifully-set table, good wine and cheese, and fine fruit.

Most people do not want more than three courses, and the hungry can always fill up with cheese and fruit at the end. So have either *hors-d'œuvre* or soup, a main dish with vegetables, and a sweet and coffee, with liqueurs if the budget allows it. Choose something which does not need last-minute attention for cooking or serving, and include some things which can be prepared well in advance, like a cold sweet and *hors-d'œuvre*.

138

The simplest dish is a casserole, which can be made more sophisticated by using wine, mushrooms, sweet peppers, or an unusual mixture of herbs and spices among the ingredients.

Choose vegetables which will keep hot without spoiling in flavour or appearance: green peas, carrots, canned corn, broad beans in a sauce, macedoine of vegetables in a sauce, vegetables *au gratin*, braised celery. Best potatoes are roast or crisps (call them game chips) and heat up packet ones; or serve boiled rice. A tossed green salad is an alternative to the vegetables. Dress it at table, having washed and dried the lettuce in advance. If you have an attractive bowl and salad servers this makes a pleasant ceremony to watch.

If your guests are foreigners serve something typically British: roast beef and Yorkshire pudding, steak and kidney pie, Scotch salmon (plain, boiled, smoked, or grilled), Dover sole (grilled), Aylesbury duckling, turtle soup with Madeira wine (canned soup is good for this), strawberries and cream, treacle tart, trifle, ice puddings and ice-cream sundaes.

EMERGENCY MEALS

The occasion may be unexpected guests, but probably more often it is something which has delayed you and kept you from preparing the meal you had planned. To be ready for these occasions you want to have some popular menus in reserve, ones that you know how to prepare in the minimum time. I think it is worth while writing these down somewhere for quick reference, perhaps including a selection of menus, plain and posh. Then be sure you keep the necessary ingredients in stock, replacing as they are used up. Include in the menus some luxury canned or frozen foods which will help to disguise the fact that it is a scratch meal.

Whether or not you have a freezer will, of course, have a lot to do with the kind of emergency meals you can plan. The following are just some ideas to start you off if you haven't already got yourself organised to cope with emergency situations.

Hors-d'œuvre or Starters

Keep some of these in your store cupboard:
Anchovy fillets to serve plain or as a garnish for eggs, potato, or Russian salad.

Artichoke hearts, canned, to be drained and dressed with French dressing.

Cod's roe, smoked, canned, to serve with thin hot toast and plenty of lemon.

Pâté in small cans. Choose from liver, smoked trout, grouse, smoked goose, prawn, and others.

Prawns, canned, to make a quick fish cocktail.

Soups

Obviously canned or packet, some of the family favourites as well as some luxury ones for special occasions, for example, turtle, *bisque d'homard, bouillabaisse*, cock-a-leekie, pheasant, or wild duck.

Main Dish

This is a bit tricky if you don't want the meal to be too obviously out of a can. Here is where the family favourites should be kept in reserve. You might choose from: canned frankfurters with canned sauerkraut to serve with it; curried eggs and rice with the curry sauce from can or freezer; frozen whole plaice *à la meunière* with slices of fresh orange of you have them; spaghetti with a meat sauce, which may be canned, frozen or made from a can of minced meat; canned chicken or turkey in a sauce or frozen chicken pie; canned or frozen steak and kidney pie. If you have a freezer, make your own single-portion favourite dishes. They heat up much faster than a larger quantity, and should be much better than the commercial articles.

For vegetables, apart from potato powder, the best in my opinion are salads, assuming you keep a supply of washed and drained salad ingredients in the refrigerator; or frozen vegetables. If you rely on canned ones keep a supply of packet sauces to serve with them, parsley, onion, cheese.

There are also plenty of good canned sauces you might choose from as a reserve for serving with quickly-cooked frozen fish or meat, for example, *Béarnaise*, lobster, Madeira wine, Newburg, Robert or Sanfayana (tomato and sweet pepper).

Sweet Course

This is easy if you have fresh fruit or cheese and biscuits in stock. Most people like canned fruit, so keep some exotic ones for special occasions, guavas, lichees, green figs, mangoes, melon cubes, ginger in syrup, pawpaw. The freezer owner can keep ready-to-bake fruit tarts, or ice-cream, while those who like something more substantial can have canned or frozen steamed puddings.

HIGH TEA

An evening meal served at approximately 6 p.m. soon after the wage-earners have returned home. It forms the chief evening meal of a large proportion of the people in Britain. It is frequently followed by a late supper before bedtime.

High tea most frequently consists of a main dish, hot or cold, with bread, butter and spreads, and sometimes cake. Tea is the usual beverage. It also forms the last meal of the day for very young children.

Nutritionally it often tends to be a somewhat unbalanced meal with a preponderance of bread and flour-confectionery, but if the main dish contains a good portion of meat, fish, eggs, or cheese, and is accompanied by vegetable or salad or followed by fruit it is of better nutritive value.

PACKED MEALS AND PICNIC MEALS

These can vary from a simple sandwich meal to a three- or four-course meal complete with wines, a folding table to serve the meal on, and chairs for the diners.

To be really nourishing the simple sandwich meal should contain plenty of protein-rich food. This means that the sandwiches should have generous fillings of cheese, eggs, meat, or fish. This should be accompanied by some fresh salad vegetables and/or raw fruit. A sweet course is an optional extra. A drink of some sort is needed, preferably a hot or cold milk drink, fresh fruit juice, tea, coffee, cocoa, or hot soup.

Alternatives to Bread Rolls of any kind, crispbread, plain biscuits, pastry as tarts and turnovers.

Filling Alternatives Instead of making bread into sandwiches, carry it as bread and butter and take any of the following separately: cubes or fingers of cheese, hard-boiled eggs (plain or stuffed), cold lamb cutlets or other chops, cold sausages, cold leg of chicken or other poultry, cold fried fish in batter, fish cakes or meat rissoles. Take paper napkins to hold them in.

141

Pastry Take any savoury pie or pastry but be sure there is the right kind of filling (some meat, fish, cheese, or eggs) and not too much pastry.

Containers for Packed Meals Light plastic boxes are the best to use. Pack each kind of food separately in either greaseproof paper, foil, or polythene bags. Drinks are best carried in thermos flasks and then can be kept really hot or chilled as needed. It is, however, much simpler to buy drinks on the spot, and these are often available when food is not.

WEDDING BREAKFAST

The bride's parents or relatives usually provide the breakfast and the guests are friends of the bride and groom and of their parents. The number of guests varies from just a few intimate friends to hundreds. Very large wedding breakfasts are usually given to professional caterers to carry out. When the approximate number of guests is known the caterer is asked to submit a quotation for the meal, the cost of which will obviously depend on the choice of food and wines, the type of meal, and the number of staff needed to serve it. The catering may be done by a local hotel or restaurant, in which case the breakfast is usually held on their premises, or it may be undertaken by caterers who have a special service of 'outside' catering, and then the breakfast may be served in a private home or in a room or marquee hired for the purpose. In either case the caterer supplies not only the food and wines, but also cutlery, china, and glasses. It is not necessary to ask him to supply the cake too. That can be home-made, or from a baker or confectioner. It is, too, often made by the bride herself or by relatives or friends. In any case, it is the bride who chooses the type of cake, and if any coloured decorations are involved these will be chosen to harmonise with the wedding clothes. It is customary to send pieces of the cake to absent friends and special small boxes are available for this.

The traditional wedding cake consists of several tiers surmounted by a vase of flowers and trailing greenery. The object of this monumental affair is decorative, to make a centrepiece which everyone can see. At a small informal breakfast, however, a single-tiered cake looks more appropriate. This can have a raised base and spray of flowers in the centre to make the table decoration. For this kind of cake a tin about

12–14 in. (30–35 cm.) in diameter (or square) is the best size, but a smaller one can look very decorative too.

The cake should be made about 3–4 weeks before the ceremony, wrapped in greaseproof paper, then in foil, and stored in an airtight tin. The icing should start at least a week in advance, as two or three days are needed between the different coatings to allow for setting.

The older type of breakfast was a sit-down meal, usually of cold meats and salad, plus the wedding cake, and this kind is still popular. It does require more space and staff to serve it than the more modern type of buffet meal.

The choice of food depends on the type of meal, but the following are popular (see also *Buffet Party*, page 137).

Savoury course   Salmon, lobster, prawns with mayonnaise and salad; cold chicken, turkey, tongue, ham, and other meats with salad; pastry such as patties, *vol-au-vents*, and sausage rolls.

Sweet course   Ices, jellies, trifles, and other cold sweets; fruit salad, pastry flans, meringues, and any popular sweets.

Drinks   Champange, hock, and other white wines, sherry; coffee.

The wedding cake is put on the table in front of the bride, or in the middle of the buffet. The usual procedure for cutting it is as follows. At the end of the breakfast speeches are made, one to propose the health of the bride and groom – usually made by the best man – and the other a 'thank you' from the groom. Then the bride cuts the cake. She usually simply puts the knife in and the cake is removed for cutting up into small pieces to distribute to the guests. After this the breakfast comes to an end and the bride and groom leave.

CATERING QUANTITIES FOR APPROXIMATELY 25 SERVINGS

(For other quantities of food to allow, see *Buying and Storing Food*, pages 48–61).

SANDWICHES (allowing 2 large rounds per person)

   4 *large* (1¾ *lb.*) *thinly-sliced loaves*
   1–1½ *lb. softened butter or margarine* (½–¾ *kg.*)
   About 3 *lb. of filling, depending on the kind* (1½ *kg.*)

CHEESE AND BISCUITS
3 *lb. cheese* (1½ *kg.*)   1½ *lb. biscuits* (¾ *kg.*)

CHEESE AND WINE PARTY
4 *lb. cheese* (2 *kg.*)   *Plenty of rolls, French bread, and biscuits*

SALAD
5 *lettuce*   1½ *lb. tomatoes* (¾ *kg.*)
3–4 *cucumbers or use alternative vegetables*
of about the same bulk

TEA (2 cups each)
4 *oz. tea* (125 *g.*) *to* 2 *gallons water* (9 *l.*)   3 *pints milk* (1¾ *l.*)
½–¾ *lb. sugar* (250–375 *g.*)

COFFEE
8 *oz. coarsely-ground coffee* (250 *g.*)   4 *pt. water* (2¼ *l.*)
8 *pt. milk* (4½ *l.*)

Put coffee and water in a saucepan and heat until it just bubbles. Remove from the heat, stir, and leave in a warm place for 5 mins. Strain into a hot jug. Heat the milk until it steams but don't allow a skin to form. Pour into hot jugs.

FRUIT PUNCH (quantities for 25 glasses)
2 *lb. sugar* (1 *kg.*)   4 *pt. water* (2¼ *l.*)

Heat together until the sugar dissolves.

6 *oranges*

Peel and remove as much white pith as possible. Cut the oranges in slices and add to the syrup.

6 *more oranges*   6 *lemons*

Extract the juice and strain it into the syrup. Instead of these fresh oranges you could use an equivalent amount of frozen juice.

4 *sliced bananas*   8 *oz. small, sweet grapes* (250 *g.*)
8 *oz. cherries, stoned* (250 *g.*)

Add these to the rest of the punch and chill it.

144

2 pt. ginger ale (1 *l.*)   1 *pt. cold weak tea* ($\frac{1}{2}$ *l.*
4 *pt. soda water* (2$\frac{1}{4}$ *l.*)

Just before serving, add these to the punch, together with some ice cubes.

WINES AND SPIRITS (approximate number of glasses per bottle)

Champagne	6–8
Wine	6–8
Sherry, Madeira and aperitifs	16
Gin	20–30 depending on whether used to make a long drink or cocktail
Whisky	20
Liqueur	30

SOFT DRINKS

Tomato juice	4–6 to 1 pt. ($\frac{1}{2}$ l.)
Fruit squashes	20–25 to 1 bottle plus 7 pt. water (4 l.)

OTHER FOODS (Quantities for 25 servings)

Rice: 2$\frac{1}{2}$ lb. raw weight (1 kg.) for a risotto, or other rice dish; 1$\frac{1}{4}$ lb. for serving with curry, etc. ($\frac{1}{2}$ kg.)

Spaghetti: 3 lb. raw weight (1$\frac{1}{2}$ kg.) for Bolognese or similar dish

Beef to roast and serve hot or cold: 5 lb. boned weight (2$\frac{1}{2}$ kg.)

Turkey, oven-ready weight: 14 lb. (6$\frac{1}{2}$ kg.)

Chicken: two 5 lb. oven-ready (2$\frac{1}{2}$ kg.)

Ham, cooked: 4 lb. (2 kg.)

Beef for a casserole or curry: 6 lb. (3 kg.)

Lamb for kebabs: 8 lb. leg (3$\frac{3}{4}$ kg.)

Fish fillets: 7$\frac{1}{2}$–8 lb. (3$\frac{1}{2}$–3$\frac{3}{4}$ kg.)

Lamb cutlets: 50.

Hamburgers: 5$\frac{1}{2}$ lb. lean minced beef or other meat (2$\frac{1}{4}$ kg.)

Soup: 8–10 pt. (5–5$\frac{1}{2}$ l.)

Sauce or Gravy: 2–3 pt. (1$\frac{1}{2}$ l.)

Potatoes, for mashed or chips: 8 lb. (3$\frac{3}{4}$ kg.)

Jelly or cold sweet: 4$\frac{1}{2}$–5 pt. (2$\frac{1}{2}$ l.)

Cream: 3–3$\frac{1}{2}$ pt. (2 l.)

Chapter Five

FOOD AND HEALTH

NUTRITION

Nutrition is the science concerned with the study of food and its relation to health and disease. Fifty years ago the factors thought to be important to health were such things as clean homes, sound drains, fresh air, rest, and recreation, moderation in all things, and enough food to fill the belly three times a day. If it could be appetising and attractively-prepared food so much the better.

The idea that there is more to choosing food than just eye and appetite appeal is a new one. It has resulted from research carried out by those studying the new science of nutrition. A great deal of the knowledge has come within recent years and much research is still going on. It is now well established that health is more dependent on a wise choice of food, properly prepared, than on any other single factor. This new knowledge is being applied on a world-wide scale to try to improve the health of all people. It is realised that freedom from hunger is not enough, that people can have enough to satisfy hunger and still be in poor health because the nutritional quality of the food is poor.

This new importance given to the subject of food is of great significance in family meal preparation. By learning a few elementary facts about nutrition it is possible for the cook to influence the health of her family to a marked degree. It gives a new interest and purpose to shopping, cooking, and eating.

The Basic Principles of Good Nutrition

1. The body needs five types of chemical substances from food (see *Nutrients*, page 148), and needs these every day in order to maintain health.
2. The simplest way of ensuring that these five are adequately provided is to have a list of foods which must be included in the daily and weekly meals, and then to add to these other foods for variety.

146

There are many lists of foods which would serve this purpose and they would vary for different countries and different food habits. There is no such thing as one perfect diet that all should eat. Good nutrition is achieved in a wide variety of ways in different parts of the world.

The list which follows is based on average British eating habits. Check your meals by this.

MILK

Children 1 pt. ($\frac{1}{2}$ l.) daily, including milk used for cooking and as drinks.

Adults $\frac{1}{2}$ pt. ($\frac{1}{4}$ l.) daily.

The following have approximately the same composition as milk and can be exchanged for 1 pt. ($\frac{1}{2}$ l.) of liquid milk.

2 oz. hard cheese (50–60 g.)
4 oz. cottage cheese (125 g.)
$\frac{1}{3}$ pt. evaporated milk ($\frac{1}{4}$ l.)
2 oz. dried milk powder (50–60 g.)
1 pt. yogurt ($\frac{1}{2}$ l.)

FATS

Some butter or margarine daily.
1 tsp. cod liver oil or its equivalent for children and teenagers.
Additional fats and oils for cooking.

MEAT, GAME, POULTRY, FISH, EGGS

One of these at two meals daily.
Children 1 oz. (25–30 g.) or more per portion according to age.
Adults 3–4 oz. (75–125 g.) per portion.
Note 2 eggs are equivalent to 4 oz. (125 g.) of meat.
Count eggs used in cooking as part of the daily quota.

VEGETABLES AND FRUIT

Two portions daily from this list, with other varieties in addition, according to needs.
Freshly-cooked cabbage, Brussels sprouts, spinach, or cauliflower
Freshly-cooked potatoes, or vitamin-enriched potato powder
Raw vegetables such as watercress, cabbage, Brussels sprouts
1 orange
1 grapefruit
1 dose of blackcurrant syrup or rosehip syrup

2 tomatoes

5 tablespoons (1 small glass) fresh, canned, or frozen orange, or grapefruit juice

$\frac{1}{4}$ pt. fresh or canned tomato juice (150 ml.)

BREAD

2–3 oz. (50–90 g.) daily for people leading sedentary lives. Children, teenagers, and active adults need more.

Cereals, cakes, and flour confectionery are extras to add variety to the diet, but should not be eaten instead of the other foods in this list.

SUGARS, PRESERVES, AND SWEETS

A little for sweetening purposes.

NUTRIENTS

These are the chemical substances of which food and the human body are made. The only source of materials for upkeep and growth are the foods eaten, hence the importance of studying the chemical composition of both, so that the body's needs can be related to the foods eaten. The sciences concerned with this study are chiefly biochemistry, physiology, nutrition, and dietetics.

The nutrients are:

1. *Carbohydrates* These come chiefly from plants, and are made by them from carbon dioxide in the air, plus water in the soil, plus the energy from the sun, the process being known as photosynthesis. The simple carbohydrate made in this way is a sugar (glucose) and plants are able to convert this into other sugars and into the carbohydrate starch which they store for future use in such parts as seeds, tubers, bulbous roots, and so on. When animals eat plants they use the carbohydrate as a fuel for energy production and store a certain amount for future use as animal starch (glycogen). Surplus carbohydrate may be converted into fat and stored.

2. *Fats and Oils* (Lipids to the chemist) Plants are able to make these from carbohydrate and store them in the seeds (e.g. nuts), and sometimes in the flesh of fruits (e.g. olives).

Animals and humans get their supplies of fats by eating plant products such as oils, or by eating the fat of other animals. Fat is used as a fuel for energy production, but is also important as part of the essential structure of body cells, as a protective covering for certain organs (e.g. the kidneys), and as an insulating layer under the skin.

3. *Proteins* These consist of the same basic elements as carbohydrates and fats (carbon, hydrogen, and oxygen), but, in addition, proteins contain nitrogen. Most plants get the nitrogen they need from the soil via manures (natural and artificial), and from decaying plant and animal matter. A few plants (legumes) can take nitrogen from the air and use it to make protein. The highest concentration of protein in plants is usually found in seeds, e.g. grains such as wheat, in nuts, in peas and beans.

Animals and humans get their protein by eating plants and other animals.

Protein is the basic substance of all cells in the body and therefore the basic substance of life itself. No growth can take place without it, nor can worn-out tissues be replaced, so that on a protein-deficient diet the young fail to grow and the adults fail to replenish their fabric and gradually deteriorate.

Because protein contains the same elements as carbohydrate and fat, it can also be used by the body as a fuel for energy production. In a normal mixed diet a certain amount of the protein eaten is used for fuel, but in poor diets all the protein has to be used thus, to maintain life, and consequently growth and replacement cease. On the other hand, even if there is adequate carbohydrate and fat for energy needs, but inadequate protein, still growth and replacement cannot take place. Fat and fluid may accumulate in the body and disguise the fact that muscle and other vital tissues are lacking.

4. *Mineral Substances* Plants obtain these from the soil and water surrounding their roots. Animals and humans get them from plants, other animals, drinking water, and from condiments such as salt. Minerals are part of the structure of the body, e.g. iron is a vital constituent of the red cells of the blood: calcium is the main ingredient which gives rigidity to bones: fluorine helps to make the enamel of teeth strong and caries-resistant. In addition, minerals exert a controlling influence over body processes such as growth and energy production, e.g. iodine in the thyroid gland. A serious deficiency of a mineral can have very grave effects on health, e.g. anaemia in iron deficiency: porous and brittle bones in cal-

cium deficiency: dental decay in fluorine deficiency: goitre in iodine deficiency.

5. *Vitamins* Those which are found in plants appear to be made by the plant, but why some plants contain rich stores of a vitamin and others little, if any, is still largely unexplained. Why, for example, does a blackcurrant contain a large amount of vitamin C while a plum has very little, or why does a cabbage have a lot and a lettuce very little ?

Animals and humans obtain their vitamins partly from plant foods and partly from other animals. Some vitamins which appear to be essential to humans are only found plentifully in animal foods, e.g. vitamin B12 and vitamin D.

Vitamins occur in foods in very small amounts and are needed in the body in only small quantities, but they are vital to human growth and life. They are important as regulators of body processes, e.g. some vitamins of the B complex play an essential part in the way energy is obtained from food, and vitamin D is essential in enabling bones to use calcium for their normal growth.

When vitamins were first discovered they were identified by letters of the alphabet, but today the chemical structures are known and the alternative chemical name frequently used instead. The chief vitamins known to be important to humans are: vitamin A and carotene (the form found in plants); vitamin C or ascorbic acid; vitamin D; vitamin E (its importance to humans uncertain); vitamin K; the vitamins of the B complex consist of B1 or thiamine, riboflavine, nicotinic acid, B12, and a number of others.

When a particular vitamin is lacking in a diet the deficiency sometimes produces very marked and obvious symptoms, e.g. lack of vitamin D produces rickets. With other vitamins the symptoms may be less well defined and it is difficult to diagnose the trouble. Reliable methods of detecting mild vitamin deficiencies are one of the developments hoped for in the near future.

CALORIES

Calories are units used to measure the energy content of foods.

The energy needs of the body for maintenance of life, for growth, and work, are also measured in calories. If a person is to maintain a normal healthy weight, his intake of energy via food must equal his output of energy. If the intake is consistently higher than the output the surplus is stored as fat. If the intake is consistently lower than the output the person will lose weight and children will stop growing. Estimating a person's calorie needs is very difficult as each individual varies, and a quantity of food which maintains normal weight in one person will make another fat, and yet another thin. Estimations of people's probable needs have to be made by those responsible for feeding large groups of people, and these estimations are usually based on tables of recommended allowances which have been drawn up by medical and scientific authorities.

Calorie values of foods are expressed either as calories per oz. or per 100 grammes ($3\frac{1}{2}$ oz.). These however can be very misleading, unless the quantity of the food eaten is taken into account and how it is served, e.g. whether it is cooked plain, or with fat or served with sugar or cream or a sauce.

The following examples show how the calorific value of foods is altered by the method of cooking.

POTATOES

A 4 oz. portion (125 g.)

Boiled or plain mashed	80 calories
Mashed with milk and butter or margarine	136 calories
Roast	140 calories
Chips	272 calories

APPLES

A 4 oz. portion of

Raw apple, 1 medium-sized (125 g.)	40 calories
Baked or stewed with 1 oz. (30 g.) sugar	152 calories
As above with cream	284 calories
Apple dumplings	228 calories
with cream	460 calories
Apple pie	216 calories
with cream	346 calories

APPETITE

Appetite is an important means by which man controls his intake of food. A poor appetite can lead to an inadequate intake and finally to malnutrition; a too hearty appetite, on the other hand, can lead to obesity and its accompanying ill health. Fortunate are those whose appetite controls intake to suit the body's needs.

Exactly how appetite control works is still largely a mystery. Appetite-depressant drugs are widely used in slimming cures, but the wisdom of this is doubtful as the drugs tend to have undesirable side effects and are not a permanent cure for the tendency to overeat. Most recent work tends to show that the part of the brain known as the *hypothalamus* controls appetite, but the controlling mechanism does not seem to work properly for everyone.

Psychological influences are important. The sight and smell of good food stimulates appetite in most people. Others eat because they are unhappy and emotionally disturbed and food is a comfort. Habit and custom also play a part. The nervous strain involved for hearty eaters who have been put on a slimming diet is considerable. It used to be thought that appetite was stimulated by exercise and that its value to slimmers was not very great, even though the exercise used up energy which might otherwise be stored as fat. Modern research suggests that, at least for some people, regular exercise does stimulate the appetite-depressing mechanism of the body and can lead to a smaller intake of food. This, plus the exercise, can have a long-term beneficial effect.

One of modern man's difficulties is that his eating habits and appetite are legacies from his forebears who, of necessity, led a much more active life.

Certain types of food seem to satisfy the appetite more quickly than others, e.g. meat is more satisfying than sugar and the person who has a big steak usually does not want to fill up afterwards with a lot of sweet things.

The appetite is stimulated by the sight and smell of good food, and even by thinking of it. Other stimulants are the extractives present in a *consommé* (clear soup), or taking a small amount of alcohol before a meal.

FEEDING PEOPLE WHOSE DIETS NEED SPECIAL CARE

INFANT FEEDING (from birth to 5 years)

The doctor's advice should be carefully followed in the early stages. Infancy is a period of very rapid growth when the foundations of good health are made and good food habits established. A baby's first food is milk and then cereals. Fruit and vegetable *purées* and egg yolk are gradually added, followed by sieved or minced meat and fish. At about one month, cod liver oil and orange juice are given. By the age of 1 year the child should be on a mixed diet and having a good general diet (see *Nutrition*, page 146) with quantities adapted to the child's needs and appetite. To reduce the labour of sieving, many infant foods are available in small cans, providing a wide variety of flavours and foods. Mechanical sieves, blenders, and mincers of various kinds are a help in making *purées* and minced food in the home.

Menu Plan Suitable for a Child of 1–5 years

ON WAKING

Orange juice in water.

BREAKFAST

Milk.
Cereal or porridge.
Half an egg or half a rasher of bacon or 1–2 Tbs. steamed fish.
Bread or rusk with butter or margarine.

MID-MORNING

Milk.

DINNER

Minced or chopped meat or flaked fish, or grated cheese or egg (according to the family meal).
Mashed potato, swede or carrot, and a green vegetable.
Milk as a drink, or included in the pudding.
Milk pudding or junket or custard, with stewed fruit, or a fruit fool, or a baked apple or a light sponge pudding.
A piece of raw fruit to end the meal, or a hard rusk.

Milk or milky cocoa.
Bread or rusk.
Butter or margarine.
Jam, jelly, honey, or vegetable extract.
Finely-grated or chopped vegetables such as tomatoes or watercress made into sandwiches.

Milky drink.

Cod liver oil at some convenient time. (Some mothers give it at bath time.) If cod liver oil or an equivalent rich source of vitamin D is not given it is important to see that there is plenty of margarine used in spreading and cooking, and that fish such as herrings, kippers, and sardines are frequently used for sandwich fillings.

OLDER CHILDREN

A similar pattern of eating should be followed, except that quantities gradually become larger and the pattern of the evening meal changes with later bedtimes. After a light tea taken on returning from school, there will be either a High Tea or Supper with a main dish of egg, cheese, meat or fish, some vegetable, salad, or fruit, and more milk as a flavoured milk or straight.

FEEDING DIFFICULTIES

Most feeding difficulties start as attention-getting gambits and are best ignored. It does not hurt healthy children to go without food for a while, and if they find their refusal to eat does not upset anybody they will soon grow tired of the act. A very young child soon discovers that to be difficult about food is one of the few weapons it has with which to oppose adult domination, and if success comes once, the same or a similar thing will be tried again, until there is danger of a whole pattern of feeding difficulties being built up.

Frequently children will refuse a particular food because they have heard an older child or adult say that they do not like it. This is a pity, but when it happens with a valuable food it is important for the mother to know something about the relative nutritive values of foods, so that an adequate substitute may be provided. For example the child who refuses to eat cooked green vegetables needs to have more fresh fruit and tomatoes added to the day's foods.

It is important that parents should encourage children to eat as varied a diet as possible and to teach them that it is normal to like and eat a wide variety of foods, to have a healthy appetite and enjoy good food. On the other hand, it is important not to over-emphasise food – a danger when the mother prides herself on her cooking and on 'keeping a good table'. It is so easy then for a pattern of overeating to develop which, in turn, can lead to obesity and its accompanying disabilities, both physical and psychological.

ADOLESCENTS

The right kind of food can make a great deal of difference to the health of adolescents during puberty, their period of most rapid growth. The usual age for the sudden spurt in growth is about 11 years for girls and 13 for boys, although quite normal individuals will differ widely from these figures, some at younger ages, some older.

The growth rate per year in puberty is often double that of the previous year. This growth involves all body tissues, blood, bones, muscle, and glands. The additional material needed to produce healthy growth can only come from food. An adolescent needs a liberal intake of all nutrients (see *Nutrition*, page 146).

Frequently adolescent girls are afraid of getting fat if they eat certain foods. Often the foods they think are fattening are not, and are precisely those they should be having in generous amounts. Milk is one example of this. Many schoolgirls refuse to drink it because they think it is fattening and yet, at the same time, they consume large quantities of sweets, cakes, and biscuits, which have a much higher calorific value than milk and do not usually contain as much protein, minerals, and vitamins, necessary for good health and good looks.

Both boys and girls frequently have fluctuating appetites and strong food aversions. The former is a normal condition, and food should not be forced on them. Like very young children, they will often be difficult about food, just to annoy and worry their parents. It is, therefore, unwise to take much notice of

155

their whims. See that good nourishing food is available, and they will eat readily enough when they are hungry again and are not badgered to do so. If they refuse certain foods, let them have more of the foods they like and, if these are nutritionally less desirable, use guile to get them to take the better foods. For example, if they refuse to drink milk but like coffee, make the coffee strongish with all milk or use some undiluted evaporated milk, or make the milk a very sophisticated 'mocha' with a mixture of soluble coffee and drinking chocolate. If they like fruit shakes, add some evaporated milk. If they do not like milk but like cheese, do not worry. Give them lumps of cheese to eat whenever they like; with fruit, for snack meals, and even for a quick breakfast.

If they are maddeningly casual and irregular about meal times do not get too worried. A hot dinner is not a necessity.

If they are getting themselves a cold snack see that there is more than tea, cake, and bread available. Leave some cold meat, canned fish, or cheese and some fruit and/or salad ingredients. The fact that they may make of it what, to you, is a revolting mixture, is unimportant – as long as the mixture contains the nutrients needed for health and growth.

Much good can often be done by drawing their attention to the eating habits of their stage or athletic heroes and heroines, details of which are frequently published and usually show a sensible if unorthodox pattern of eating.

THE SEDENTARY

A large number of people today lead very sedentary lives with machines to do the hard physical work of most jobs, cars to transport them from door to door, spectator rather than active sports, and little exercise taken, unless it is deliberately planned.

For a sedentary life the energy-producing foods needed are much less than for an active life, but many people's appetites do not automatically control intake to fit the body's needs. The two most noticeable effects of this on the sedentary are obesity, with its accompanying troubles, and indigestion through overloading the intestines with food too rich and difficult to digest for someone leading an inactive life.

A diet consisting of foods low in calorific value yet containing adequate amounts of other nutrients should be aimed at. Foods which provide nothing but energy should be reduced to the minimum, e.g. sugars and sweets, oils and fats (except for 1–1½ oz. (30–45 g.) butter or margarine daily (see *Nutrition*, page 146), fatty meats, fatty methods of cooking like frying, pastry, and suet puddings.

Milk, cheese, eggs, lean meat, plenty of fresh fruit and vegetables, and some bread and butter should form the basis of the diet, and simple cooking methods should predominate.

THE VEGAN

A person who eats only vegetable foods. This can be an adequate diet if the vegetables are carefully chosen for their nutritive value, but it is more difficult to have sufficient good-quality protein, iron, and vitamin B12. Vegans tend to suffer from protein deficiency, and from iron-deficiency anaemia.

Most people are vegans for religious reasons, but some believe it is a more healthy diet for humans although there is very little reliable evidence to support their theories. On the other hand, most people who adopt vegan or vegetarian diets are more interested in the connection between food intake and health, and may eat a better diet than some others for that reason. This does not, however, prove that good health could not be achieved with a well-chosen diet containing meat and other animal foods.

THE VEGETARIAN

This originally meant a person who ate only vegetable foods but has come to mean people who eat no meat. Most people who call themselves vegetarians do in fact consume milk and cheese and sometimes eggs as well, hence the adoption of the word 'vegan' to distinguish the true vegetarian. Sometimes the milk-drinking vegetarians are referred to as 'lacto-vegetarians'. The lacto-vegetarian has, on the whole, a more nourishing diet than the vegan because milk and cheese are an excellent source of good-quality protein likely to be lacking in the diet of a vegan. There is still, however, the problem of iron consumption (see *Vegan*, above).

PRESERVED FOODS

People in Britain are more healthy today than they have ever been, and this is at least partly due to a better state of nutrition. There would not be enough foods to achieve this if it wasn't for modern methods of preserving, so that the food can be

157

brought from far-away places in good condition. We just can't grow enough here to feed everyone adequately with locally-produced and unpreserved food. And, while it is true that all preserving produces some loss of nutritive value, it is also true that modern methods reduce this to a minimum and in certain cases actually improve the nutritive value. In the section on 'The Nutritive Value of Foods', pages 161–72, I have mentioned many preserved foods, and explained how the preserving affects the food value and its nutritional significance.

'HEALTH' FOODS AND 'NATURAL' FOODS

There is no such thing as a health food. There are healthy diets and unhealthy diets, but no single food can rightly be claimed to promote health.

Buying expensive 'health' foods by no means ensures that the consumer will be more healthy, and spending the same money on a well-chosen diet of ordinary foods might easily produce better results.

There is a widespread belief that 'natural' foods – meaning unprocessed foods – are more healthy than processed and manufactured ones. The argument seems to be that nature cares more about the welfare of the human race than man himself.

In fact, the composition of processed foods is closely controlled by law and they are most unlikely to contain any toxic substances, whereas natural foods quite easily can, especially if they have not had any inspection or testing before being sold. To take a few examples; honey can be poisonous if the bees have gathered the nectar from certain flowers; members of the *brassica* (cabbage) family contain goitrogens which, under certain conditions, can induce goitre in humans; water taken from a well or clear mountain stream can be much less safe to drink than the treated and processed water from a city supply; certain fungi contain deadly poisons; some fish and shellfish are toxic even when taken from uncontaminated waters; fungal contamination of natural foods like cereals produces poisons. Many natural foods are harmful when they become stale, and one of the things done to food during processing is to prolong its life as a safe food to eat.

It is a good thing that the public should be critical of the kind of food processing we have, but to make sweeping general-

158

isations that all processed food is bad and all natural food good shows a lack of understanding of the true nature of food, and of modern food technology.

One should view with scepticism the pronouncements of people who grow rich on selling 'health' foods, just as much as one should not accept uncritically all that a manufacturer of processed foods tells us about his products.

The consumer in Britain is protected by many laws controlling the manufacture and sale of foods, and there is no food sold legally which does not come under some form of control.

The major laws are Acts of Parliament – important general laws which it is a criminal offence to break, and for which the offender can be prosecuted in the Magistrates' Court. An Act gives power to the appropriate Government Department to pass other types of law – Statutory Regulations and Orders – which are laws controlling the details of Acts, are constantly under review and altered and added to as the need arises.

The Government Department concerned with the majority of laws regarding food is the Ministry of Agriculture, Fisheries, and Food.

Among the important Acts affecting the consumer very closely is the Food and Drugs Act of 1955, which controls the composition of a large number of manufactured and packet foods, lays down rules for the labelling of foods, and controls the hygiene of food handling in shops and restaurants.

A more recent Act is the Weights and Measure Act of 1963, which is primarily designed to protect the customer against a trader who might use inaccurate scales or give short measure. Weighing, measuring, or counting the goods must be carried out in the presence of the customer. It also makes it compulsory for net weights of certain foods to be printed on the labels on containers. In the case of some fruits and vegetables, such as those which are pre-packed, a scale must be provided for the purchaser to weigh the goods and the container.

Under the laws which control the labelling of pre-pracked foods, the label must give the name and business address of the packer or labeller, or a registered trade mark. When the composition of these foods is not already controlled by law, the Labelling of Food Order requires the ingredients to be listed in descending order, according to the proportions by weight, unless the actual quantities of each ingredient are listed. Water need not be declared as an ingredient.

The use of any false or misleading trade description is prohibited, and the use of a label or advertisement which falsely describes a food or misleads as to its nature, substance, or quality, including its nutritional or dietary value, is prohibited. It is also an offence to sell unsound food.

Anyone who has occasion to think that food sold to them is defective in quality, weight, or composition, should regard it as a duty to report the matter to the local Council Office, where there are officials responsible for seeing that the Acts are complied with.

Obviously the details of such Acts are too numerous to be listed in a book of this nature, but copies of all Acts can be purchased from Her Majesty's Stationery Office, and some are available in local reference libraries.

The controls concern such things as the composition of flour and bread, the production and designation of milk, the addition of vitamins to margarine, the colourings which may be used in food, the amount of fish in a fish cake, the size of stamped eggs – and a host of other items.

In certain respects some people feel that the laws are not strict enough, or that there is no control where there should be some. One example is the use of awkward weights of foods in a packet which seems to be designed to confuse the housewife, and to make it almost impossible for her to compare prices of different brands. Others would like to see it made compulsory for all perishable foods to be stamped with the date by which they should be used; and that meat and other foods packed for sale in supermarkets should be clearly labelled with names of cuts and price per pound. Some shops and some manufacturers already give this kind of service, and the housewife can help by giving her custom to such places and buying such foods, whenever she has a choice.

Some of the problems which confront our food law makers are very complex, requiring much research, and are today studied on an international level by the Food and Agricultural Organisation and the World Health Organisation, who issue reports on their findings from time to time. These, too, are obtainable through Her Majesty's Stationery Office. Among the subjects that they deal with are the use of chemicals in foods, and the safety of food colourings.

THE NUTRITIVE VALUE OF FOODS

As I have said earlier, the nutritive value of individual foods in the diet is less important than the composition of the diet as a whole. To eat a wide variety of foods is one of the best ways of ensuring good nutrition, for then some foods supplement the nutritive value of others to make a good total diet. To worry about the individual composition of this or that food tends to produce food fads – which will not necessarily result in good nutrition.

Provided that a good general pattern of eating is followed (such as that outlined under 'The Basic Principles of Good Nutrition', pages 146–8), there is little need to worry about the choice of individual foods.

But for those who like to know more about nutritive values, I include some information about the most important groups of foods, and the most common in these groups

MILK AND ITS ALTERNATIVES

Milk contains some of all the nutrients known to be needed by man. The amounts of iron and vitamin C, however, are very small. For this reason it is unwise to give children so much milk that they cannot take enough of the foods which will supply iron and vitamin C. This can happen when people become over-enthusiastic about giving children large amounts of milk. In the average diet, the most important nutrients present in milk are the protein, calcium, and riboflavine. Other vitamins present in useful amounts are B1, nicotinic acid, A, and D. The fat (cream) in milk is in a finely emulsified form and is easy to digest. The carbohydrate is a sugar, lactose. When milk is pasteurised there is a reduction of 20 per cent of the vitamin B1 and 20 per cent of the vitamin C but this loss is far out-weighed by the benefits of having safe milk. Sterilised milk loses 30 per cent of the vitamin B1 and 50 per cent of the vitamin C. In drying and canning milks there are similar losses of these two vitamins. In some cases they are 'restored' by adding vitamins after processing.

Skimmed milks are usually labelled 'unfit for babies'. This is because the cream, and vitamins A and D, have been removed, and these are essential in milk for infants. The skimmed milks are still excellent value for adults and older children who can

161

get their vitamins elsewhere. The skimmed milks are a rich source of protein, calcium, and some of the B vitamins.

Cheese

The main variation in nutritive value is in the fat content, according to whether the milk is skimmed or whole, whether it had added cream or whether it is all cream. The calorie value is 100–110 per oz. (or 30 g.), the harder cheese being the more concentrated, and the softer having more water – and, therefore, a lower calorie value, e.g. cottage cheese made from skimmed milk.

All cheese is an excellent source of protein, and one of the cheapest available. It is also a rich source of calcium, riboflavine, and vitamin A, more in cheese made during the summer months. Its nutritive value is not affected by cooking.

Except for some Norwegian cheeses which have added sugar, there is no carbohydrate present.

When cheese is being substituted for meat in a main meal, 2 oz. (60 g.) cheese is equal to 3–4 oz. (90–125 g.) of meat as far as protein is concerned.

Yogurt

Being made from milk, it has the same nutritive value, except for sugar, which is less in yogurt than in milk. During the process of fermentation some of the sugar in the milk is converted to lactic acid – which gives the sharp taste to yogurt (and also to sour milk and cream).

Many claims have been made regarding the therapeutic value of yogurt, but there is no reliable evidence that it is any more beneficial than an equivalent amount of fresh milk or cheese.

FATS

Fat is a concentrated source of energy, giving twice as much per gramme as carbohydrate and protein. Fat stored in the body helps to protect it from the cold, and also to cushion organs such as the kidneys. Too much stored fat, on the other hand, is a hindrance to movement and to the circulation.

Fat takes longer to digest than other foods and this makes the satisfying feel of a meal containing fat greater than a fatless one. But too much fat delays digestion, and can cause great discomfort and even vomiting.

162

Butter and margarine contain fat-soluble vitamins A and D. Butter usually has more vitamin A, and margarine more vitamin D. The quantity of vitamins in margarine is controlled, but that in butter varies with the season, the kind of cow, its diet and living conditions.

MEAT, GAME, POULTRY, FISH, AND EGGS

Bacon

Bacon is a good source of protein, fat, and vitamins of the B complex, especially vitamin B1, and is a better source of B vitamins than beef, lamb, or chicken. Very fat bacon tends to have proportionately less of the protein and vitamins than the leaner cuts, with lean gammon having the highest content. Fat bacon, on the other hand, has a higher calorie content.

Beef

Beef is a valuable source of protein, iron, and vitamins of the B complex. With the exception of offal, beef contains more iron than any other meat, corned beef being the richest. The nutritive value of beef is not very much affected by cooking, except when meat is canned. Then a lot of the vitamin B1 is lost. In corned beef the B vitamins are very largely lost due to expression of juice, and losses occur when there is a lot of 'drip' from defrosted frozen meat.

There is no difference in nutritive value between an expensive fillet steak and the cheaper stewing steak, so with the cheaper meat you get more food value for your money.

Chicken

It is a good source of protein, having approximately the same amount per oz. (30 g.) as other lean meats. The fat content is lower than most meats, and the calorie value too. Chicken contains small amounts of calcium, iron, and vitamins of the B complex, expecially nicotinic acid.

Chicken breast cooked and served simply is regarded as a very easy meat to digest, and is a favourite food for sick people.

Eggs

Eggs contain some of most nutrients except carbohydrate and vitamin C. They are a good source of high-quality protein, of iron, and of vitamins A and D. They contain some vitamin B1 and riboflavine. They are not a rich source of nicotinic acid, but do contain tryptophan, from which it is made. They are, on the whole, easily digested, unless cooked to make them tough. Hard-boiled eggs are more easily digested when mashed or chopped, and this is the better way of serving them to the very young and old, and to invalids.

Raw eggs are less well digested than lightly cooked ones and, in addition, they contain a substance called 'avidin' which, in the raw state, makes the vitamin Biotin unavailable to the body. It is, however, unlikely that this would matter in the quantities in which most people are likely to eat raw eggs.

Fish

Fish is a good source of protein containing approximately the same amount per oz. (30 g.) as the average meat. It provides some calcium and vitamins of the B complex, while oily fish and fish livers are a good source of vitamins A and D.

Most of the nutrients are retained during canning and curing, and canned fish is a better source of calcium than fresh fish, as the bones are softened enough to eat, and these supply calcium. Fish roes are a better source of B vitamins than the flesh.

White fish is easily digested, and forms an important item of the diet for sick people.

Herrings are best value for money, and should appear in some form on the menu at least once a week (for alternatives, see page 154). This is to ensure a good intake of vitamin D, which is not found in appreciable amounts in many other foods.

Lamb and Mutton

Both are a good source of protein and fat. Each contains less iron than beef, about the same amount of vitamin A, more vitamin B1, and about the same of the other B vitamins. Because of their high fat content lamb and mutton are sometimes more difficult to digest than leaner meats, but the surplus fat is easy to remove, either before or after cooking.

Offal

This includes organs like liver, heart, kidney, pancreas (sweetbreads), brains, tripe; and also feet, whole heads, and tails. Of these, the most valuable nutritionally are liver, kidney, and heart. Liver is the best nutritive value for money of any

164

part of an animal, being a rich source of protein, vitamins A and B, iron, and some vitamin D. Both kidney and heart contain good amounts of protein, vitamins A and B, and iron. The other kinds of offal provide much smaller quantities of nutrients, and are no better than meat muscle. Tripe is an exception, in that it is a good source of calcium as well as protein, because lime is used in cleaning the tripe during its preparation for sale.

Pork

Weight-for-weight, it generally contains less protein and more fat than beef, and more fat than lamb. The calcium content is small, and there is less iron than in beef. But pork is a very good source of vitamin B1, much better than either beef or lamb, and it is a good source of the other B vitamins. It contains no vitamin A, C, or D. Because it has a high fat content, pork tends to be more difficult to digest than the leaner meats, so ideally the foods served at the same meal should have a low fat content to compensate.

Sausages

Their food value depends on the kind of meat used, and the amount. Preservatives are allowed to be used in sausages, and a sulphur compound is the usual one. This has a destructive effect on vitamin B1, so that pork sausages have less of this vitamin than would be obtained from an equal weight of fresh pork. Although sausages provide some of all nutrients except vitamins A, C, and D, they are not particularly good for providing any one nutrient.

Veal

This is similar to beef, but has less fat, iron, and vitamin A. It is a good source of protein and vitamins of the B complex. Many people think veal is indigestible and should not be given to invalids. There is no evidence to support this theory. Veal does need thorough cooking, and should never be served rare, like beef.

FRUIT AND VEGETABLES

Fruit

Fruit is important in the diet as a source of vitamins, especially vitamin C, and, to a lesser extent, carotene. Fruit also contains considerable amounts of cellulose, which is useful in providing bulk to the diet and aiding peristalsis. Raw fruit, especially apples, is excellent for exercising the teeth and gums, and for cleaning the teeth after sticky, sweet foods have been eaten. Children should be taught to end a meal with a piece of raw fruit to clean their teeth.

The best fruits for vitamin C are rosehip syrup, black-currants, oranges, lemons, grapefruit, strawberries, green gooseberries, other fresh currants, loganberries, raspberries, and some varities of apple. Some imported tropical fruits are also a good source whether they are fresh or canned, e.g. guavas, goldenberries or cape gooseberries, tree tomatoes. Candied, *glacé*, and dried fruits usually contain no vitamin C. Accelerated freeze-dried fruits retain the vitamin as do frozen fruits. Canned fruits are also a good source if the original fruit was good, and many of the fruit juices are excellent sources of this vitamin (orange, grapefruit, guava, black-currant).

Vegetables

In the average family the most important contribution vege-tables make to the nutritional value of the diet is vitamin C, and the chief ones providing that are potatoes, green vegetables, and tomatoes. These are not the richest sources of the vitamin, but they are the ones eaten in largest amounts regularly. Because bad cooking and serving can cause large losses of this vitamin it is very important for the home cook to learn how to handle vegetables carefully.

Beans

Young green beans in pods, e.g. French beans, contribute small amounts of many nutrients, including vitamin C, but they are not outstanding in any way. All dried beans are a good source of vegetable protein, carbohydrate, and of B vitamins. When beans are allowed to sprout the shoots provide vitamin C. Dried beans do, however, contain much coarse cellulose, and tend to produce flatulence when eaten by some people. They are usually more easily digested when thoroughly cooked and then sieved.

Dried beans of all kinds are a cheap source of protein and energy, and when mixed with small amounts of milk, cheese, or eggs are equal in value to meat protein.

166

Brussels Sprouts

They are one of the best green vegetables for vitamin C, 3 oz. (90 g.) of boiled sprouts (a small helping) providing the day's minimum needs for this vitamin. They also contain small amounts of B vitamins and carotene, together with small amounts of all other nutrients except vitamin D.

Cabbage

Cabbage is a valuable food because when properly cooked and served, it supplies useful amounts of vitamin C. Four ounces (125 g.) of boiled cabbage will supply the daily needs of this vitamin for the average adult. If raw cabbage is eaten, $1\frac{1}{2}$ oz. (45 g.) would supply the same amount of vitamin, but, since this is rather a lot to eat, on the whole cooked cabbage is a more useful regular item in the diet.

Cabbage also supplies some carotene, some B vitamins, calcium, iron, a little protein, and plenty of cellulose.

Carrots

They contain more sugar than most other vegetables, except sugar beet, though not enough for them to be classed as a high-carbohydrate food.

Their most outstanding contribution to the diet is carotene, from which vitamin A is made in the body. Carrots are one of the richest sources of this subtance, which is more readily absorbed from cooked carrots than from raw ones. Raw carrots are, however, valuable for children, to make them chew, and to clean their teeth. Give a piece of one at the end of a meal.

Cauliflower

An important source of vitamin C, provided that the cauliflower is freshly cooked and is not kept hot or reheated. It contains small amounts of vitamins of the B complex, calcium, iron, protein, and carbohydrate, but no fat, carotene, or vitamin D.

Peas

All peas contain more protein than most other vegetables, processed and mature dried peas having most, and very young

167

green peas the least. They all contain some carbohydrate, more in mature peas in the form of starch, while young peas contain sugar, hence their sweet taste. The sugar changes to starch as they mature. All peas contain some calcium, iron, and carotene, but are not important sources of these nutrients. They also contain vitamins of the B complex, fresh green peas having most. Processed and dried peas usually lose much of the vitamin B1 during processing. Fresh green peas, frozen, and modern dried peas have small amounts of vitamin C, but mature dried and processed peas have none.

Potatoes

Potatoes contain small amounts of protein, calcium, iron, vitamins of the B complex, and vitamin C. They also provide starch used as a source of energy, but are not as rich a source as bread and cereals. Unless they are fried or roasted, potatoes are comparatively low-calorie foods. In the average diet in Britain they are most important for their vitamin C content, providing more than 50 per cent of the daily total. This is because of the regularity with which they are eaten, and the amounts consumed. Preserved potatoes, like flakes and powder, which do not contain as much vitamin C as freshly-cooked potatoes, are not an adequate substitute in this respect, and people who use them for reasons of convenience should take more of the other foods providing vitamin C. This also applies to people who regularly eat in large catering establishments where the potatoes are liable to have lost most of the vitamin by the time they reach the customer.

During storage, the vitamin C content diminishes, and is at its lowest at the end of the winter before the new potatoes arrive.

Salads

Some people seem to equate salads with good nutrition, and to think that they are essential items in a diet. This is not true. They are certainly desirable, but there are other foods which can take their place nutritionally – fruits for example, and in some climates these are far safer to eat than vegetables, which can more easily be contaminated with disease-producing organisms.

The nutritive value of the salad obviously depends on the choice of ingredients. It is common for a cooked portion of green vegetables to be a better source of vitamin C than a portion of the vegetables raw, simply because it is possible to eat three or more times as much of the cooked vegetable.

Salads are important for providing fresh crisp foods to give variety of texture, and also for their attractive appearance. Raw vegetables and fruit need more chewing than cooked ones, and this gives the teeth important exercise.

Tomatoes

They contain small amounts of all nutrients except fat and vitamin D. They have a fairly high content of carotene, and a useful amount of vitamin C. (Two average-sized tomatoes will supply the minimum day's need of an adult.) Some of the vitamin C is lost in cooking and canning (approximately 40–50 per cent), and when canned tomatoes are heated for service, the loss is greater still. If canned tomatoes are to be a main source of vitamin C in the diet, use canned tomato juice, and do not heat it.

BREAD, FLOUR, AND CEREALS

Bread and flour are a useful source of protein, iron, calcium, vitamin B1, and nicotinic acid, as well as of calories. Wholemeal bread and flour contain more vitamin B1 and nicitonic acid than white bread and flour, but the amount of calcium is less. Calcium, iron, vitamin B1, and nicotinic acid are added to white flour and bread.

The germ of the wheat is removed when low-extraction flours are made, and this is rich in protein and B vitamins. It is used to make germ meals (white flour plus germs) or sold separately as wheat germ. The outer branny layers of the wheat grain are also removed in low-extraction-rate flours. These consist very largely of cellulose. Bran is used for some breakfast cereals, and also for feeding animals. Herbivorous animals have the power to digest cellulose and obtain energy from it, but man cannot do this. Opponents of this policy say it is unnecessary to have so much calcium in the diet and why remove the most valuable parts of the grain and then put back some of the nutrients into the white flour?

Controversy regarding the relative values of white and brown bread has gone on for many years, and is likely to continue for many more. The protagonists sometimes seem to forget that the composition of the diet as a whole is the important thing, and, in a country with a wide choice of foods such as we have, the kind of bread eaten is relatively unimportant.

Cakes and Biscuits

Their value depends to a certain extent on the ingredients, although the bulk of these are fat, flour, and sugar so the carbohydrate and calorie content is always high. If the fat used is either butter or margarine this will provide some vitamin A and D, and there will be B vitamins from the flour and some protein, calcium, and iron.

Nutritionally, cakes and biscuits should be looked on as luxuries to have in small amounts, and not as an important item in the diet.

Oat Products

Oats contain some of most nutrients, except vitamins A, C, and D. When compared with wheat products, the protein content is about the same as for wholemeal flour, but there is considerably more fat in oatmeal. This accounts for the fact that oat products have a tendency to develop a rancid flavour when stale. There is less calcium and more iron than in wheat flour. The B vitamin content is approximately the same as for wholemeal flour, except for much less nicotinic acid. When oat products are eaten regularly they make an important contribution to the nutritive value of the diet.

Pasta

Pasta is made from the same part of the wheat grain as white flour and has a similar composition, the most important nutrients being protein and carbohydrate. There are small amounts of calcium and iron and B vitamins. As a staple article of diet it is not as good nutritionally as the sort of white bread which is a staple in Britain, but the cheese, meat, and other similar ingredients usually eaten with it make up for its deficiencies to a certain extent.

Pastry

The value depends on the ingredients used but, as fat and flour are the basis, pastry is a food of high calorific value, definitely not for slimmers.

Pastry made with butter or margarine contains some vitamins A and D, and indeed, this sort of pastry contains some of all the important nutrients except vitamin C. If the filling is a fruit rich in this vitamin then the pie or tart can be said to be of very good nutrutive value for the active and the slim.

Rice

The main nutrient is carbohydrate (starch), but rice also contains some protein, and a little fat, calcium, iron, and vitamins of the B complex. Parboiled and brown rice contain more of the minerals and vitamins. When rice is boiled in large amounts of water the water-soluble B vitamins are largely dissolved out into the cooking liquid, which is often discarded. It is better to cook rice in a small amount of water which is all absorbed by the end of the cooking time. Compared with wheat flour, the nutritive value of rice is not so good, and it does not make as good a basic cereal on which to build nutritionally-sound diets.

SUGARS, PRESERVES, AND SWEETS

Sugar and Sweets

Nutritionally, sugar is a poor food. It provides only one nutrient, carbohydrate. The best way of eating sugar, therefore, is as part of a meal where the other foods help to make up for the deficiencies of the sugar. The worst way of using it is as sweets between meals. Black treacle and molasses contain calcium and iron, but unless large amounts of them are eaten this is not important in the day's total intake of nutrients. Brown sugar has no advantage over white, nutritionally.

Chocolate

Chocolate has a high carbohydrate value from the sugar added, and a high calorie value from the sugar and fat – approx. 166 calories per oz. (30 g.) Milk chocolate contains more protein than plain chocolate but neither is a particularly rich source of this nutrient. You would have to eat almost the whole of a 4 oz. (125 g.) bar of chocolate to get as much protein as is contained in one egg but you would get 640 calories from the chocolate and only 92 from the egg. Chocolate contains a fair amount of calcium and iron, small amounts of carotene, and of vitamins of the B complex.

171

Honey

Honey contains mainly sugars (glucose and fructose), and small quantities of various vitamins, but the amounts are so small that it is not possible for honey to be an important source of any of them in the diet. Many people ascribe magical health-giving properties to honey, yet science has failed to find anything in it to account for this reputation. All that can be said for it is that it has a much nicer flavour than white sugar, and that it is a more versatile sweetener, being suitable for use in cooking and as a spread.

Jam and Marmalade

Jam is chiefly a source of carbohydrate, the main ingredient being sugar. If it is made with a fruit rich in vitamin C, there will be some in the jam, but even with blackcurrant jam this is not more than approximately 6 mg. vitamin C per oz. (30 g.).

FOOD HYGIENE

Food and kitchen hygiene are important health factors about which many people are careless. The end result is frequently food poisoning, characterised by attacks of diarrhoea and/or vomiting.

Foods most frequently the cause of this are meat dishes, especially reheated and cooked meat, meat pies, and stews.

Sometimes the bacteria which cause food poisoning are already in the meat, and sometimes they arrive there as a result of bad hygiene in the home, e.g. not washing the hands after visiting the toilet, blowing the nose, or handling animals. Bacteria also come from dust and flies to which the meat has been exposed.

Do not let flies in your kitchen or on food. They are dirty, disease-bearing insects because they feed on excreta and refuse, and then come straight on to the food, bringing germs attached to the fine hairs on their legs and in the saliva they secrete copiously as they feed. There are so many ways of protecting food from flies, and modern sprays for dealing with them, that there is no excuse for having them in the house at all. When using any sprays or repellents, be sure to follow the manufacturer's instructions for their safe use.

Cooked meat which is not to be eaten at once should be

cooled rapidly and then stored in a cold place, preferably in the refrigerator. Meat that is being reheated should be brought to the boil and not just warmed up.

Meat pies and cooked cold meats should be used up on the day they are bought, and home-made ones should be stored in a refrigerator.

For recommended safe storage times for different foods, see pages 101–14.

Nothing containing meat should ever be allowed to stand in a warm kitchen or dining room. And the same applies to things containing cream and gelatine.

Be particular, too, about the shops that you patronise, and do not use dirty ones with dirty assistants, ones where animals are allowed to roam about, or ones where the assistants handle cooked meat in their hands, and where cooked meat is not kept in a refrigerator or in a refrigerated display cabinet. Do not buy cooked meat from a butcher where the same assistant handles raw meat as well. And do not buy cream cakes which have been displayed on a counter where people can cough and breathe over them.

WASHING-UP

Keeping utensils and cutlery really clean is of vital importance to health. The most hygienic way of doing the dishes is in a good dish-washing machine, but there is no reason why hand-washing should not be hygienic too, and it is often kinder to delicate china and glass than a machine. One of the reasons why a machine is so good is because really hot water is used, and the dishes are properly rinsed in clean water.

The first important step in hand dish-washing is to scrape or rinse all food from utensils before beginning to wash up; either under the cold tap for all except greasy articles, or use paper towels to wipe off the food residues. If you fail to do this the washing-up water soon gets like soup, and the utensils are not cleaned properly. As you remove the food, stack the utensils in neat piles ready for the real washing. It is a good idea to stand cutlery in a jug or jar of cold water to loosen any food left on it, before washing. Always put cold or hot water in a saucepan as soon as you have finished with it, and leave it to soak. Remember that cold water is the best for soaking all but greasy utensils.

If you have twin sinks, fill the second one with very hot water for rinsing the utensils after they have been washed. Some people keep the hot tap running slowly and rinse under that as they go. Another way, when all the utensils have been washed, is to put them in the drying racks in the sink after it has been emptied, and then to pour very hot water over them as a rinse. For this you need either a swivel arm to the taps or a short length of hose, preferably with a spray end.

Always wear rubber gloves when washing up as you can then stand hotter water than is possible with bare hands. Thick gloves are better than the very thin ones.

Plastic-coated draining racks are the best, as they can be washed more easily than wooden ones, and are light to lift. Leave the rinsed dishes to drain dry. If they need it, rub them up with a clean dry tea towel as you put them away. Some people prefer to dry glass and cutlery as it is washed, but it is essential to use a clean dry cloth or paper towels; a damp, used towel can be full of germs.

To wash up properly is more bother than to do a really dirty job, but the result is worth while, because it helps to ensure that your family eats from really clean plates and with really clean cutlery, and that the tools that you cook with are really clean.

WASTE DISPOSAL

A waste-disposal unit fitted to the sink waste pipe should be used in accordance with the manufacturer's instructions and local authority regulations.

There are, however, many other methods of dealing with kitchen waste. Some of it can be used for animal feeding, or go on the compost heap for garden use, or in the incinerator. But for many city dwellers all waste goes into one receptacle, to be removed by the council employees.

For disposal in sacks and bins, all kitchen waste should first be wrapped in paper. This serves two purposes. If the waste is going into a bin, wrapping helps to keep the bin clean, or, if a paper or polythene sack is being used, it prevents sharp things from cutting the sack, and discourages animals from trying to claw their way in. If you use a bin this should be washed out when it gets dirty and occasionally disinfected, especially during the warmer months, when flies and bacteria breed fast.

174

If you use a small pedal bin in the kitchen and throw waste straight into this, tip the waste onto paper and wrap it before finally disposing of it. Wash out the soiled bin straight away. Paper and polythene sacks for lining these bins are a great convenience, as are the small bag units for fixing on a wall or the side of a kitchen unit.

Before throwing away empty cans, rinse them to remove food residues and smells. Jagged tops should be wrapped in paper; this is especially important if you are using a sack for waste disposal.

Be sure to keep outside bins covered to prevent animals from climbing in, and, in the summer, to keep out flies and other pests. Powdered disinfectant helps to discourage them.

KEEPING THE KITCHEN CLEAN

How much daily care the kitchen needs depends on how much use it gets. Things which usually require daily attention include wiping over the bench tops and cooker after use, making sure that the sink is left clean, emptying out the day's food waste, putting things away, cleaning out ashes from a boiler, changing the tea towels, checking food in larder or refrigerator to see what needs using up right away (or what should be thrown out).

Things needing weekly or periodical cleaning include a thorough cleaning of the cooker, refrigerator, larder and/or food cupboards, the floor, the surrounds of the cooker and kitchen units, windows, and ventilators.

Six-monthly or annual cleaning should include all walls and the ceiling, cupboards and drawers, the freezer, cleaning behind all movable equipment, any curtains or blinds, and extractor fans or other ventilating arrangements.

For cleaning, use hot water and a detergent which is also a good grease solvent. Change the water frequently, as soon as it gets dirty.

CLEANING THE COOKER

Be sure to turn off the gas or electricity before you do anything other than just wiping over the top or outside.

Regular care should include wiping over the top after use, cleaning up any spills as soon as possible, and wiping out the oven while it is still warm.

For a special clean, remove the racks and other loose parts, and put them in the sink to soak in hot water and detergent. Use steel-wool pads for light cleaning of the inside of the oven, drip trays, and so on. For heavier dirt use a proprietary oven cleaner, following the directions carefully.

The chief sources of dirt in an oven are fat spluttering or things boiling over or being spilt. You can cut down the rate of soiling by covering meat when it is roasted, or by using low-temperature roasting methods. When putting pies or milk puddings to cook, put the pie-dish or casserole on a baking tray to catch spills. Do this for anything that is likely to bubble over or to spill when it is moved about.

CLEANING THE REFRIGERATOR

Regular care should include wiping up spills as soon as they occur, and wiping dirty marks from the handle and door.

Occasional special cleaning is necessary depending on individua' use. Switch off, pull out the plug, and defrost *before* washing the racks and other removable parts in warm water and detergent, then rinse and dry. Wipe out the interior with a cloth, using plain hot water, then dry thoroughly. For anything which resists this treatment use a little detergent on a cloth, but be sure to rinse it away well. Wash the outside with detergent, wipe dry, and apply a little liquid polish to protect the surface. Occasionally remove dust from the back, using the brush attachment of the vacuum cleaner.

CLEANING THE FREEZER, see page 209 (Defrosting a Freezer)

HOW TO CLEAN MATERIALS COMMONLY USED IN KITCHEN FITTINGS AND EQUIPMENT

ALUMINIUM

It is easy to clean by ordinary washing methods and when it needs scouring use either a nylon pad or impregnated soap pads made of steel wool. Copper cleaning pads tend to cause pitting and washing soda or caustic cleaners should be avoided, as they cause corrosion. Aluminium utensils should always be dried before storing, as dampness causes pitting of the surface.

CHINA

Soak if necessary, otherwise wash in hot water and detergent. To remove stains on tea or coffee cups, rub with a little salt or bicarbonate of soda on a damp cloth.

CHROMIUM

Wipe with a damp cloth and then dry. If it is really dirty, wash it with warm water and detergent. Wipe dry, and if necessary, clean it with a special chrome polish.

COPPER

Wash with a detergent and dry thoroughly. If it is tarnished, clean it with a mixture of salt, lemon juice, and vinegar.

EARTHENWARE

Avoid plunging very hot dishes into water. If food sticks, either leave the dishes to soak in water and detergent, or else scour with steel-wool soap pads.

ENAMEL

Avoid scouring enamel with any material which might scratch the surface. If food has been burnt in an enamel saucepan, boil salt water in it several times until the burnt food can be easily removed.

With the heavy enamelled iron pans, any chipped, exposed iron should be dried thoroughly before the utensil is put away. If it is used infrequently, rub a little oil over the iron to protect it.

GLASS

Rinse glass in cold water before washing it in hot water and detergent, then rinse again in hot water.

To clean a decanter, put a chopped potato inside with an equal quantity of vinegar and water. Shake well. Empty, rinse and then hold it upside down under the cold tap. Leave it to drain and then polish the outside with a clean tea towel or paper kitchen towel.

If food sticks to heat-resistant glass during cooking, soak it in warm water and detergent before washing. If necessary, clean with soap-impregnated steel-wool pads. Don't plunge hot dishes into cold water.

Glass-ceramic cooking utensils should be treated in the same way as heat-resistant ones.

LINOLEUM
Wipe up spills as soon as possible. Wash with detergent and water. Avoid harsh scouring and, when the floor is dry, protect the surface with a liquid polish.

NON-STICK UTENSILS
Follow the makers' instructions. Usually washing in hot water and detergent is sufficient. Do not scour.

PAINT WORK
Wipe with a damp cloth and detergent. When dry, protect the surface with a little liquid furniture polish.

PLASTIC
Wipe or wash in warm water and detergent. Dry. If not coming into contact with food, protect with a layer of liquid furniture polish. Kitchen ware which becomes stained can be treated with a weak solution of a household bleach. Rinse well and dry.

Remove tea and coffee stains from cups by rubbing with bicarbonate of soda on a damp cloth or use detergents; severe staining can be removed by soaking in a weak solution of bleach. Avoid any abrasive cleaners which will roughen the surface.

SILVER WARE
Regular use and washing with hot water and detergent keeps silver clean and bright. Pieces which are only used occasionally should be wrapped in polythene or tissue paper to protect them from the tarnishing effects of exposure to air. When necessary, clean with a proprietary silver cleaner and wash, rinse, and dry any which come into contact with food.

STAINLESS STEEL
Wash with water and detergent. If it becomes discoloured clean it with a very fine scouring paste or powder, or with steel-wool soap pads. Avoid prolonged contact with either salt or vinegar, as this can cause corrosion.

TILES

Wash with hot water and detergent. Remove any stains with fine abrasive powder. Unglazed tiles can be treated with special seals and emulsion polishes. Glazed wall tiles can be given a finish of liquid polish. Other varieties of tiles should be washed with water and detergent. Use only the recommended polishes, and read the labels on the polish first.

TIN

Wash in hot water and detergent. Put in a warm place to dry out completely before storing away. Try to avoid harsh scouring or scratching which may break the tin coating and lead to rusting of the steel underneath.

WOOD

Untreated wood should be wiped over, or washed with cool water and detergent. If it is very dirty, scrub it with cool water and detergent, or with steel-wool soap pads. Rinse well, and leave it to dry before putting it away.

Wood with a varnished or treated surface should be wiped over with a damp cloth, and a little detergent, if the surface is sticky or greasy.

Chapter Six

PRESERVES, BOTTLING, AND FREEZING

CAUSES OF FOOD SPOILAGE

Food spoils because of the action of enzymes within the plant and animal cells, and the action of micro-organisms such as bacteria, yeasts, and moulds which can be present within the food, or arrive from outside contamination.

In order to preserve food, the conditions of storage must be unfavourable to the growth of organisms which cause spoilage.

For normal growth these organisms need:
MOISTURE;
WARMTH; and
TIME TO GROW.

If any one of these conditions is made unsuitable, preservation will be affected.

Consuming the food soon after killing or harvesting is the obvious solution, but not a practical one for large urban populations, or when the food is a seasonal variety.

The food itself can be made unsuitable for the growth of organisms by the addition of such agents as salt (e.g. salt fish), sugar (e.g. jams), acid (e.g. vinegar in pickles), or by the use of chemical preservatives (as in sausages).

If sufficient moisture is removed and the food stored in dry conditions, this will preserve. Sun-drying of food is one of the oldest methods of preserving used by man. Modern processes are the quicker dehydrating, and accelerated freeze-drying.

To heat the food enough to destroy micro-organisms is well known in the pasteurisation of milk and in bottling and canning. This must be combined with an airtight seal to prevent re-contamination.

To keep food cold is an old as well as a new method. The modern methods of chilling, freezing, and refrigeration all preserve because they reduce the temperature below that which is needed for rapid growth of micro-organisms, and they can be low enough to prevent growth completely.

This section deals with long-term methods of preservation used in the home. The short-term storage of food, and refrigeration, will be found in the chapter on 'Buying and Storing Food', pages 101–14.

MAKING JAM

A mixture of fruit and sugar boiled to give a sugar concentration (60 per cent) which will be sufficient to allow keeping for long periods. Most people like jam to be firmly set. Setting is brought about the the presence of pectin, a carbohydrate in fruits which forms a 'gel' when the fruit is cooked with acid and sugar. Some fruits do not contain enough natural acid and pectin to make a good set, and these may have commercial pectin added, or be mixed with a fruit with a high pectin and acid content. The missing acid can be added by using lemons or citric or tartaric acid. In order to keep, it is not necessary for a jam to be firmly set, and many people prefer certain jams not to be set. As long as the sugar content is adequate a runny jam keeps satisfactorily.

Important Steps in Making Jam

Suitable Equipment

A preserving pan or a large wide saucepan is required. A proper preserving pan is best because it is very wide in relation to its depth and this allows rapid evaporation and quick cooking, which helps to give a good flavour and colour to the jam. The pan should be made of either stainless steel, aluminium, or unchipped enamel. Copper and brass pans cause destruction of vitamin C in the fruit. The pan should be large enough not to be more than half full when the fruit and sugar are added, otherwise the vigorous boiling needed will make the jam froth over the top. This means that if 5 lb. (2½ kg.) jam is being made a pan of 8 pt. (4½ l.) capacity will be needed.

A long-handled wooden spoon or stirrer is also essential. If stone fruit is being cooked, a utensil is needed for removal of stones as they rise. This may be a perforated spoon or a special little wire basket made to fit on the side of the preserving pan.

Clean glass jars and covers are needed too. Packets of covers are sold in 1 lb. (½ kg.) and 2 lb. (1 kg.) sizes, complete with

181

waxed discs, rubber bands, and transparent top covers. Labels are usually included too.

Choosing the Fruit

For a jam to set well the fruit needs to be firm-ripe. Over-ripe fruit will not set so well because it will contain less pectin, and the jam will also tend to be of a poorer colour and flavour. Bruised and damaged fruit can be used, provided that the bad bits are first cut out.

Fruits which usually make a good set because they contain plenty of both acid and pectin are cooking apples, black and red currants, damsons, gooseberries, and most plums. Fruits of medium setting quality are apricots, blackberries, green-gages, loganberries, and raspberries.

Fruits of a poor setting quality are cherries, pears, peaches, strawberries, marrow, rhubarb, pumpkin, and green tomatoes.

Preparing the Fruit   See *Individual recipes*

Preliminary Cooking

This is usually carried out before the sugar is added, and the object is to soften the fruit. If sugar is added first, it tends to make the skins tough and the fruit does not break down to give a smooth jam. If, however, jam is preferred with whole fruit, the sugar is added at the beginning of cooking and in some cases the fruit and sugar are mixed together and left to stand over-night. But it is not wise to add sugar to gooseberries and black-currants before the fruit has been softened, as the skins of these fruits will become very tough. The amount of water needed is given in the individual recipes.

Using the Pressure Cooker

This cuts down the pre-cooking time of the fruit. Use 15 lb. pressure and only half the usual amount of water, and do not have the cooker more than half full. *Times:* apricots and black-currants 3 mins.; damsons and plums 5 mins.; cherries, just bring to pressure. When cooking is finished, cool the pan quickly under cold water. After the sugar is added, the jam is finished in the open pan without pressure.

The Sugar

Use either granulated or loaf sugar and, if the jam is to keep well, there should not be more than 5 lb. (2½ kg.) finished jam produced for each 3 lb. (1½ kg.) sugar used (60 per cent sugar). If less sugar is used (and some people like less sweet jam) the jars will have to be airtight like those used for bottling fruit, or the jam may be sealed in cans.

Removing the Stones and Scum

Remove the stones as they rise to the top (see *Equipment*). Do not remove any scum until the jam is finished. The scum contains sugar, and it is a waste to remove this in the early stages. It will quite likely all disappear during subsequent cooking.

Testing for Setting Point

(a) *The Flake Test* Lift out the wooden stirring spoon with some jam adhering to it. Turn it round slowly to allow to cool a little and then let the jam fall off the edge. If the jam is ready the drops will run together and break off as separate flakes.

(b) *The Cold Plate Test* Remove jam from the heat. Put a little on a very cold plate and leave in a cold place for a few minutes. Push the blob with the little finger and if the jam is ready the surface will wrinkle.

(c) *The Temperature Test for Sugar Content* Use a sugar thermometer and dip it into hot water and then into the jam. If the jam is ready it should register 220–222° (104–105°C.) Replace thermometer in hot water to soak off the jam.

(d) *Volume Test for Sugar Content* Before starting operations, consult the recipe to see how many pounds of finished jam there should be. Fill a 1 lb. (450 ml.) jam jar this number of times with cold water and empty into the preserving pan. Take a clean stick or stirrer with a flat base, and stand it upright in the water. Make a notch at water level. Tip out the water and make the jam. When it is ready for testing, remove the pan from the heat and allow bubbling to stop. Stand the stick upright in the jam and see if the level is as marked.

Potting and Covering

Jars should be clean, dry, and warm. Fill them just short of overflowing. The simplest way of doing this is to use a cup or small jug and a saucer. Dip the jug into the jam and when it is lifted out hold the saucer under it to catch drips. Pour jam into jars. While the jam is hot place waxed discs on top, pressing down to remove all air bubbles. This helps to prevent the entry of moulds. Wipe the jars and either cover while hot or leave to become quite cold – not warm. If the jam has large pieces of fruit in it, these may tend to rise to the top if it is potted at once. Leave it to cool in the pan until a skin begins to form on top, then give it a good stir, and pot as before.

Storing Jam
Labelit with the variety and date and store in a dark, dry, airy, cool place. Sometimes crystals form with keeping and this may be due to several factors. Large crystals are usually caused by insufficient boiling and too little acid, while small crystals may be due to over-boiling and the presence of too much acid.

APPLE AND GINGER JAM
Quantities for 5 lb. (2½ kg.)

3 *lb. apples* (1½ *kg.*)

Peel and core apples and tie the peel and cores in clean muslin and hang in the pan. Place apples in preserving pan with

1 *pt. water* (500 *ml.*)   2 *Tbs. ground ginger*
Grated rind and juice of 2 lemons

Cook until the fruit is tender. Remove the muslin bag and squeeze out the juice.

3 *lb. sugar* (6 *c. or* 1½ *kg.*)

Add to the pan and stir until the sugar dissolves. Boil rapidly until setting point is reached.

BLACKBERRY JAM
Quantities for 5 lb. (2½ kg.)

3 *lb. blackberries* (1½ *kg.*)

Pick over the fruit removing all stalks and leaves and any mouldy berries. Put in the pan with

4 *Tbs. water and 2 Tbs. lemon juice*

Boil gently until the fruit is soft.

3 *lb. sugar* (6 *c. or* 1½ *kg.*)

Add to the fruit, stir until it boils, and boil rapidly until setting point is reached.

BLACKBERRY AND APPLE JAM

Quantities for 5 lb. (2½ kg.)

2 *lb. blackberries* (1 *kg.*)   ¼ *pt. water* (150 *ml.*)
1 *lb. cooking apples* (½ *kg.*)

Pick over the blackberries removing all stalks, leaves, and mouldy fruit. Peel, core, and slice the apples. Cook these separately with half the water in each until the fruit is tender. Then combine the pulps.

3 *lb. sugar*   (6 *c. or* 1½ *kg.*)

Add to the fruit and stir until it boils. Boil rapidly until setting point is reached.

BLACKBERRY AND ELDERBERRY JAM

Quantities for 5 lb. (2½ kg.)

2 *lb. stemmed elderberries* (1 *kg.*)   ½ *pt. water* (300 *ml.*)

Cook together until fruit is soft. Rub through a sieve to remove the seeds.

2 *lb. blackberries* (1 *kg.*)

Add to elderberry juice and boil for about 10 mins. or until the fruit is soft.

3 *lb. sugar* (6 *c. or* 1½ *kg.*)

Add to the fruit, stir until it boils, and boil rapidly until setting point is reached.

BLACKCURRANT JAM

Quantities for 5 lb. (2½ kg.)

2 *lb. blackcurrants* (1 *kg.*)   1½ *pt. water* (1 *l.*)

Remove the currants from the stalks. Wash if necessary. Put in a pan with the water and boil gently until the fruit is soft, stirring frequently to prevent burning.

3 *lb. sugar* (6 *c. or* 1½ *kg.*)

Add sugar, stir until it dissolves, and boil rapidly until setting point is reached.

DAMSON JAM

Quantities for 5 lb. (2½ kg.)

2½ *lb. damsons* (1¼ *kg.*)   1 *pt. water* (600 *ml.*)

Wash the fruit and stew it with the water until it is soft and well broken down.

3 lb. sugar (6 c. or 1½ kg.)

Add to the fruit, stir until it boils, and boil rapidly until setting point is reached. Remove the stones as they rise to the surface.

DRIED APRICOT JAM
Quantities for 5 lb. (2½ kg.)

1 lb. dried apricots (½ kg.)   3 pt. water (6 c. or 1¾ l.)

Wash the apricots and soak them in the water for at least 24 hrs. Then boil gently for 2 hrs., or until a thick pulp. Watch for catching and add a little more water if necessary.

3 oz. almonds (90 g.)   3 lb. sugar (6 c. or 1½ kg.)
Juice of 1 lemon

Blanch the almonds and cut them in quarters lengthwise. Put all the ingredients in the preserving pan, stir until the sugar dissolves, and then boil rapidly until a little sets when tested. Cool until it begins to thicken, stir well. Pour into jars and tie down when cold.

Pressure-Cooker Method   Use 1 pt. (½ l.) water and pressure cook 10 mins., add sugar, and proceed as above.

ELDERFLOWER AND RHUBARB JAM
Quantities for 5 lb. (2½ kg.)

3 lb. rhubarb (1½ kg.)   3 lb. sugar (6 c. or 1½ kg.)
2 <i>oz. elderflowers</i> (60 <i>g.</i>)</p>

Wash the rhubarb and cut it in pieces about 2 in. (5 cm.) long. Put it in a bowl. Wash the elderflowers and tie them in muslin. Bury this in the middle of the rhubarb. Strew the sugar over the top. Cover and leave for 24 hrs., stirring occasionally. Put in the preserving pan and heat up slowly but do not allow to boil. Turn back into the bowl for another 24 hrs. Remove the elderflowers and add

Grated rind and juice of 1 lemon

Return to the preserving pan and bring to the boil. Boil rapidly until setting point is reached.

GOOSEBERRY JAM

Quantities for 5 lb. (2½ kg.)

2¼ *lb. gooseberries* (1¼ *kg.*)   ¾ *pt. water* (450 *ml.*)

Wash the fruit and top and tail it. Put it in a pan with the water and boil gently until the fruit is quite soft and well broken down.

3 *lb. sugar* (6 *c. or* 1½ *kg.*)

Add to the fruit, stir until it boils, and boil rapidly until setting point is reached.

GREENGAGE JAM   See *Plum Jam*

LOGANBERRY JAM

Quantities for 5 lb. (2½ kg.)

3 *lb. loganberries* (1½ *kg.*)

Pick over the fruit and remove stalks and hulls and any mouldy berries. Wash and put in the pan. Cook slowly with constant stirring until the fruit is thoroughly softened.

3 *lb. sugar* (6 *c. or* 1½ *kg.*)

Add the sugar, stir until it boils, and boil rapidly until setting point is reached.

MARROW AND GINGER JAM

Quantities for 5 lb. (2½ kg.)

3 *lb. marrow, prepared weight* (1½ *kg.*)
3 *lb. sugar* (6 *c. or* 1½ *kg.*)
Grated rind and juice of 2 lemons

Peel the marow and remove the seeds and pith. Cut in ½ in. (1 cm.) cubes. Weigh at this stage. Put in a pan with the sugar and lemon and leave to stand overnight.

4 *oz. crystallised ginger* (125 *g.*)

Chop the ginger coarsely and add to the marrow. Bring to the boil, stirring all the time, and boil steadily until setting point is reached.

PEAR JAM OR PEAR GINGER

Quantities for 5 lb. (2½ kg.)

> 6 *lb. pears* (*Williams are best*) (3 *kg.*)
> 3 *lb. sugar* (6 *c.* or 1½ *kg.*) 3 *lemons*
> 3 *oz. crystallised ginger* (90 *g.*)

Peel the pears, core, and chop or mince coarsely. Put in a pan with the chopped ginger, sugar, and the lemons finely minced or chopped.

Leave to stand overnight. Bring to the boil and cook gently until the correct yield is obtained. This jam does not set stiffly.

PLUM JAM

Quantities for 5 lb. (2½ kg.)

> 3 *lb. plums* (1½ *kg.*)   ¼–¾ *pt. water* (150–450 *ml.*)

Wash the fruit and remove any stalks. Add the water, using the smaller amount if the plums are ripe and juicy. Cook together gently until the fruit is quite soft.

> 3 *lb. sugar* (6 *c.* or 1½ *kg.*)

Add to the fruit and stir until it boils. Boil rapidly until setting point is reached. Remove the stones as they rise to the surface.

QUINCE JAM OR 'CHEESE'

Quantities for 5 lb. (2½ kg.)

> 2 *lb. quinces, prepared weight* (1 *kg.*)   2 *pt. water* (1¼ *l.*)

Peel and core the fruit and mince it coarsely. Put in a pan with the water and stew gently until it is quite tender.

> 3 *lb. sugar* (6 *c.* or 1½ *kg.*)

Add the sugar and stir until it boils. Boil steadily until setting point is reached. The jam should be a rich orange-red colour.

RASPBERRY JAM

Quantities for 5 lb. (2½ kg.)

> 3 *lb. raspberries* (1½ *kg.*)

Pick over the fruit and remove all leaves and stalks and any mouldy fruit. Put in a pan, stir until the juice runs, and boil gently for about 10 mins.

                    3 lb. sugar (6 c. or 1½ kg.)
Add sugar, stir until it boils, and boil hard for 2 mins.

RHUBARB AND FIG JAM
Quantities for 5 lb. (2½ kg.)
       8 oz. dried figs (250 g.)   *1½ pt. water (1 l.)*
Wash the figs and chop or mince coarsely. Add water and soak
overnight.
                    2 lb. rhubarb (1 kg.)
Wash rhubarb and cut up small, add to the figs, and cook
together until soft.
       3 lb. sugar (6 c. or 1½ kg.)   *Juice of 2 lemons*
Add sugar and lemon juice to the fruit, stir until boiling, and
boil rapidly until the correct yield is obtained.

STRAWBERRY JAM
Quantities for 5 lb. (2½ kg.)
4 lb. hulled strawberries (1¾ kg.)   *4 lb. sugar (8 c. or 1¾ kg.)*
Put the berries and sugar in a basin in layers. Leave for 24
hrs. Bring to the boil and boil for 5 mins. Return to the basin,
cover, and leave for 48 hrs. Put in the pan and bring to the
boil and boil rapidly for 10–20 mins. or until setting point is
reached. Allow to cool until a skin begins to form on top.
Stir and pot.

MARMALADE

The name was originally used for preserves made of a thick
fruit pulp and is said to have originated in Spain as a quince
preserve (Spanish for quince – *memelo*). In Britain the word
is usually taken to mean a special preserve made from citrus
fruit and eaten at breakfast.

Tastes in marmalade vary from those who like a sweet
jelly with a few wisps of peel in it to those who like their
marmalade thick and dark and stiff with fruit, such as the
famous Dundee and Oxford marmalades. These are usually
quite bitter in flavour. The traditional marmalade is made
with Seville oranges, very bitter, imported from Spain from
the end of December to February with January being the main
marmalade-making month.

The basic methods used in making marmalade are the same as for jam (see *Jams*, pages 181–4).

Cutting up the fruit can be a tedious job, but various methods can be used to make it less so. Fine shredding is the most time-consuming of the methods, but there are machines and gadgets available for shredding foods and some are suitable for marmalade. An alternative is to cook the fruit whole (see *Quick Method*, below) and shred the peel when it is soft and much easier to handle.

If it does not matter to you whether the peel is in bits instead of in shreds, mincing is one of the best and quickest methods (preferably a power-driven mincer). An electric blender can be used to produce a pulpy marmalade which is in fact more like the kind of preserve known abroad as 'marmalade'.

Easiest of all is to buy the cooked pulp in tins and merely add the sugar and proceed from there to give a very good marmalade.

Cooking the shredded or minced peel is a fairly slow process and fills the kitchen with the smell of marmalade making. The use of a pressure cooker reduces the time this takes (see *Pressure-Cooker Method*, below).

METHODS OF MAKING

1. *Standard Method*

Wash the fruit and cut in half. Squeeze out the juice, and strain out the pips. Slice or mince the peel and put in a pan with the juice, acid if used, and the water. Leave to soak overnight. Next day cook the fruit by boiling gently until the peel is softened, about 1½–2 hrs.

Add the sugar and stir until it dissolves, then boil rapidly until setting point is reached.

2. *Quick Method*

Wash the fruit and put it whole into a pan with the water. Boil gently for 2 hrs. with the lid on the pan. Test to make sure that the fruit is tender.

Lift out the oranges on to a plate and leave until cool enough to handle. Cut in half and remove the pips. Shred the peel. Put peel, cooking water, and sugar in the pan and stir until it boils. Boil rapidly until setting point is reached.

3. *Pressure-Cooker Method*

This is a useful method for cutting down the time required for softening the peel from 1½–2 hrs. to 20 mins. After that the marmalade is finished with the sugar in an open pan as for other methods. Preliminary soaking overnight to soften the peel is not necessary. Any recipe can be used but the amount of water should be reduced by half.

Some cooker manufacturers recommend processing at 15 lb. pressure which gives a temperature of 252°F. or 122°C., while others recommend 10 lb. pressure which gives a temperature of 240°F. or 116°C. The lower temperature is said to be better because there is less chance of the pectin being broken down and the set will be better. After cooking the peel, the pressure must be reduced slowly at room temperature otherwise frothing may take place.

It is most important that the pressure cooker should not be more than half full of fruit and water.

4. *Electric-Blender Method*

Use the *Quick-Method* recipe and, after removing the pips from the oranges, cut them up roughly and process them in the blender with only as much of the liquid as is needed. Then return the pulp to the remaining liquid and finish as before.

GRAPEFRUIT MARMALADE (jelly)

Quantities for 5 lb. (2½ kg.)

> 2 *lb.* (1 *kg.*) *fruit to include some lemon*
> (*e.g.* 2 *grapefruit and* 3 *lemons*)

Wash the fruit and peel it. Cut about 4 oz. (125 g.) of the peel into very fine shreds and tie in a muslin bag. Cut up the rest of the fruit coarsely.

> 4½ *pt. water* (3 *l.*)

Put fruit and water in a pan, with the shredded peel, and cook gently in a closed pan for 2 hrs. Remove the bag of peel after 1 hr. or when it is tender. Pour fruit and water into the jelly bag and allow to drip for 10–15 mins. Then put the pulp back in the pan and add another pint of water, cook for further 20 mins., and strain.

3 lb. sugar (6 c. or 1½ kg.)

Put juice and sugar in a pan and stir until the sugar dissolves, bring to the boil, add shreds of peel, and boil rapidly until setting point is reached.

The recipe can also be made with the pressure cooker for the first cooking of fruit and shredded peel but use only 2½ pt. (1½ l.) of water. When the juice is strained there should be about 1¾ pt. (1 l.). If necessary either reduce it by boiling hard or add some more water to the pulp to make up to 1¾ pt. (1 l.) and reboil; strain. Finish as before.

GRAPEFRUIT MARMALADE (thick)
Quantities for 5 lb. (2½ kg.)

1½ lb. grapefruit (¾ kg.)   3 pt. water (1¾ l.)
Juice of 2 lemons   3 lb. sugar (6 c. or 1½ kg.)

Make either by the *Standard*, *Quick*, or *Pressure-Cooker Methods*, reducing the water to half for pressure cooking.

LEMON OR LIME MARMALADE
Quantities for 5 lb. (2½ kg.)

1½ lb. lemons or limes (¾ kg.)   3 lb. sugar (6 c. or 1½ kg.)
3 pt. water (1¼ l.)

Make as for thick grapefruit marmalade or use the *Quick Method* or the *Pressure-Cooker Method* (reduce water to half for pressure cooking).

SEVILLE ORANGE MARMALADE (dark, thick)
Quantities for 5 lb. (2½ kg.)

1 lb. Seville oranges (1½ kg.)   3 lb. sugar (6 c. or 1½ kg.)
1 small lemon   3 pt. water (1¾ l.)
½ oz. black treacle added with the sugar (1 Tbs. or 15 g.)

Make by the *Standard Method* as for thick grapefruit marmalade or use the *Quick Method* or the *Pressure-Cooker Method* (reduce water to half for pressure cooking).

SEVILLE ORANGE MARMALADE (jelly type)
Quantities for 5 lb. (2½ kg.)

2 lb. Seville oranges (1 kg.)   Juice of 2 lemons
4½ pt. water (3 l.)   3 lb. sugar (6 c. or 1½ kg.)

Make in the same way as grapefruit jelly marmalade.

SEVILLE ORANGE MARMALADE (standard type)

Quantities for 5 lb. (2½ kg.)

1½ *lb. Seville oranges* (¾ *kg.*)   *Juice of* 1 *lemon*
3 *pt. water* (1¾ *l.*)   3 *lb. sugar* (6 *c. or* 1½ *kg.*)

Make in the same way as thick grapefruit marmalade.

SWEET ORANGE MARMALADE

Quantities for 5 lb. (2½ kg.)

2 *lb. sweet oranges* (1 *kg.*)   *Juice of* 2 *lemons*
3 *pt. water* (1¾ *l.*)   3 *lb. sugar* (6 *c. or* 1½ *kg.*)

Make by any of the methods for thick marmalade.

JELLIES

Pectin, acid, and sugar are all needed in the correct proportions for jelly making (see *Jam*, page 181–4). The best fruits for
jellies are crab apples, black or red currants, gooseberries,
loganberries, quinces, and cooking apples, though the latter
usually need some additional flavouring such as cloves, mint,
or geranium leaves. Apples can be mixed with fruits such as
blackberries, bilberries, or elderberries, as the apple juice
helps these to set well and they add flavour and colour to the
juice.

Cooking the Fruit

Fruit should be firm-ripe. Wash it and remove any damaged
parts, but it is not necessary to peel, core, and remove other
waste parts, and is undesirable as these help to provide pectin
needed for setting. They are all strained out when the juice is
made. The fruit and water (see amounts in recipes) are boiled
together gently until the fruit is thoroughly broken down.
This is essential to extract all the pectin and acid; time required
is usually ¾–1 hr.

Straining the Juice

Special felt or flannel jelly bags can be purchased for this,
complete with stands to hold the bag. Otherwise use several
thicknesses of butter muslin and fasten the four corners to the
legs of an upturned stool or chair, with a bowl beneath to

catch the juice. Scald the bag with boiling water, fasten in position, and put in the cooked pulp and juice. Leave to drip overnight. Do not squeeze the bag or the juice may become cloudy.

Adding the Sugar

Juices from the list of best fruits for jelly making take 1 lb. ($\frac{1}{2}$ kg.) sugar to 1 pt. ($\frac{1}{2}$ l.) juice, while less good ones should have $\frac{3}{4}$ lb. (360 g.) sugar to 1 pt. juice, but if these are mixed with apple juice or have lemon juice added, they will take the larger amount of sugar. See recipes. Bring the juice to the boil before adding the sugar, stir until it dissolves, and then boil rapidly for 10 mins. or so until setting point is reached. Best tests for this are temperature tests plus the flake test (see *Jam*, page 183).

Potting, Covering, and Storage   See *Jam*, pages 183–4.

APPLE AND BLACKBERRY JELLY

4 *lb. blackberries* (1$\frac{3}{4}$ *kg.*)   2 *pt. water* (1 *l.*)
2 *lb. cooking apples* (1 *kg.*)   *Sugar*

Wash the berries, wash and cut the apples, removing any damaged parts. Make as Apple Jelly, adding 1 lb. sugar ($\frac{1}{2}$ kg.) to 1 pt. ($\frac{1}{2}$ l.) juice.

APPLE AND MINT JELLY

3 *lb. cooking apples*, (1$\frac{1}{2}$ *kg.*)   *Juice of* 1 *lemon*
3 *or* 4 *sprigs fresh mint*   *Sugar*
Water to cover   *Green colouring*

To get a jelly with a good colour use apples with bright green skins.

Cook as for apple jelly, adding the mint and lemon juice to the apples during cooking. Strain and add 1 lb. ($\frac{1}{2}$ kg.) sugar to 1 pt. ($\frac{1}{2}$ l.) juice. If desired, add a few drops of green colouring, but if a stronger mint flavour is wanted, hold a bunch of fresh mint leaves in the jelly for a little while when it is boiling with the sugar. Finish as above. Alternatively, to give the extra mint flavour, add a little chopped mint to the finished jelly.

APPLE JELLY

3 lb. (1½ kg.) cooking apples, crab apples, or japonica apples:
Cloves or root ginger or lemon rind
1½ pt. water (¾ l.)   Sugar

Wash the fruit and cut it in small pieces, removing any bad bits. Put in a pan and just cover with water. Add 2 or 3 cloves or a piece of bruised root ginger or the thin yellow peel from a lemon. Boil gently for 1 hr. or until well mashed down. Strain, measure the juice, and add 1 lb. (½ kg.) sugar to 1 pt. (½ l.) juice. Finish as described above.

BLACKCURRANT JELLY

4 lb. blackcurrants (1¾ kg.)   Sugar
3 pt. water (6 c. or 1½ l.)

Wash the blackcurrants on the stalk and put in a pan with the water. Proceed as above, adding 1 lb. (½ kg.) sugar to 1 pt. (½ l.) juice.

BRAMBLE JELLY (Blackberry)

4 lb. blackberries (1¾ kg.)   ¾ pt. water (5 dl.)
Juice of 2 lemons   Sugar

Wash the berries and add lemon and water. Proceed as described above, adding 1 lb. (½ kg.) sugar to 1 pt. (½ l.) juice.

GOOSEBERRY JELLY

4 lb. green gooseberries (1¾ kg.)   Sugar
3 pt. water (6 c. or 1½ l.)

For method, see above. Use 1 lb. (½ kg.) sugar to 1 pt. (½ l.) juice.

LOGANBERRY JELLY

4 lb. loganberries (1¾ kg.)   Sugar
1 pt. water (½ l.)

For method, see above. Allow 1 lb. (½ kg.) sugar to 1 pt. (½ l.) juice.

QUINCE JELLY

2 lb. quinces (1 kg.)   Sugar
3 pt. water (1½ l.)

Wash the fruit, cut up, add water, and proceed as above. If the fruit is very ripe add the juice of 1 lemon to the quinces during cooking. Use 1 lb. ($\frac{1}{2}$ kg.) sugar to 1 pt. ($\frac{1}{2}$ l.) juice.

REDCURRANT JELLY

3 lb. redcurrants (1$\frac{1}{2}$ *kg.*)   *Sugar*
1 pt. water ($\frac{1}{2}$ *l.*)

Wash the fruit on the stalks and proceed as above. Use 1 lb. ($\frac{1}{2}$ kg.) sugar to 1 pt. ($\frac{1}{2}$ l.) juice.

CHUTNEY

Chutney is made from fruit and vegetables cooked with spices, salt, sugar, and vinegar until the mixture looks like thick jam. It is the presence of the acid in the vinegar, together with the salt, sugar, and spices, which makes the chutney keep, even for 2 or 3 years. It is bottled in glass jars and stored for at least 3 months before use to allow the flavours to mellow, even longer is better. Chutney is chiefly used to serve with cold meats or with bread and cheese for a snack meal but also to give zest to many savoury dishes. It is one of the accompaniments usually served with curries and similar hot dishes.

Although it is possible to buy a wide variety of ready-made chutneys, many housewives prefer to make their own, either to have a product a little different from the shop one, or else to use up surplus garden produce, especially gluts of apples, plums, and green tomatoes.

Chutney requires long, slow cooking, and the smell in the kitchen is very strong and penetrating. Today electric extractor fans can help to remove the smell to a large extent and certainly prevent it from penetrating throughout the house. The use of a pressure cooker to carry out preliminary softening of the fruit and vegetables can reduce the cooking time by about $\frac{1}{2}$ hr. and the use of a thermostatically controlled oven for cooking the chutney means it can cook without attention throughout the whole period.

Chutney should be cooked in either aluminium, steel, or enamel-lined pans (not chipped). It is not wise to use iron, brass, or copper, as vinegar reacts with these metals.

Any glass jars can be used to hold the chutney. If metal lids are used they must be protected from contact with the chutney by lining the lids with several layers of wax paper or by using special lining discs sold for the purpose. Chutney can be bottled hot or cold, as convenient.

Keep it in a cool dry place and inspect it occasionally to see it is keeping satisfactorily, and that the covers are sufficiently airtight to prevent undue evaporation.

APPLE CHUTNEY
Quantity 4–5 lb. (1¾–2¼ kg.)

     5 lb. apples (2¼ kg.)   *1 lb. onions (½ kg.)*

Peel, core, and cut up the apples into small pieces. Skin and slice the onions finely. Alternatively, put both through a coarse mincer.

1½ lb. brown sugar (3 c. or	*2 cloves garlic, chopped*
¾ kg.)	*1 pt. vinegar (½ l.)*
¼ tsp. cayenne pepper	*4 oz. crystallised ginger,*
1 Tbs. salt	*chopped (½ c. or 120 g.)*

Method 1

Boil the apple, onion, and garlic with a little of the vinegar until the mixture is fairly thick. Add sugar, ginger, and seasonings and cook for 20 mins. Add remaining vinegar and cook until the mixture has the consistency of thick jam.

Method 2   Use ½ pt. vinegar only (¼ l.)

Put all the ingredients into a pressure cooker but be sure it is not more than half full. Cook at 15 lb. pressure for 15 mins. Reduce pressure with cold water. Remove lid and continue cooking until the chutney is the right consistency.

ELDERBERRY CHUTNEY
Cooking Time 1–2 hrs.   *Quantity* about 2 lb. (1 kg.)

  2 lb. elderberries weighed after removing the stalks (1 kg.)
  1 medium onion   *1 green apple*

Peel and chop the onion and apple, or mince coarsely.

1 tsp. peppercorns or mustard seed	*1 small bay leaf*
1 tsp. allspice	*6 cloves*

Tie these in a piece of muslin having the string long enough to come over the side of the pan (for easy removal). Add to the fruit.

     1 pt. vinegar (½ l.)

Add to the fruit and boil gently for 20 mins.

4 *oz. brown sugar* ($\frac{1}{2}$ *c. or* 120 *g.*) *or golden syrup* (4 *Tbs.*)
1 *tsp. salt*

Add to the other ingredients and boil gently until the mixture is like thick jam.

Pour into hot jars and cover when cold.

GREEN TOMATO CHUTNEY

Quantity 3–4 lb. (1$\frac{1}{2}$–1$\frac{3}{4}$ kg.)

2 *lb. green tomatoes* (1 *kg.*)	4 *oz. sultanas or dates* (125 *g.*)
$\frac{1}{2}$ *lb. apples* ($\frac{1}{4}$ *kg.*)	8 *oz. onions* ($\frac{1}{4}$ *kg.*)

Peel the apples and chop all the fruit (stone dates) and vegetables or put them all through a coarse mincer.

$\frac{1}{4}$ *oz. dried root ginger* (10 *g.*)	$\frac{1}{4}$ *oz. salt* (10 *g.*)
6 *red chillies*	$\frac{1}{2}$ *pt. vinegar* ($\frac{1}{4}$ *l.*)
8 *oz. brown sugar* ($\frac{1}{4}$ *kg.*)	

Bruise the ginger and chillies and tie them in a muslin bag. Put all the ingredients in a pan and simmer gently until the chutney is like thick jam. Remove spices and bottle the chutney.

MINT CHUTNEY

Quantity 2–3 lb. (1$\frac{1}{2}$–1$\frac{3}{4}$ *kg.*)

2 *lb. apples* (1 *kg.*)   4 *oz. raisins* ($\frac{1}{2}$ *c. or* 125 *g.*)

Peel and core the apples and mince them with the raisins, or chop both finely.

1 *tsp. dry mustard*	4 *oz . brown sugar* ($\frac{1}{2}$ *c. or*
$\frac{1}{4}$ *pt. chopped mint* ($\frac{1}{2}$ *c. or*	125 *g.*)
1$\frac{1}{2}$ *dl.*)	2 *tsp. salt*
$\frac{3}{4}$ *pt. vinegar* (1$\frac{1}{2}$ *c. or* 5 *dl.*)	$\frac{1}{2}$ *tsp. pepper*

Put all the ingredients in a pan and cook until it is the consistency of thick jam.

PLUM CHUTNEY

Quantity 6–7 lb. (2$\frac{3}{4}$–3$\frac{1}{4}$ kg.)

1 *lb. onions* ($\frac{1}{2}$ *kg.*)	2 *lb. apples* (1 *kg.*)
3 *lb. plums* (1$\frac{3}{4}$ *kg.*)	1 *lb. raisins* ($\frac{1}{2}$ *kg.*)

Peel the onion. Peel and core the apples. Stone the plums. Put all through a coarse mincer or chop finely.

1 *lb. brown sugar* (2 *c.* or ½ *kg.*)	2 *tsp. ground ginger*
2½ *pt. vinegar* (1½ *l.*)	3 *chillies, chopped*
2 *tsp. ground allspice*	2 *oz. salt* (60 *g.*)
Pinch of cayenne pepper	½ *tsp. ground cloves*
½ *tsp. dry mustard*	½ *tsp. ground nutmeg*

Put all the ingredients in a pan and boil gently until it is of the desired consistency.

SWEET INDIAN CHUTNEY
Quantity about 3 lb. (1½ kg.)

8 *oz. apples* (¼ *kg.*)	1½ *lb. ripe tomatoes* (¾ *kg.*)
6 *oz. raisins* (180 *g.*)	2 *oz. onions* (60 *g.*)

Peel and core the apples and peel the onions. Put all through a coarse mincer or chop finely.

1 *tsp. ground ginger*	2 *Tbs. salt*
1 *lb. brown sugar* (2 *c.* or ½ *kg.*)	½ *pt. vinegar* (¼ *l.*)
1 *tsp. pepper*	2 *chillies, chopped*

Boil all the ingredients together gently until it is of the consistency of thick jam.

PICKLES

These are usually fruit and vegetables preserved in vinegar, after brining with salt to draw out some of their moisture. Herbs and spices are added for flavouring. Pickles are sharp and harsh in flavour but are a popular British food to eat with bread and cheese and cold meats. The sweet fruit pickle is milder in flavour.

Most of the common pickles are available in shops and it is not worth while preparing home-made ones unless there is surplus garden produce to be used up.

Vinegar for Pickles
Bottled vinegar is the best to use as it is stronger than draught vinegar. White or distilled vinegar is used for white pickles, *e.g.* small onions for cocktail purposes. Spices are usually added before the vinegar is used. Mixed pickling spices can be purchased by the ounce but some people prefer to make

their own blends, e.g. using more or less of the hot chillies. The spices most commonly used are cinnamon bark, cloves, whole allspice, mace, peppercorns, cayenne pepper, or chillies. For each quart (1 l.) of vinegar allow 1 oz. (30 g.) of spices (3 Tbs.). Put spices and vinegar in a covered pan and bring to the boil. Remove from the heat and leave to stand for 2 hrs. to infuse. Strain and use as required. If you are going to do a lot of pickling it is a good idea to make up a lot of spiced vinegar and put it back in the bottles for later use.

Utensils for Use

Do not use anything made of iron, brass, or copper, nor chipped enamel, as the vinegar attacks these. Glass, aluminium, or steel are the safest.

Choice of Vegetables

They should be fresh and not too mature and fibrous otherwise the pickle will be poor.

Brining

Most vegetables contain 80 per cent or more water and the object of brining is to draw out some of this water otherwise it dilutes the vinegar and the pickle keeps badly. The vegetables are prepared and then either soaked in a solution of salt and water to cover (1 lb. salt to 1 gal. water) ($\frac{1}{2}$ kg. to $4\frac{1}{2}$ l.) or sprinkled generously with dry salt (4 oz. to 2 lb.) (125 g. to 1 kg.). Ordinary household cooking salt should be used. Leave them for 12–24 hrs. Then wash and drain thoroughly.

Bottling and Covering

Any kind of glass jar can be used. Wash well and dry. Pieces of plastic material tied tightly are suitable or plastic-lined metal tops. Metal must always be protected from the vinegar in some way and the tops should be as tight as possible to prevent evaporation.

Storing Pickles

Label and date them and store in a cool, dry place. Most pickles improve with keeping for at least several months before using. Some are at their best 1–2 years after making.

MIXED PICKLES

The vegetables usually preferred are cauliflower sprigs, small onions, gherkins or small cucumbers, French beans. Cut the vegetables in pieces and brine in dry salt for 48 hrs. Wash, drain, and pack in jars. Cover with vinegar and store as usual.

PICCALILLI or Mustard Pickles

3 *lb. vegetables* (1½ *kg.*)

The vegetables are usually some marrow, cauliflower sprigs, beans, onions, cucumber, and green tomatoes. Prepare them and cut in small pieces. Put them in brine to cover and leave for 24 hrs. Drain.

1½ *pt. white vinegar* (¾ *l.*)   4 *oz. sugar* (½ *c. or* 120 *g.*)

Keep back a little of the vinegar and heat the rest with the sugar and vegetables. Simmer for 20 mins. Drain vegetables and pack into jars.

½ *oz. dry mustard* (1½ *Tbs. or* 15 *g.*)   ¾ *oz. flour* (1½ *Tbs. or* 10 *g.*)
¼ *oz. turmeric* (½ *Tbs. or* 10 *g.*)   ½ *tsp. ground ginger*

Blend these with the rest of the vinegar, add to the hot mixture, stir, and boil for a minute and then pour over the vegetables. Cover and store as before.

PICKLED BEETROOT

Cook the beetroots. When they are cold, skin and slice them. Pack into jars and cover with cold spiced vinegar. A sprinkling of grated horseradish throughout the jar is an improvement. Do not pack the beetroot too tightly or there will not be enough vinegar to preserve it.

PICKLED CUCUMBERS

The thick field or ridge cucumbers are the ones usually pickled. Wash and cut in cubes or pieces and brine them. Wash, drain, and pack in jars, leaving room for at least ½ in. (1 cm.) vinegar on top. Pour in the cold spiced vinegar, cover, and store.

PICKLED EGGS

12 *eggs*

Hard-boil the eggs and shell them.

> 1 *qt. vinegar* (1 *l.*)   ½ *oz. allspice* (1 *Tbs. or* 15 *g.*)
> ½ *oz. black peppercorns* (1 *Tbs. or* 15 *g.*)
> ½ *oz. root ginger* (2 *pieces or* 15 *g.*)

Boil these together for ½ hr. Add the eggs and boil gently for 10 mins. Put the eggs in a hot jar and pour the vinegar and spices over them. Leave to cool, cover, and store in a cool place (but not in the refrigerator). They will be ready for use in 4 days but will keep for several weeks. Use to garnish salads and other savoury dishes or as part of an *hors-d'œuvre*.

PICKLED FRUIT (Sweet Pickle)

Suitable for small whole apples or crab apples, pears, peaches, plums, damsons, blackberries, quinces.

> 4 *lb. fruit* (1¾ *kg.*)

Peel apples and remove stalks. Peel, core, and halve or quarter the pears; skin peaches and remove the stones, quarter if large; wash and remove stalks from damsons; wash and pick over blackberries using only firm ones.

> *Rind of* ¼ *lemon*   2 *lb sugar* (4 *c. or* 1 *kg.*)
> 1 *piece of root ginger*   ½ *Tbs. cloves*
> 1½ *pt. vinegar* (¾ *l.*)   1 *Tbs. allspice*
> ½ *a piece of stick of cinnamon*

Crush the spices and tie them loosely in a piece of muslin. Put in a pan with the sugar and vinegar and heat until the sugar dissolves. Add the fruit to this and simmer until it is tender. Drain and pack the fruit in warm jars. Boil the vinegar to evaporate some of the water and make it syrupy. Pour the hot vinegar over the fruit having about ½ in. (1 cm.) of vinegar above the top fruit. Cover and store. These pickles improve with long keeping, becoming more mellow in flavour.

PICKLED GHERKINS

Wash the gherkins and brine them for 3 days. Drain well and pack into jars. Pour hot spiced vinegar over them, cover, and keep in a warm place for 24 hrs. Drain off the vinegar and boil it again. Pour over the gherkins and store as before. Repeat this process until the gherkins are a good green colour. More vinegar may need to be added finally to provide enough to cover them completely. Store in the usual way.

PICKLED ONIONS OR SHALLOTS

Small onions or shallots are used. Skin them under water using a stainless knife to prevent them turning black. Put in brine to cover and leave for 3 days. Drain and pack in jars. Cover with cold vinegar and store as before.

PICKLED RED CABBAGE

Use only fresh cabbage of a good colour. Remove any discoloured outer leaves. Shred the cabbage, removing any very coarse stalks. As it is shredded put it in a bowl, sprinkling each layer with salt. Leave 24 hrs. Rinse and drain and pack into jars, but only loosely or there will not be room for enough vinegar to preserve it. Cover with cold spiced vinegar and store as before. This is at its best from a week to 3 months. After that it becomes flabby.

PICKLED WALNUTS (Green)

Test the walnuts by pricking them with a steel needle or silver fork and only use those with no sign of a hard shell inside. Cover the nuts with a brine (1 lb. salt to 1 gal. water) ($\frac{1}{2}$ kg. to $4\frac{1}{2}$ l.) and soak for several days.

Drain and spread on dishes in a single layer and put in the sun until they turn black, about a day.

Pack in jars and cover with cold spiced vinegar. Cover and keep for at least a month before using.

PRESERVED EGGS
See also *Freezing*, page 215

Only really fresh hens' eggs should be preserved. Ducks' eggs are too often infected to be very satisfactory although some people have successful results. Hens' eggs should be about 48 hrs. old before preserving to make sure they are cooled right through because they are warm when laid. Dirty eggs should be wiped with a damp cloth.

There are several ways of preserving eggs: using waterglass; dipping in special liquids to coat and seal them; or rubbing with a specially prepared grease which seals the pores of the egg. Whichever method is used, follow the makers' instructions carefully. All the methods are designed to seal the pores of the egg-shell and so prevent evaporation of moisture from inside the egg and prevent bacteria from passing inside.

Preserved eggs are best used in cakes and other cooking.

BOTTLING FRUIT

Of the many methods which can be used for bottling the oven method or the pressure cooker are the best for general family use. The preparation of fruit, jars, and syrup is the same for both. The three most important points in bottling are:

1. To have fruit in good condition, not bruised and over-ripe, because then it will have so many micro-organisms in and on it that the processing is unlikely to destroy them all and the fruit will not keep well.

2. To heat or process it sufficiently to destroy organisms which cause spoilage.

3. To have an airtight seal so that air and organisms cannot get into the sterile contents and cause spoilage during storage.

Jars for Bottling

Special preserving jars are sold for this purpose and consist of jar, lid, a rubber band, and a clamp or screw band to hold the lid on. The device for holding the lid is put on loosely during the processing of the fruit so as to allow for expansion of the contents of the jar. After processing it is tightened up and as the contents cool, they shrink and if the jar is airtight a vacuum is created and this holds the lid on well enough to make an airtight seal. When they are quite cold, jars should be tested by removing the clamp and holding them up by the lid. If the lid comes off, either the jar is defective or your method of using it was faulty.

Always examine the edges of jars and lids to make sure there are no chips on either. It is a wise precaution to fill jars with water, seal them, and turn upside down when bad fits will be shown by the water leaking out.

It is not wise to use the same rubber band more than once, though some do take a chance, but it is not worth the risk.

Preparing the Fruit

Most fruits should be just fully ripe, otherwise the flavour will be poor. Gooseberries are the exception to this, and are best bottled green and hard. Pick over all fruit carefully and discard

204

bruised or over-ripe ones. Berries should go from bush to bottle as fast as you can because, if left in piles in warm weather, they deteriorate very rapidly. Some people do actually pick clean raspberries straight into the preserving jars. You can do the same thing with cultivated blackberries.

To prevent browning of fruits like apples and pears, put them in cold salted water as you peel them and keep a plate on top to make them stay under the water. When ready for packing in the jars, drain and rinse them. These hard fruits pack better if they are blanched in boiling water for a minute or two to make them soften and shrink, then plunge in cold water, drain, and pack. Tie them in muslin or put them in a strainer to facilitate handling.

Very hard cooking pears and quinces should be stewed before bottling, otherwise prepare the fruit as for stewing.

Making the Syrup

Plain water can be used if you prefer but the flavour is better if some sugar is added. The amount depends on personal taste. The usual amount is 4–8 oz. per pt. (110–220 g. per ½ l.) of water. Heat together, stirring until the sugar dissolves, and then boil for 2–3 mins.

For tomatoes, add 1 Tbs. salt and 1 Tbs. sugar to each 2 pt. (1 l.) of water used. Heat to dissolve the sugar.

Packing the Jars

Pack the fruit as tightly as possible without squashing it. Shake down berries and use the handle of a wooden spoon to work larger fruits into position, blanch hard and difficult ones (see *Preparing the Fruit*). From here the methods differ.

OVEN METHOD OF BOTTLING

Cooking Time 2 hrs.   *Temperature* E.200–250° (95–120°C.), G. ¼

Fill the jars to within ¼ in. (6 mm.) of the tops with cold syrup. Put on the rubber bands and the lids. Clamp or screw down. With screw bands loosen slightly by giving a half-turn backwards. This is necessary to allow for expansion. With other types there is sufficient play in the clamp to allow for this. Stand the jars in the meat tin or other baking tin in about 1 in. (2½ cm.) of water and put in the bottom of the oven (or other position recommended by the manufacturer's instruction book). Cook in a slow oven.

Remove the jars from the oven on to a wooden board or table. Tighten screw bands immediately. Leave for 24 hrs. and then test the seal before storing away.

PRESSURE-COOKER METHOD OF BOTTLING

Cooking Time 1 min for most fruits; 3–4 mins. for peaches or pineapple; 5 mins. for tomatoes. *All at 5 lb. pressure.*

Make sure the jars are not too tall and likely to block the pressure outlet on the cooker.

Have jars and syrup hot and pack and fill quickly. Loosen screw bands as before. Keep the jars standing in hot water as they are packed and until ready for the cooker. Place the jars on the rack in the bottom of the cooker, and do not allow them to touch each other or the sides of the cooker.

Use 1 in. (2½ cm.) of water in the pan – 1–4 pt. (½–2¼ l.) depending on size. Add a little vinegar to stop the pan from blackening. Bring the water to the boil before adding the jars. Put on the lid and process at 5 lb. pressure, bringing up to pressure quickly (5–10 mins.). Close the vent immediately steam begins to escape. If these precautions are not taken the fruit may be over-cooked.

Remove cooker from heat and allow to cool for not less than 10 mins. before opening. Lift jars out on to a wooden board or table and tighten screw bands. Leave to become cold and test the seal next day.

BOTTLING FRUIT PULP OR *PURÉE*

This is an economical way of getting a lot of fruit into the jars and is useful to have for making fools, whips, and other dishes needing a *purée*. Stew the fruit to a pulp with sugar to taste, and as little water as possible. Pour the hot pulp into hot jars and close as for the other methods. Place the jars on a rack or folded cloth in a pan with boiling water to cover and boil for 5 mins. Remove and screw down as before.

STORING BOTTLED FRUIT

Wipe the jars, label them, and store in a cool place away from the light. Screw bands and clips which are not needed once the jars are sealed should be removed, cleaned, and oiled lightly. Either store separately or put back in position, but do not screw bands down tightly. Look over the store occasionally to make sure all are keeping satisfactorily. One jar fermenting for a long time can make a terrible mess of the store.

FREEZING

Freezing takes place when a liquid is cooled sufficiently to turn it into a solid, thus water to ice. All food contains a high percentage of water and most food will freeze at between 32° and 27° (0° to −3°C.). This temperature, however, is not low enough to prevent deterioration in quality. Micro-organisms and enzymes cause changes and when the food is defrosted liquid is lost and, with it, flavour and nutritive value.

Deep-freezing is freezing food at a temperature of 0° to −10° (−18 to −23°C.) which is a low enough temperature to keep food in good condition. This is the temperature of most home freezers. At this temperature, food will freeze in about 6–7 hrs.

Quick-freezing is the method used commercially. The food is forzen at temperatures below −20° (−29°C.), which takes about ½ hr., and the food is then stored at 0° (−18°C.). The quicker the freezing the better the results because the minimum damage is done to the cells of the food. If the storage temperature is allowed to go above 5° (−15°C.) the food will begin to spoil, so keep a freezing thermometer in the cabinet as a check.

BUYING FROZEN FOOD FOR STORING IN A FREEZER

It is useless to buy frozen food for storing any length of time unless you have a freezer which will stay at 0° (−18°C.). Food can then be kept for periods of 1–12 months, depending on the type. For keeping times in 1-, 2-, and 3-star freezing compartments, see pages 103–4.

It is essential to buy frozen food from a dealer who looks after his stock properly, keeps it at 0° (−18°C.) and does not stack food up above the safety line on the freezing cabinet. It is no good trying to refreeze food which has already softened. If you do, the quality will be poor.

The following are approximate storage times for frozen food at 0° (−18°C.):

1 *month*   Ices and frozen sweets, bacon, shellfish, pre-cooked meals.

2 *months*   Sausages, salmon steaks, sponge cakes, bread and rolls.

3 *months*   Doughnuts, minced meat, offal, ham, fish.

6 *months*   Pieces of chicken, fruit pies, peas and beans, asparagus, game, pork, veal, chops and steaks.

12 *months*   Raw fruit, fruit juices, large pieces of meat, whole chicken.

CHOOSING A FREEZING CABINET

New models are constantly coming on the market, and old ones being improved, so that information on this subject soon becomes out of date. When choosing a freezer there are, however, several points to check on regardless of the make.

First make sure it is one which will maintain a temperature of 0° (−18°C.). Some of the freezing compartments of refrigerators fail here and are therefore not suitable for freezing raw food and will not keep frozen food for more than 2–3 weeks (see pages 103–4).

Next, be sure the freezer will go in the space available and that, within these limits, it is as big a one as you can afford. Make sure too that it is going to fit in a suitable place, not next to the cooker or central-heating radiator, or some other warm place. For details of use and care of the freezer follow the maker's instructions.

CONTAINERS FOR FREEZING

The essential for good storage is a moisture- and vapour-proof container, needed to prevent the escape of liquid and to prevent the drying of foods, which takes place very rapidly at low temperatures.

Polythene and plastic containers should be the kind specially made for use in a freezer, and oblong and square boxes are amongst the best, because they are economical of storage space and can be washed and used many times, thus making the higher initial cost worth while. Waxed tubs and cartons come in a variety of shapes and sizes, and with care these can be used several times. (Cottage cheese and ice-cream cartons are not suitable.)

Liquids expand when they freeze, so containers should leave room for this (especially important for glass). Leave ½ in. (1 cm.) head room for small containers of $\frac{1}{2}$ pt. ($\frac{1}{4}$ l.) and 1 in. (2$\frac{1}{2}$ cm.) for larger ones. Tight-fitting lids do not need any other sealing, but others should have the special sealing tape put round the joins.

Polythene sheets and bags should be of the special quality made for deep-freezing.

Lined bags are useful for chicken and other meats. Aluminium foil of special quality is one of the best wrappers. Household foil can be used double. Polythene bags can be sealed by gathering the ends together and folding over to secure with plastic-coated wire. Or they may be sealed by using a warm iron, first protecting the polythene with paper. Before sealing bags, squeeze out as much air as possible.

When food is being wrapped in sheets of material, either do it up like a parcel, or wrap as a butcher does meat, making sure the food is well inside the wrapper.

DEFROSTING A FREEZER

A good freezer properly used should not need defrosting more than once a year. Frost which forms on doors and walls should be scraped off regularly while it is still a thin layer. Do this with a wooden or plastic scraper, but not with anything sharp which is likely to scratch the cabinet. If the freezer doors are too frequently opened and if the food is not properly wrapped, frost will soon get too thick and defrosting be needed. It is a good idea to defrost when stocks are low. Remove all the food, wrap it in newspaper or put it in the refrigerator, and defrost as quickly as possible. Wipe the inside of the cabinet dry and run at very cold for 15–20 mins. before returning the food. Wipe water from the containers before putting them back. For the actual defrosting process, follow the maker's instructions.

LABELLING FOOD FOR THE FREEZER

All packages should be labelled clearly. Ordinary stick-on labels are no use, but special ones can be bought for use in the freezer. Grease pencils are used for writing on packages and coloured tape for marking.

LOADING THE FREEZER

The maker will recommend the maximum load which can safely be frozen at one time. This is usually 2–3 lb. (1–1$\frac{1}{2}$ kg.)

of food per cubic foot (28 litres) of capacity per 24 hrs. Overloading slows down freezing and produces poor results. Packets freeze fastest if put in contact with freezing coils or the sides of the freezer. As packets are being prepared, store them in the refrigerator until they are all ready to go into the freezer in one load. This avoids constant opening of the freezer door.

THE FREEZER IN POWER CUTS

When fully loaded, a properly insulated freezer will protect food for 1–2 days, provided the freezer door is kept shut. If the freezer is less than half full, the food will keep only about 24 hrs. If foods become partially thawed but still have ice crystals in them they may be refrozen, but the quality will be damaged and they should be used up as soon as possible.

DIRECTIONS FOR FREEZING FRUIT

Adding Sugar

Use caster or granulated at the rate of 4–6 oz. (125–175 g.) per lb. ($\frac{1}{2}$ kg.) of fruit. Sprinkle it over the fruit and mix in gently until the sugar begins to dissolve in the juices.

Using Syrup

Boil the sugar and water until the sugar is dissolved. Use cold. For sliced apples use $\frac{1}{2}$ lb. ($\frac{1}{4}$ kg.) of sugar per qt. (l.) of water; stone fruit 1 lb. ($\frac{1}{2}$ kg.) of sugar per qt. (l.) of water; soft fruit 2 lb. (1 kg.) of sugar per qt. (l.) water. In each case use $\frac{1}{2}$ pt. ($\frac{1}{4}$ l.) of syrup per lb. ($\frac{1}{2}$ kg.) of fruit.

Apples Use good-quality cooking apples. Peel, core, and slice or cut in rings. To keep them a good colour slice directly into a salt solution made with 2 Tbs. salt per gallon of water. Leave for 15–20 mins. Strain, and scald in boiling water until they are just pliable. Cool in cold water, drain, and pack plain or in syrup. For serving apples raw, slice directly into cold syrup and freeze.

Apples and Blackberries Prepare the apples as above and mix with the unscalded backberries. Freeze plain or in syrup.

Berries (except strawberries) Remove stalks and hulls. Either sprinkle with sugar, cover with cold syrup, or freeze plain.

Cherries (dark ones)   Remove stalks also stones (if desired), freeze in syrup or sugar. (Morellos) mix sugar at rate of 1 lb. (½ kg.) per 5 lb. fruit (2½ kg.).

Citrus Fruit Segments   Freeze with sugar.

Currants   As berries.

Damsons   Remove stalks, wipe off bloom, rinse, and freeze in syrup or sugar.

Gooseberries   Top and tail, wash, freeze with syrup or plain.

Grapes   Leave whole or cut to remove pips. Freeze in syrup.

Greengages   Remove stalks and wash, freeze with syrup or plain.

Juices   Freeze in small cartons leaving ½ in. (1 cm.) head room.

Melon   Freeze slices or cubes with sugar.

Mulberries   As other berries. Freeze firm ones only.

Peaches   Skin, slice, and freeze in syrup.

Pineapple   Freeze slices plain with cellophane between slices.

Plums   Remove stalks, wash, and wipe bloom from dark ones. May be stoned and frozen in syrup. Make good frozen *purées*.

Purées   Make in the usual way and sweeten to taste. Do not make in the electric blender as this mixes in too much air.

Raspberries, see *Berries*.

Rhubarb   Cut in pieces 1–2 in. (2½–5 cm.) long and pour hot syrup over it. Leave 8–12 hrs. before packing. Can also be frozen plain.

Strawberries   Hull and wash in cold water. Best crushed or sliced and frozen with sugar. May also be done in syrup.

DIRECTIONS FOR FREEZING VEGETABLES

Most vegetables need to be blanched (scalded) before packing. The scalding time is counted from when the water boils after the vegetables have been added. The water should be boiling when they are added. Then plunge them in ice-cold water until they are cold right through, drain, and pack.

Asparagus   Grade according to the thickness of the stalks. Wash and scrape the lower ends. Cut in even lengths to fit the containers. Scald 4 mins. for thick pieces, 2 mins. for thin.

Beans, Broad   Pod, and grade. Use only very young beans. Scald 3 mins.

Beans, French or Runner   Use only young and stringless ones. Leave French beans whole, slice or cut runners. Scald 2–3 mins.

Beetroot   Use small young ones only, or cook larger ones until tender, peel, and cut up. Scald small ones 20 mins. or until the skin will rub off.

Broccoli, Sprouting   Use only young tender stalks. Cut in lengths to fit the container. Scald 3 mins.

Brussels Sprouts   Use only small firm ones, trimming off any loose outer leaves and the stalks. Wash, and scald 3 mins.

Carrots   Very small ones whole, others sliced or diced. Remove tops and wash well. Scald 5 mins. and rub off skins. Then cut large ones.

Cauliflower   Break into flowerets 2 in. (5 cm.) across. Scald 3 mins.

Celery   Only suitable for cooking. No need to blanch.

Herbs   Wash, drain, and freeze. Chop while frozen.

Mushrooms   Use button ones only. Wash, trim, and freeze unscalded.

Onions   Peel, chop, and freeze in small packets.

Parsley   Wash, drain, chop or leave in sprigs and put in small packets.

Parsnips   Peel and slice $\frac{1}{2}$ in. (1 cm.) thick. Scald 2 mins.

Peas   Use young ones only. Shell, and scald 1–2 mins.

Potato Chips   Fry, drain well, cool, and freeze. To heat, spread on baking trays in a hot oven E.400° (200°C.), G.7 for 5–10 mins. Salt and serve.

Spinach   Blanch 2 mins.

Sweet Peppers Wash, remove seeds and stem. Halve or slice or dice and freeze in small lots.

USING FROZEN VEGETABLES

Beetroot, herbs, and peppers are defrosted and used without heating. Other vegetables are cooked while still frozen. Boil in a little salted water until just tender.

DIRECTIONS FOR FREEZING MEAT AND FISH

Beef If freshly killed, refrigerate it for 5–7 days to allow it to mature before freezing. When freezing steaks or other small pieces put wax paper between layers. Thaw beef in its wrapper in the refrigerator, 8 hrs. for steaks and not less than 5 hrs. per lb. ($\frac{1}{2}$ kg.) for large pieces. Cook as soon as it is thawed.

Chicken Clean, pluck, wrap giblets separately. Thaw 24–36 hrs. in the refrigerator or 6–8 hrs. at room temperature. Thaw joints 6 hrs. in the refrigerator or 3 hrs at room temperature. Cook as soon as thawed.

Chicken, Fried Fry until it is browned but not cooked. Freeze. Thaw and then bake in a shallow pan in a moderate oven E.350° (177°C.), G.3 for 30–45 mins. or until tender.

Duck As Chicken.

Fish Steaks and fillets, put waxed paper between layers. Cook while still frozen. Large pieces and small whole fish, clean and freeze, dip in ice water and freeze, repeat until a layer of ice is formed all over the fish, then wrap. Defrost in the refrigerator for 12–24 hrs. and cook partly frozen.

Goose As Chicken.

Lamb If freshly killed refrigerate 1–2 days to allow it to mature before freezing. Put wax paper between chops and small pieces. Thaw and use as for beef.

Pheasant As Chicken.

Pork As Lamb.

Roast Meat Roast, cool rapidly, and remove as much fat as possible. Wrap and freeze. Thaw in the refrigerator for 5–6 hrs. per lb. ($\frac{1}{2}$ kg.).

Turkey   Freeze as chicken. Thaw small turkeys 2 days in the refrigerator; large ones 3–4 days.

Turkey, Roast   Roast and cool as rapidly as possible. Remove meat from bones and remove fat. It keeps best if covered with turkey stock. Thaw 5–6 hrs. and use cold or reheated.

Veal   As Lamb.

Wild Duck   Clean but do not pluck until it has been in the refrigerator for 2–3 days. Then dry-pluck and freeze. Thaw 10–12 hrs. in the refrigerator or 5–6 hrs. at room temperature.

DIRECTIONS FOR FREEZING BAKED GOODS

Biscuits and Cookies   Bake and freeze, or shape into a roll and freeze unbaked. Thaw cooked ones 2–3 hrs. at room temperature. Thaw, uncooked until soft enough to slice the roll, then bake.

Bread   Freeze sliced, as it is then easy to remove only what is wanted. Do not keep more than 2 months. Thaw at room temperature or toast slices while still frozen. Rolls, heat E. 350° (180°C.), G.4 for 15–20 mins.

Breadcrumbs   Freeze plain or buttered, in small packs.

Cakes   Freeze whole (iced if wanted) or in portions with waxed paper between layers. Thaw at room temperature, whole cake up to 12 hrs., pieces 2–3 hrs.

Cream Puffs and Éclairs   Freeze unfilled. Thaw 5–10 mins. at room temperature. Or freeze uncooked, thaw 15–20 mins. then bake as usual.

Pastry, Flans   Freeze baked or unbaked. Thaw baked at room temperature 1 hr. Bake raw flans while frozen, cook at E.400° (200°C.), G.6.

Pies, Fruit (double crust)   Freeze in the raw crust and do not cut any vent holes in the top. Bake while frozen, and cut a vent hole before baking. Bake 15–20 mins. at E.400° (200°C.), G.6 and then reduce heat to E.350° (180°C.), G.4 for 20–30 mins. more.

Scones   Cook, cool, and freeze on trays. Remove and pack in bags. Heat while frozen at E.400° (200°C.), G.6 until well heated through.

FREEZING OTHER FOODS

Casseroles Cook as usual but undercook the vegetables and omit potatoes. Make sure the meat is covered by the sauce and freeze in rigid containers. Place in a pan of cold water and thaw enough to remove from the container. Heat in the top of a double boiler or in a moderate oven for $\frac{3}{4}$–1 hr.

Cream Use only double cream. It can be frozen on cake or pudding, or pipe in rosettes and freeze separately. Thaw at room temperature. Put rosettes on pudding to thaw, about 15 mins.

Eggs Shell and beat to mix but not aerate. Put in containers with 1 in. ($2\frac{1}{2}$ cm.) head room for expansion. Before freezing add 1 tsp. salt per pt. ($\frac{1}{2}$ l.) or 1 Tbs. sugar per pt. Egg yolks the same. Egg whites, freeze plain. Eggs can be frozen in cubes in the ice tray, 1 egg per cube, and then stored in bags. Defrost completely before use.

Gravies Use cornflour or rice flour for thickening. Freeze in tubs. Heat in double boiler, stirring well.

Sandwiches Use day-old bread. Fill, wrap individually, freeze flat, and then stack. Thaw 1–2 hrs. Do not keep more than 2 months and do not fill with either hard-boiled egg, salad vegetables, salad cream, or mayonnaise.

Sauces As Gravies, or thaw in the refrigerator and use cold.

Soups Make as usual but with less liquid. Omit milk or potatoes and freeze in tubs or similar containers. Add liquid and heat over direct heat or in a double boiler, stirring frequently.

Steamed Puddings Steam, cool, and freeze. Thaw 6 hrs. at room temperature and then steam until hot. Will keep a year.

Stock Boil stock to concentrate it, cool, and remove fat. Freeze in ice-cube trays, then put in packets.

215

Chapter Seven

A.B.C. OF COOKING TERMS AND METHODS

À LA

Meaning 'with' or 'in the manner of', e.g. '*à la crème*' meaning 'with cream', and '*à la Grecque*' meaning 'in the Greek manner'.

AMERICAN TERMINOLOGY

TERMINOLOGY	*English names*
American cheese	Cheddar
biscuit	scone
broil	grill
confectioner's sugar	icing sugar
cornstarch	cornflour
cracker	water biscuit
farina	semolina
French fried potatoes	chips
Graham flour	whole wheat flour
ground	minced
mince	chop finely
molasses	black treacle
pan frying	shallow frying
pie	open tart
double pie	two-crust pie or plate pie
deep dish pie	pie
skillet	shallow pan with a lid
Swiss cheese	Emmental

AMERICAN EQUIVALENTS

1 square of chocolate	1 oz. (25 g.)
1 cake of compressed yeast	$\frac{2}{3}$ oz. (20 g.)
1 envelope of gelatine	$\frac{1}{3}$ oz. (10 g.)
Cans No. 1 size	16 oz. (454 g.)
No. 2 size	20 oz. (567 g.)

ANGLAISE OR À L'ANGLAISE

To cook plainly in water, or to coat with egg and breadcrumbs before frying.

ASPIC JELLY

A clear, savoury jelly made from meat, fish, or vegetable stock, with gelatine to make it set. It is used for masking cold meats and fish or other savoury dishes, for cocktail savouries, lining moulds for savoury jellies, and in many other ways.

Aspic jelly may be purchased ready-made in crystal form, but this is not generally of very good quality. It can be improved by the addition of Madeira or brandy. Better than this are the aspic jellies sold in jars, in jelly form, to be melted and used as needed. They are usually fairly expensive, but so are home-made aspic jellies using a good meat stock, and the latter is hardly worth while in the average home when only small quantities of the jelly are needed at a time.

Quite a good jelly for the same purpose is made by using any of the meat cubes which can be relied on to give an obsolutely clear liquid. Set it with gelatine. In the same way a can of *consommé* may have gelatine added to make it set more firmly, only about a quarter of the amount you would need for a liquid which had no jellying capacity of its own.

Fish and vegetable aspics are both made in the same way, using clear fish or vegetable stocks with gelatine.

AU BEURRE NOIR

Served with brown butter, made by heating butter until it turns nut brown.

AU FROMAGE

With cheese.

AU GRATIN

This refers to a covering of breadcrumbs dotted with fat. It is used as a finish for many savoury dishes. The food being cooked 'au gratin' is usually in a sauce which may contain cheese, and grated cheese may be mixed with the breadcrumbs. The top is browned under the grill or in the top of a hot oven. It is usually served in the dish in which it is cooked.

BAIN-MARIE

A shallow container of hot water in which saucepans are stood to keep hot without further cooking, e.g. keeping sauces hot. For one sauce a double boiler can serve the same purpose provided the water in the lower half is not allowed to boil.

BAKING

Any food cooked in the oven may be called 'baked', but the term is generally used for cakes and pastry.

BARBECUE SAUCE

A sauce used for brushing meat, poultry, or fish prior to and during grilling. It may also be used as a marinade. Usually made with oil, spices, herbs and other flavourings.

BARDING

Is tying a thin sheet of fat bacon or fat salt pork over meat, usually the breast of a bird or lean meat like veal, to act as a self-basting device. It also adds flavour. It is usually removed before serving, but sometimes is left on small game birds like woodcock and pheasant. If the piece of fat is thick it will have to be removed before the end of the cooking time to allow the meat to brown.

BASTING

Is keeping the surface of food moist by spooning a liquid or melted fat over it at frequent intervals during cooking. It is used in cooking many kinds of foods, either to help keep the surface moist or to give extra flavour; for example, basting with wine or a barbecue sauce.

Basting meat during roasting is not as important today as it used to be because there is better control over temperatures than in old ovens, and less tendency for the meat to become dry; but basting is still done for purposes of flavouring.

BATTERS

Are mixtures of flour, liquid, eggs, and sometimes other ingredients. They are sufficiently soft to be beaten or 'battered'. They are used in English cookery for such things as Yorkshire puddings, pancakes, for coating fried fish, fritters, and drop scones. Batters may be divided into two main groups according to their consistency. A thin batter is like thin cream, flows easily when poured and is the consistency for pancakes and batter puddings. A thick batter pours sluggishly and spreads slowly when dropped from a spoon and is the consistency for drop scones, Scotch pancakes, pikelets, fritters, and frying batters.

BEATERS
Kitchen utensils used for beating include cutlet bats used for flattening meat and many types of egg whisks (see pages 21 and 28).

BEATING
Is vigorous mixing with a wooden spoon or an egg-whisk to make a mixture smooth and beat air into it.

BEIGNETS are fritters.

BEURRE MANIÉ
A mixture of butter and flour in equal quantities, worked together to make a paste and used for thickening liquids at the end of a cooking process rather than at the beginning as with a *roux*. The *beurre manié* is dropped in the boiling liquid and whisked until blended and the liquid thickened.

BINDING
Adding egg, melted fat, or a liquid to dry ingredients to hold them together.

BISQUE
A thick soup usually made from a *purée* of shellfish but other fish are also used.

BLANC
A French cooking term for a variety of different cooking liquids such as a *court bouillon*, which is water flavoured with vegetables and herbs; or a white stock.

BLANCHING
Is a preliminary stage in many cooking operations, used to help remove skins of tomatoes, or remove some salt from pre-

served foods, to remove a strong or bitter taste, or to help keep food a good colour.

Sometimes the food is simply treated with boiling water by putting it in a bowl, pouring the water over it and leaving for a few minutes. Other foods are put in cold water, brought to the boil, and cooked for a few minutes or even half-cooked. The recipe should indicate which method to use. The first is usually for removing skins from fruit and nuts or salt from bacon rashers, the longer method is used for preparing things like brains and sweetbreads or for the preliminary cooking of a piece of salty meat. In all cases the water used for blanching is discarded before cooking continues with some fresh liquid.

BLANQUETTE

A white stew where the meat and vegetables are cooked in a white sauce. Cream or egg is added to the sauce just before serving.

BLENDING

Is the thorough mixing of ingredients to give a smooth texture or an even consistency. It can be used to describe mixing dry ingredients with a liquid to give a smooth paste, or for mixing two dry or two wet ingredients together.

A blender is a machine for blending ingredients at very high speed, either to produce a liquid or to make a pulp or *purée*.

BLIND

Baking blind means baking flan cases without a filling. To keep the pastry in shape the inside is filled with a piece of crumpled foil until the pastry is set. This is then removed for the cooking of the pastry to continue.

BOILING

Boiling point is the temperature at which a liquid most rapidly changes to a vapour, the process being accompanied by violent agitation due to bubbles of vapour escaping through the surface. With water at normal atmospheric pressures boiling takes place at 100°C. (212°) at sea-level. If the pressure above the liquid is increased it will boil at a higher temperature as in pressure cooking, and if the pressure is reduced, as in a vacuum, boiling will take place at a lower temperature as is done in the

220

evaporation of moisture to make dried milk and other modern dried foods.

Violent boiling does not raise the cooking temperature but it does increase the speed of evaporation. It should, therefore, not be used in ordinary cooking but only when rapid concentration of a liquid is wanted. Rapid boiling of things like potatoes does not hasten the cooking, it only makes them break up, due to the mechanical effect of the large vapour pockets being formed.

Many foods which are called 'boiled' are in fact best cooked at a temperature below boiling point – that is, simmering.

BOLOGNA

A town in Italy famous for the invention of a smoked sausage made from various kinds of meat and spices. The sausages are usually cooked before smoking and are then suitable for eating cold without further cooking.

BONING

This is cutting flesh away from bones, either before or after cooking. Special thin pointed knives are used, and skill and experience are needed to do it without damaging the flesh or leaving a lot of waste on the bones. Most butchers and fishmongers will do boning for you if you ask them. If you want to do it for yourself the most important thing is to find the position and shape of the bones, and to cut close to the bone with a scraping action which does not tear the flesh. To watch an expert do it is the best way of learning.

BORDER

In many recipes food is either cooked in a border mould or shaped into a border in some other way, to make a circle with a hole in the middle. The hole is frequently filled with another type of food, e.g. a border of rice filled with fish in a sauce. Border moulds for baking in usually consist of tinned steel or aluminium and come in a variety of sizes, some plain and some fluted. Moulds for setting jellies are usually either tinned copper or aluminium. Rice and similar food may be pressed in a mould after cooking and then turned out while still hot. Alternatively, the border may be shaped on a serving dish using spoons to pile it up. Mashed potato borders may be piped, and this is the best way for individual-sized ones.

BOUCHÉES
Are little patties made from puff pastry and filled with a savoury mixture. They are usually served at cocktail parties, buffets, and in *hors-d'œuvre*.

BOUDINS
French variety of Black Pudding.

BOUILLABAISSE
A Mediterranean fish soup which depends on local fish for its flavour.

BOUILLON
Is the French name for stock.

BOUQUET GARNI
Is used for flavouring stocks, sauces, and many other savoury dishes. The one most commonly used consists of a bay leaf, a sprig of thyme, and a sprig of parsley, all tied together with white cotton, or, if dried herbs are used, tied in a small piece of muslin. Ready-made bouquets in muslin bags can be purchased from many shops selling herbs. As the bouquet is always removed before serving it is a good plan to leave the tying thread long enough to hang over the edge of the cooking vessel. Mixtures which are strained before serving can obviously have the herbs put in loose.

A wide variety of other herbs is used in a bouquet, and sometimes a small piece of celery is tied with the herbs.

BRAISING
The term is used to cover two different types of dish. One consists of pieces of meat cooked in a thickened sauce with vegetables, much the same as making a stew or cooking a casserole, the other and older meaning applies to cooking large pieces of meat. The latter is an excellent way of dealing with the tougher cuts of meat, as an alternative to slow roasting

For this you want a pan with a tight-fitting lid, preferably one which can be used on top of the stove as well as in the oven. Prepare enough finely sliced vegetables to make a layer about 2 in. (5 cm.) thick on the bottom of the pan. Best vegetables to use are onions, carrots, celery, turnips, and parsnips.

Trim excess fat from the meat and fry it brown all over. Lift out of the pan and pour off excess fat. Put in the layer of vegetables and put the meat on top of them. Season with salt and pepper and add a *bouquet garni*. Put on the lid and cook in a slow oven, E.300–350° (150–180°C.), G.2–3, using the higher temperature for smaller pieces of meat.

Times   Chops ¾ to 1 hr.

Pieces of steak 1½–2 hrs.

Larger pieces 40–45 mins. per lb. (½ kg.)

Braised meat looks best if cut in slices for serving, arranged on a meat dish, and garnished with vegetables. For a gravy, use either the strained liquid from the cooking, skimming off excess fat if necessary, or thicken the liquid with some *roux*, or put vegetables and liquid in the electric blender when the pulverised vegetables act as a thickening agent. In all cases the *bouquet garni* is removed before making the gravy.

BREADCRUMBS

Buttered Crumbs are made from fresh breadcrumbs coated with melted butter or margarine. They are used for gratin dishes and for a topping for many sweet and savoury dishes. For every pint of breadcrumbs (½ l.) melt 1 oz. (25 g.) of butter or margarine and stir the crumbs round in it until they are coated. If these are then dried in the oven they will keep well in a covered container; or, without drying, in the freezer.

Dried Crumbs are made from bread dried in the oven until crisp. White bread dried very slowly will produce white crumbs, otherwise they will be light brown. The simplest way of making the crumbs is to break the bread in small bits and feed them into the blender with the motor running but keep your hand over the top or the crumbs will fly out. They can also be made by mincing with a bag tied over the end of the mincer to collect the crumbs; or crush them with a rolling pin and sieve to remove coarse pieces. Dried crumbs are used for coating food before frying, and it is generally considered that white ones are the best for deep fat frying as the others tend to turn very dark during frying.

Fresh Crumbs are made from the crumb of stale but not hard bread. The quickest way of making them is to use an electric blender; alternatively use a grater, or rub through a sieve.

BRINE
A solution of salt and water used in many types of food preparation, especially for pickling meat and making bacon. To the brine is added saltpetre, which turns the meat pink during cooking, and a variety of spices is also used. Brine is also used in pickle-making and for brushing on bread before baking in order to make the crust crisp. It is also an important beverage for people doing heavy work under hot conditions when they sweat a lot and lose dangerous amounts of salt and water from their bodies. A weak brine is drunk, $\frac{1}{2}$ level tsp. salt to 1 pt. ($\frac{1}{2}$ l.) water.

BROCHETTES
Fine long skewers for threading small pieces of meat on for grilling, the French version of a kebab or shashlik. Many of the skewers have ornamental heads, and when these are used the meat is often cooked first and then threaded on the skewers for serving.

BROILING is grilling.

BROSE
Is a Scottish term used to cover a wide variety of dishes made from oatmeal, Atholl brose, which contains whisky, being one of the most famous.

BROTH
Is variously described as the liquid in which meat has been boiled or a soup made from meat and/or bones and vegetables.

BRUSHING, see *Glaze*, page 237

BUTTERSCOTCH
Is a toffee containing butter, but the name also refers to the flavour obtained when butter and brown sugar are cooked together. Some butterscotch-flavoured packet and frozen foods are on the market.

CARAMEL

When sugar is heated to a high temperature it begins to undergo a chemical change, a change in flavour, and a change in colour; first to a light brown, then amber and finally dark brown to black, after which it burns leaving carbon as a black residue.

The amber-brown colour is used extensively in sweet dishes. Although dry sugar can be melted and cooked to a caramel, better results are obtained if a little water is added first to make the sugar into a syrup (2 Tbs. of water to 2 oz. (50 g.) of sugar). Then the syrup is boiled hard, without stirring, until the colour changes to amber. If the colour is too pale the flavour will be poor, and if too dark it will be bitter.

Caramelising takes place during roasting, frying, and baking, and is responsible for some of the flavour of foods cooked by these methods, e.g. roasted onions and parsnips, or baked apples.

CARVING

To become a good carver requires a certain amount of experience, but to start right is important. The knife should be really sharp, the kind of knife being less important than its sharpness. It should be sharpened every time it is used and, if the knife is stainless steel, be sure that you have the correct kind of sharpener for it. An alternative to an ordinary knife is an electric carving knife which many people find easier, especially if they like the meat cut very thinly.

Most meat should be cut across the grain, that is, across the meat fibres. If cut the other way, with the fibres, the shape of the fibres can be clearly seen. The reason why across the grain is considered to be the best way is that, unless the meat is very tender, it is very difficult to chew the long fibres. In most cases cutting across the grain means cutting at right angles to the bone. In rolled joints it usually means carving across the already cut ends. Carving should be a sawing action, with long light strokes backwards and forwards, and on as even a plane as possible, so that the surface remains flat; otherwise the carver soon finds that only scrappy bits are coming off each time, because of the bumps and hollows formed by the crooked carving.

Use a fork with a thumb guard and, if possible, do the cutting away from yourself.

Exceptions to the rule for cutting across the grain are with:

Saddle of Mutton

This consists of two loins joined together in the middle, so, in this case, carving is done in slices parallel with the backbone.

Legs of Lamb or Mutton

These are also sometimes carved parallel with the bone.

Game and Poultry

These are carved by first removing the legs at the joint nearest the body. The simplest way is to hold the end of the leg in one hand and pull the leg slightly away from the body while severing the joint with a knife or poultry scissors. If desired, the leg may be cut into two portions at the joint. Next remove the wing, together with a small portion of the breast. Then remove the wish-bone by slicing down across the breast at the neck end. The breast is carved in slices, cutting downwards.

CASSEROLE COOKING

Any oven-proof dish can be used as casserole, either with its own lid, or with a foil one. Any food which is suitable for cooking in a saucepan, at simmering point, can equally well be cooked in the oven in a casserole. The temperature will vary with the recipe, but it is usually in the range of 250–350° (120–180°C.), G.$\frac{1}{2}$–4. It should be remembered that a casserole takes time to heat through, and that the thicker it is the longer it takes before the contents actually start to cook. To bring the contents to simmering on top of the cooker cuts down the total time required, otherwise you need to add anything up to $\frac{1}{2}$ hr. to the cooking time to allow the contents to heat up. Alternatively, the casserole can be put in a much hotter oven than is required for the actual cooking, and the heat at once turned down to the correct cooking temperature.

CASSOLETTES

Small dishes made of fireproof porcelain, heat-resistant glass or metal, and used to serve *hors-d'œuvre* or individual savoury or sweet dishes.

CEREALS

The edible seeds of grasses, chiefly rice, wheat, and sweet corn, or maize, oats, barley, rye, millet, and buckwheat. A wide variety of foods is made from cereals, for example, flours, meals, breakfast cereals, and *pasta*.

CHARCOAL

The black residue formed when animal or vegetable matter is heated to drive off volatile substances, but is not actually burnt. It consists of carbon.

That used as a fuel for cooking is made from wood, and is used for certain types of grills and for barbecue fires.

Charcoal also has the property of absorbing odours and gases, and biscuits containing charcoal have long been sold as palliatives for indigestion.

CHAUDS-FROIDS

A very elaborate French dish consisting of *fricassée* of meat or game served cold, the sauce being set with aspic jelly and used to mask the meat. In many cases the dish is elaborately garnished with truffles and other edible decorations, all masked with a final layer of clear aspic. Unless it is very expertly done it is apt to look pretentious and unappetising. Because of the time and handling involved in the preparation of such dishes, the consumer runs a considerable risk of getting food poisoning.

CHINING

This is sawing through the rib bones of a loin or best end of neck joint to separate the backbone and make for easier carving. The butcher will do it for you. It is a much better method than the more usual chopping between the rib bones.

CHITTERLINGS

The small intestine of any animal. Used chiefly as sausage casings, but sometimes cooked as a separate dish.

CHOPPING

This can be done with a long pointed knife, with a curved knife in a wooden bowl, or in an electric blender (see *Choppers*, page 24).

CHOWDER

A thick American soup containing beans and vegetables, and frequently fish as well. It is more like a stew than the usual soup, and is substantial enough to form a main dish for lunch or supper.

CITRIC ACID

An organic acid which is found in citrus fruit and in many other fruits, e.g. gooseberries, currants, and cherries. Citric acid is added to some non-acid fruits when they are being made into jam or jelly; it is also used in making lemonade and other beverages, and in certain boiled sweets such as acid drops.

CITRUS FRUIT

Oranges, lemons, grapefruit, limes, and so on.

CLARIFIED BUTTER

When salted butter is used for frying and the dish would be spoilt by the butter going brown it must be clarified before use. To do this, heat the butter to melt it and then continue to heat while removing any scum which rises to the top. Don't heat enough to colour the butter. Strain it through a nylon sieve, or pour off the clear butter, leaving the sediment behind. The clear butter is then ready for frying. The scum and sediment from the clarifying can be used in cooking, for example, dressing vegetables.

COATING – TO COAT

To cover one food with a thin layer of another in liquid form. Usually applied to food dipped in beaten egg or in a batter. Also used to describe the stage at which an egg custard sauce has thickened, when, instead of running off the wooden stirrer it stays on in a thin coating. Sauces are frequently used to coat food when served, and a 'coating' consistency is one of the standard sauces.

Various coatings are used for food which is to be fried. Coating fish with seasoned flour and then dipping it in milk is one of the simplest and best ways of preparing it for shallow frying. Egg-and-breadcrumb coatings are used for shallow or deep fat frying. The food is coated with seasoned flour, then dipped in beaten egg and finally in fine white breadcrumbs.

When a batter coating is used the food should first be coated with seasoned flour. This treatment makes the subsequent coatings adhere better.

CODDLING

This is a method of cooking eggs which takes a little longer than boiling, but gives a more tender egg. The eggs are put into boiling water to cover to the depth of about 1 in. (2½ cm.). Cover the pan and stand it in a warm place for 7–9 mins., depending on the size of the eggs, or 20 mins. for hard-boiled.

COMPOTE

This is made with fresh or dried fruit stewed slowly in a syrup. The cooking is gentle, so that the fruit does not lose its shape and break up. When cooked, the fruit is lifted into a serving dish and the syrup is boiled hard to reduce and thicken it. It is then poured over the fruit, which is left to become cold. Sometimes brandy and liqueur are added to the syrup before pouring it over the fruit, or when it is cold. Alternatively, add spice or grated orange or lemon rind to the syrup.

CONCASSÉ

Means roughly chopped.

CONFECTIONERY

The branch of cookery dealing with cakes, pastries, and sweets or candies.

CONSISTENCY

A term which describes the thickness of a batter or cake mixture. A thin batter is like thin cream and will flow readily from a jug; a thick batter will flow, but is thick and sluggish; a dropping consistency is a soft cake mixture which drops easily from the mixing spoon; a stiff cake consistency is thick enough to stand up in rocky lumps; a soft dough is thicker still, and is stiff enough to handle and roll out, but is still soft to touch; a stiff dough has the minimum amount of water added to bind the ingredients together, and is firmer and drier than a soft dough.

CORN MEAL

A coarse meal (like coarse semolina) made from corn or maize and used in Europe and America for a number of traditional dishes, including corn bread.

COURT BOUILLON

Flavoured water (usually with vegetables and herbs, possibly wine), used for boiling and poaching meat, fish, and vegetables. In French cookery salted water is often referred to as a *court bouillon.*

CREAMING

This term is usually applied to a mixture of fat and sugar which is beaten until so light and soft that it looks like whipped cream. It is quite hard work by hand, but easy with an electric beater. Some fats are much easier to cream than others, for example, soft margarines, but others can be warmed a little to soften but not melt them; or the mixing bowl can be warmed beforehand.

CREÇY

This usually means cooked with carrots as an important ingredient.

CRÈME DE MENTHE

The name of a liqueur flavoured with peppermint; and also a name used for sweets flavoured with peppermint.

CRIMPING

To gash the sides of whole fish at intervals; or to pinch the edges of a pie for decoration.

CROISSANTS

Crescent-shaped French rolls eaten fresh with breakfast coffee. They are made from a yeast dough, into which butter is worked in much the same way as with flaky patry. *Croissants* are sold by some English bakers.

CROQUETTES

A time-consuming method of using up left-overs of fish, meat, or vegetables. The food is minced or chopped finely, combined with a thick sauce, chilled until firm, and then coated with egg and breadcrumbs and fried in deep fat.

Potato croquettes are made more simply, by combining mashed potato with the left-overs and seasonings.

CROUSTADES

Cases made to hold meat or fish, combined with a sauce, and similar to patties or *vol-au-vents*. They are usually made from stale bread or rolls hollowed out in the middle, with a small piece cut for a lid. They are then fried in deep fat, filled, and served hot. Very small ones are used for *hors-d'œuvre* or cocktail savouries, and the larger ones for main dishes.

CROÛTES

Either the same as *croustades*, or as *croûtons*.

CROÛTONS

Small cubes or squares of toasted or fried bread used for garnishing soup and savoury dishes. The crispness makes a pleasant contrast of texture with the liquid and soft foods that they accompany.

CUITE AU BEURRE

Means cooked with butter.

CURD

The solid part of milk, formed when it sours or is clotted by adding rennet. The term is also used for some kinds of preserves, e.g. lemon curd.

CURED

Curing is a process which involves salting, drying, and smoking in order to preserve meat and fish, for example, bacon or kippers. The degree of salting usually determines how long the food will keep. The smoking is mainly important for the flavour it imparts.

CUT AND FOLD

A method used to combine ingredients gently to retain air which has been beaten in, for example, folding flour into beaten eggs and sugar when making a sponge. A metal spoon is used and one mixture is folded over the other gently, with the spoon being used to cut through the mixture to the bottom to lift up the lower layers and fold, until all is blended.

CUTLET

A name used for a variety of preparations. It may be a piece of a rib of an animal (lamb cutlet or veal cutlet), or the same kind of piece with the bone removed. Many mixtures made with left-overs are shaped like cutlets before they are fried, and there are special cutters for shaping them. In vegetarian cookery pulse and vegetable mixtures are shaped in a similar way – e.g. lentil cutlet.

DECANTING

Necessary with an old wine or port which has a sediment in the bottle. Before decanting leave the bottle standing upright for 12–24 hrs. Remove the cork very gently, wipe the inside of the neck, and pour gently and steadily into the decanter. Stop pouring as soon as any sediment appears in the neck of the bottle. The dregs can be filtered or used in cooking. The sediment is harmless but it spoils the wine if disturbed.

DEGLAZING

When meat has been fried or roasted there is usually some sediment stuck to the pan, and this consists of dried meat juices. They are dissolved by adding stock, wine, or other liquid while stirring and heating. The liquid is either poured over the meat, used as a gravy, or added to a sauce to be served with the meat.

DEGRAISSER

A French word meaning to remove fat from the top of stock or a soup. The melted fat can be poured off gently, or skimmed off, or the mixture can be allowed to become cold when the fat will rise to the top and solidify, when it can easily be lifted off (see *Skim*, page 254).

DEVILLED

A method of grilling when the meat is treated with a mixture of oil, mustard, and other seasonings. It is similar to a barbecue sauce, but the meat is usually a left-over, for example turkey or chicken legs. The meat is scored and the seasonings rubbed in.

DICE

Small cubes obtained by cutting a food in strips and then cutting the bundles of strips across to make small pieces.

DISSOLVE

When a solid mixes with a liquid so that no traces of the original solid remain, for example, sugar and salt will dissolve in water. Some solids dissolve in cold water, while others need to be heated to make this happen. It is a term much misused in recipe writing, usually when 'mix' is meant.

DOUGH

A mixture of flour, liquid, and other ingredients, the result being thick enough to be shaped by hand or rolled out and cut to shape. A soft dough is used for scones and bread, while a stiff dough is used for pastry and most biscuits (see *Consistency*, page 229).

DREDGING

Sprinkling lightly with either flour or sugar. Special containers with perforated lids are sold for the purpose, but many cooks dredge by hand.

DRIPPING

Fat which has dripped from meat during cooking or fat melted from separate meat-fat, cooked specially for the purpose of providing dripping. The process of producing this sort of dripping is called 'rendering'. The simplest way of doing this is to cut the fat in small pieces and put it in a pan in a slow oven. As the fat melts out of the tissues it is strained into a basin. The process is continued until only small pieces of dried tissue remain. Care should be taken to see that the fat does not become too hot, or there will be danger of fire and the dripping will be spoiled.

Dripping which comes from roasting meat and other cooked meat often has stock and particles of other foods mixed with it. To make it suitable for use in cooking it needs clarifying. To do this, put the dripping in a pan and cover with water. Bring to the boil and boil for 2–3 mins. Strain it into a clean basin, and leave for the fat to set. Lift off the cake of fat, scrape any bits from the bottom, and heat it gently in a pan until all bubbling stops. This indicates that all the water has been driven off and the fat is ready for use for frying or other cooking.

DRY INGREDIENTS
Ingredients such as flour, sugar, raising agents, spices, salt, and so on.

DRYING
The removal of moisture from a food. If sufficient is removed the food will keep indefinitely in a dry place. It is one of the oldest methods of preserving food, the drying originally being done by the sun. It is still used for pulses, dried fruits, dried fish, and herbs. More modern and improved methods are called 'dehydrating'.

EMULSION
This is a suspension of a light substance like oil in a heavier substance like egg. Mayonnaise is an emulsion where the oil is held in suspension by the egg yolk.

The stability of an emulsion can be upset by extremes of temperature and it is important when making one to have all the ingredients at room temperature.

A creamed mixture of fat, sugar, and eggs is another example of an emulsion. Adding cold eggs to a creamed fat and sugar mixture can prevent the emulsion from forming.

Cream is an emulsion of fat globules held in suspension by the protein in milk. If milk is allowed to freeze and is then heated it will be seen that the emulsion has broken and globules of fat separate out on top of the milk.

ENTRÉE
This is the third course served in an old-fashioned formal meal of many courses. It is a savoury dish, usually of meat served in a sauce, but may also be a fish dish or a cold dish.

ESCALOPE
A very thin slice of meat without bone, e.g. veal *escalope*.

FAGGOTS OR SAVOURY DUCKS
Ball- or loaf-shaped objects made from a mixture of cooked pig's liver, pork fat, breadcrumbs, and herbs, and baked in a

covering of pig's caul. They are either baked in individual wrapped portions or in a large tin with the caul as a covering They are popular in the north of England and are eaten cold with salad, or reheated and served with vegetables and gravy, and sometimes apple sauce.

FILLET
A piece of meat or fish without bone. Fish fillets are usually half the fish with the backbone removed, and are long narrow pieces.

FINES HERBES
A mixture of finely-chopped fresh parsley, chervil, tarragon, and chives in about equal quantities. Used for flavouring omelets and other egg dishes, for salads, sauces, and fish.

FLAMBÉ
A French word meaning to add spirit to a dish and set it alight, either during the cooking process, or at the time of serving (for example, the rum or brandy on the Christmas pudding). For good results the spirit should be warm before it is ignited; either light it and pour it over the food, or pour the warm spirit over the food and then ignite it. The first method is the better one if there is a lot of sauce or other liquid with the food, as this tends to dilute the spirit and prevent a good *flambé*.

FLORENTINE (À LA)
A dish served with spinach and cheese.

FOIE GRAS
A paste made from the livers of specially fattened geese.

FREEZING (see pages 207–15).

FRICASSÉE
This is like a *blanquette* (see page 220), but the meat is fried before being put in the sauce to cook. In English cooking a *fricassée* often means cooked meat reheated in a sauce and served with bacon rolls.

FRIT
Means fried.

FRYING

This is probably the most popular of all methods of cooking, whether it is shallow frying (in just enough fat to prevent sticking), or deep-fat frying (in a large amount of fat), or oven frying (similar to shallow frying). The French *sauté* is a shallow fry, done in a special *sauté* pan (in a fry pan with rounded sides) and the pan is frequently shaken and banged about on top of the stove to make the food turn itself by jumping about (*sauter* – to jump). Shallow frying is not as good a method of cooking as deep fat frying, and it should be reserved for use as a preliminary browning operation for other methods of cooking, such as casseroles, or for cooking foods like pancakes and similar foods.

Deep frying is better because, if properly carried out, the food is less indigestible and greasy. Greasy, badly-fried food is hard to digest without discomfort which is why fried foods are usually forbidden in the diets of people suffering with digestive troubles, ulcers, etc. Food properly fried in deep fat is not greasy, and is very delicious, but it is rarely to be found in restaurants and probably not very often in the home either. The chief reason for this is that few people bother to use a thermometer to test the heat of the fat or oil, and many try to fry too much food at a time in too little fat. The final result is usually that the food cooks at too low a temperature, soaks up fat, and becomes greasy instead of being crisp and succulent. Another common fault in frying is dirty fat, which imparts a disagreeable flavour to the food, and often discolours it. Fat should be strained carefully each time it is used.

GALANTINE

A piece of boneless meat, spiced, or stuffed and rolled up into a thick sausage shape. It is wrapped in a cloth or foil, and boiled, then pressed and glazed.

GARNISHING (see page 126).

GIBLETS

The livers, hearts, gizzards, feet, and necks of poultry.

GIGOT

The Scottish or French name for a leg of lamb, mutton, veal, or pork.

GLAZE

A liquid used to brush over food to give it a shiny surface, using a pastry brush or a small new paint brush. The most common types of glaze are:

Egg glaze which is egg or egg yolk beaten with a little water and brushed over the tops of scones and pastry prior to baking. Alternatively use cold milk.

Sugar glaze, which may be simply a sprinkling of icing sugar on the food – which is then heated under a fierce grill until the sugar caramelises. It is used on custards, sweet omelets, and fruit dishes. Sugar glazes for buns and yeast mixtures are generally made by boiling 2 Tbs. of sugar with 2 Tbs. of water until the sugar is dissolved. The food is brushed with this mixture as soon as it comes out of the oven.

Glaze for cold meat dishes is made from melted aspic jelly brushed over the food. Hot meat dishes are glazed with a meat stock which has been boiled hard to reduce it to a thick shiny liquid.

GLUCOSE OR DEXTROSE

A simple sugar which is formed in green plants from carbon dioxide of the air and water from the soil with the aid of sunlight and chlorophyll. The energy from the sun is stored in the glucose molecule and released when glucose is oxidised in the body. All plants contain glucose, and it is the chief carbohydrate in the blood of animals. Insulin is needed for its complete metabolism. Excess glucose is converted by the body to a starch (glycogen) and stored as such in muscle and liver, or it may be converted to fat and stored. Two forms of glucose are used in cookery, powdered and liquid.

GOULASH

A Hungarian meat stew, flavoured with paprika pepper.

GRATING

A conventional grater is a metal utensil with ragged perforations. Food is rubbed over the surface and broken up into small pieces. A very fine grater is used for nutmegs, for making onion juice, and for the zest of citrus fruits; a medium-size for orange and lemon rind, cheese, and breadcrumbs; a coarse one for vegetables and suet.

Other graters are operated by turning a handle, to rub the food between plain metal and the grating surface. These are easy to use and protect the fingers from damage. There are also electrically-driven graters, and an electric blender will do many of the grating jobs faster than any other piece of kitchen equipment.

GRILLING

Grilled food is cooked by direct, radiant heat. It may be heat from a charcoal, coal, or wood fire, from gas or electricity, or infra-red. It is one of the most popular ways of cooking small pieces of meat and fish, and is much more appetising than most fried food because it is less greasy and of a better flavour.

Only tender cuts of meat are suitable for grilling (see page 48), but any small fish and fish steaks or cutlets, or thick pieces of fillet, are suitable. Vegetables and fruit can also be grilled as accompaniments or as part of a kebab, shashlik, or brochette.

Before grilling, the food should be brushed with oil or melted butter or other fat. When a barbecue sauce is used, this is brushed over the food during grilling.

Cooking times vary with the kind of grill and the intensity of heat, so it is best to follow the advice of the maker of your particular grill.

GRISSINI

Italian breadsticks. Pieces of bread dough about 10 in. (25 cm.) long and ½ in. (1 cm.) wide, baked until brown and very crisp. Sold by bakers and delicatessens.

GROATS

Are ground oats.

238

HOMINY

Coarsely-ground sweet corn or maize. Used in Italian cookery and in America. Uses are similar to those for semolina.

HOMOGENISE

To blend mixtures so that the two make one smooth homogeneou mixture (see, for example, *Homogenised milk*, page 61).

HORS-D'ŒUVRE

The first course of a luncheon or dinner and consisting of small dishes of very savoury and colourful foods. In modern English, called 'starters'. The *hors-d'œuvre* may be just one item such as smoked salmon or a choice from a wide variety as offered in a restaurant. They are usually cold dishes but in some countries hot ones are included as well. They may be served in many small dishes or as individual portions of mixed *hors-d'œuvre*.

INFUSION

To make an infusion, flavouring materials such as herbs or onion are put in a liquid (usually hot) and left until the liquid is well flavoured. The liquid is then used to make a sauce, or used as the liquid in which to cook other foods.

JARDINIÈRE (À LA)

Garnished with vegetables cut in small balls, dice, or fancy shapes. They are cooked separately and arranged around the dish of meat in heaps. The vegetables most often included are carrots, turnips, peas, cauliflower, and French beans.

JUGGED

A method of cooking game in a jar or jug – nowadays, in a casserole. It usually contains red wine, and is highly flavoured with herbs and spices.

JULIENNE

A method of cutting food into fine strips or shreds, usually vegetables used for garnishing. *Julienne* are about matchstick size.

JUS

French for gravy. A dish served '*au jus*' is with its own gravy or cooking liquid.

KABOB, KEBAB, KEBOB

Different spellings of Indian, Turkish, and Persian cooking. Small pieces of meat are put on skewers and grilled. Shish kebab is a Turkish method of cooking mutton or lamb on skewers, and Shashlik is the Russian name. The meat is usually served with a traditional rice dish, and in Britain it is often garnished with items such as grilled mushrooms, tomatoes, sweet peppers, and bacon.

KISSEL OR KEESSIEL

A Russian sweet made from fruit juice sweetened and thickened with potato flour. Similar dishes are also made in other countries, sometimes served as a sweet soup.

KNEADING

This is done to make a bread dough elastic, which helps it to rise and give a good loaf, and also to produce a fine, even texture. Insufficient kneading produces a coarse open texture. Each time that a dough is kneaded some of the gas (carbon dioxide) produced by the yeast is lost, and a further rising period is required to make it light again. Kneading is a stretching and folding process done with the palms of the hands and is continued until tiny bubbles are seen beneath the surface, and the dough is springy and elastic when pressed with a finger.

Sometimes a recipe advises you to knead a pastry or scone dough. This means just to make it smooth. Prolonged kneading will ruin these foods.

LACTIC ACID

An organic acid found in milk and in meat muscle. In milk it is produced by the action of bacteria (called lactic bacilli) which break down milk sugar (lactose) into lactic acid. This gives the milk a sharp taste and, when enough of it has been produced to make the milk curdle, it is called sour milk. During pasteurisation of milk, these bacteria are destroyed. Thus, souring is prevented, but finally putrefaction takes place and the milk goes bad.

Cheese may be made from sour milk or may have lactic acid added with the 'starter'.

Some butters are made from soured cream and are known as 'lactic' butters.

Commercial rennet used for making junkets usually contains lactic acid.

Lactic acid is sometimes used as a preservative, e.g. it is formed during natural fermentation in making sauerkraut. It is also added to fats to prevent oxidation, which causes fat to turn rancid.

In muscle, lactic acid is produced during the complicated chemical changes by which energy is produced from carbohydrates (glucose and glycogen). Glycogen is animal starch and forms the chief reserve of energy in the animal body. When an animal is killed the glycogen present in the muscles is gradually changed to lactic acid. This helps to improve flavour and keep the meat in good condition. An animal which is either hunted, exercised a great deal, or starved before it is killed, will have used up its store of glycogen, and the meat will be of inferior quality. The proper treatment of animals before slaughter is, therefore, a very important part of the production of good-quality meat.

Lactic acid is manufactured for commercial use by bacterial fermentation of starch.

LACTOSE

This is the sugar present in milk, and forms the only source of carbohydrate for the young of milk-fed animals. It is a disaccharide composed of two monosaccharides, glucose and galactose. It is less sweet than other sugars and is sometimes used in therapeutic diets in place of sugar where a high calorie intake is desirable without undue sweetness. The quantity of lactose thus used has to be limited to about 2 oz. (50 g.) per day as it has a laxative effect. Artificially soured milks like yogurt, have some of the lactose converted to lactic acid by the bacteria with which they have been inoculated and they therefore contain less carbohydrates than fresh milk.

LARDING

A process whereby strips of pork fat are threaded through lean meat to give it moistness and flavour during cooking. A special needle (a larding needle) is used for this job. *Barding* (see page 218) is an easier method of preparing meat than larding, but not so good for large thick joints of lean meat.

LIAISON
Binding and thickening ingredients added to soups and sauces, e.g. butter and cream liaison; egg yolks or whole eggs; flour, cornflour, or arrowroot; *roux*.

LYONNAISE
Means to be cooked with onion.

MACÉDOINE
A mixture of different kinds of fruits or vegetables, raw or cooked.

Macédoine of Raw Fruits (*Fruit Salad*).

Macédoine of Cooked Fruits (*Fruit Compote*).

Macédoine of Vegetables The vegetables are cut into dice about the size of a large pea. They are usually cooked and served with a white or *Béchamel* sauce, sometimes enriched with egg yolk and cream, or they may simply be tossed in melted butter. This last method is used for garnishing purposes.

Cold *macédoine* is used for salads and *hors-d'œuvre*, either dressed with French dressing or with mayonnaise (often called Russian Salad).

MALT
This is barley which has been allowed to ferment when the diastase enzymes present in the grain convert the starch to maltose and dextrin. Fermentation is stopped by raising the temperature to stop further activity of the enzyme. The malt is then dried and crushed and is used in the preparation of beer, stout, and whisky. It is also used to flavour malted milk drinks.

MALT EXTRACT
Is made by steeping the malt in water and then concentrating it in a vacuum when it produces a thick brown syrup. It is used for flavouring malt breads and for medicinal purposes, particularly for mixing with cod liver oil.

MARINADE

A highly-seasoned liquid used to give flavour to meat and fish by steeping them in it before cooking and then basting them with it during cooking. The liquids used are oil, vinegar, wine, and fruit juices, with herbs, spices, and onion for flavourings.

MARMITE

A covered French cooking pot for use on top of the stove.

Petite marmite is a clear soup served in an individual pot with a lid, like a little hotpot.

MASHING

This is beating and pulverising a food to break it up into a smooth mixture, e.g. mashing potatoes. Special utensils are made for the purpose but a strong kitchen fork is suitable for mashing small quantities of food and a small wire egg-whisk will deal with things like stewed apple for apple sauce. Mashing does not always give a completely smooth mixture, sieving or putting in an electric blender is needed for this.

MASKING

Covering food with a layer of sauce thick enough to stay on and hide the surface.

MEAT EXTRACTS

Meat extracts are an important by-product of the corned-beef industry. The liquid left after the meat has been pressed for canning is evaporated to give a thick brown substance which keeps indefinitely. It is invaluable for use as a concentrated meat stock. A real meat extract is very expensive, but for cheaper products it is mixed with other ingredients and made into dried cubes, meat cubes, or *bouillon* cubes. As well as a little meat extract these products contain hydrolysed protein, flour, yeast extract, caramel, fat, dried meat, and flavourings. They make quite a good stock substitute provided they are not the only flavouring used.

MEAT TENDERISERS

These are devices for making tough meat tender.

A metal meat tenderiser consists of a heavy base to which are attached thick metal needles. The meat is prodded all over with the needles and this breaks up the connective tissue and makes it more tender. This is quite an effective measure.

The other useful method is to paint or sprinkle the meat with a liquid or powder containing lactic acid and papain enzymes which digest and soften protein. Care must be taken not to exceed the quantities and times recommended by the makers, or the meat will fall to pieces and be tasteless.

For lactic acid uses, see page 241. Papain is an enzyme extracted from the leaves of the pawpaw plant, these leaves being used by local people as a wrapper when cooking meat to make it tender.

MENU

A list of the dishes to be served at a meal or a list of dishes available in a restaurant from which the customers can choose. Many of these menus are in French when the dishes so described are not in any way French. Restaurant owners seem to take the view that giving a dish a French name automatically elevates it into the *haute cuisine* class, at least in the estimation of the customers.

MEUNIÈRE (À LA)

A method of frying fish. The fish is coated with seasoned flour and fried in hot butter.

MILDEW AND MOULDS

These are caused by micro-organisms which grow on food and produce the greenish-coloured growths known as moulds. Most of these are harmless (some like penicillin are even beneficial), but they produce a 'mouldy' taste and thus spoil the food. Their presence also indicates that the food is old or has been badly stored. If jam has a little mould on top it is possible to remove enough of the top layers to get rid of the taste and the rest of the jam can be safely used. Similarly when cheese and bread are affected the mouldy part can be cut away and some salvaged but this must be done quickly, as the mouldy flavour very soon spreads. Containers which have had mouldy food in them should be thoroughly scalded and then left out in the fresh air until all traces of the smell have gone. With some types of container this may take several days.

MINCED

Chopped up into small pieces either by using sharp cook's knives or in a mincing machine. Known in American cookery as 'grinding', hence 'ground meat' for 'minced meat' or 'mince'.

MIREPOIX

A mixture of diced vegetables cooked in butter and used for flavouring certain dishes in French cookery.

MIXED GRILL

A mixture consisting of grilled lamb cutlet, a piece of grilled liver, a kidney, a sausage, a piece of bacon, mushrooms, and tomatoes. Usually served with chip potatoes and a garnish of watercress.

MORNAY (À LA)

Served with a cheese sauce or *Mornay* sauce which is *Béchamel* sauce with Parmesan cheese added.

MOUSSE

A name used for a variety o f cold savoury and sweet dishes which are made frothy and foamy by beating in air, egg whites, or whipped cream.

MUFFIN

A yeast preparation like a crumpet with eggs in it. Muffins used to be sold by street traders known as muffin men, but they are not often obtainable today. They are usually served hot toasted. Special silver muffin dishes with a lid used to be part of elegant tea services.

In the U.S.A. a baking-powder mixture is called a muffin, is cooked in small patty tins, and eaten hot with butter. In New Zealand a similar mixture is called a 'gem', and is baked in pre-heated heavy iron pans, not unlike the shape of bridge rolls. These too are eaten hot with butter.

NAVARIN

A stew, most frequently made with lamb or mutton and containing garlic, onions, and potatoes.

NEAPOLITAN

Usually applied to ices, cornflour moulds, and jellies made of three or more layers differently flavoured and coloured.

NECK

In poultry and game it forms part of the giblets, while with other meats it is one of the cheaper cuts used for stewing. Best end of neck of lamb and mutton includes part of the rib cage as well as the neck.

NOGGIN

A small measure (usually of alcohol), equal to ¼ pt. or 5 fl. oz. (1½ dl.).

NOISETTE

These are pieces of lamb from the best end of neck. A best end is purchased, chined, but not separated into cutlets. Remove all meat from the bone, roll it up and tie with fine white string at intervals of 1½ in. (4 cm.). The meat is then cut through half-way between each tie and the pieces cooked in the same way as cutlets.

NOODLES

Flat *pasta* containing egg.

OFFAL

The organs of an animal, liver, heart, kidney, pancreas, and also tail, feet, and head.

ONE-STAGE METHOD OF MIXING

Everything put together at once and mixed smooth. Used in making cakes, pastry, and sauces in the minimum time.

OXALIC ACID

An acid found in spinach, rhubarb, and some other plants. It combines with calcium and iron in foods to make insoluble compounds – which is why spinach has lost some of its reputation as a good source of iron. Too much oxalic acid is poisonous so don't eat rhubarb leaves; they contain a lot.

PANADA

A name given to a wide variety of preparations. It can mean a soup thickened with bread or a thick bread-and-milk mixture used as a basis for stuffings, or a thick flour, fat, and water mixture used for the same purpose. Sometimes a very thick *roux* is called a panada.

PARMENTIER

Cooked with potatoes as part of the dish.

PAPILLOTTE (EN)

Cooking food in an envelope of foil or thick paper. Chiefly used for small pieces of fish and meat.

PARBOILING

Boiling for part or half of the normal cooking time.

PASTA

Includes macaroni, spaghetti, vermicelli, noodles, lasagne, and so on. They are made from flour and water and some have egg and other materials added.

PÂSTE

A term used in a variety of ways. Pastry is sometimes called a paste. Savoury spreads for toast and bread are pastes, e.g. anchovy paste.

When dry starch is blended with liquid this too is frequently called a paste. Before the days of foil, flour-and-water pastes were used to enclose certain meats to keep them moist during cooking, e.g. in baked ham.

PÂTÉ

French for 'pie'. In English cookery many people use the word for what is really a *terrine* in French cookery. A French pie is shaped like an English raised pie, but the pastry is usually better, containing butter and egg. Sometimes it is made like a large plate pie or turnover.

PATISSERIE

A confectioner's shop, also the French name for pastry confections in general.

PESTLE AND MORTAR

The mortar is a bowl, usually made of either hardwood or tough earthenware. The pestle is a long-handled tool used for pounding the food. They are used by chemists for mixing powders and in the kitchen for pounding ingredients to a paste or powder. Although an electric blender does these jobs much more easily than a pestle and mortar, a small one is still a useful tool for pounding very small quantities, too small for most blenders.

PETITS FOURS

Very small fancy cakes, biscuits, and marzipan sweets served at the end of a formal meal with coffee. *Petits fours* can be purchased ready-made but good ones are always expensive because of the labour involved in making them. Any mixture which can successfully be made into cakes or biscuits not more than about 1 in. (2½ cm.) in diameter, is suitable.

PIPING

This is the process of decorating food with icing, whipped cream, meringue, mashed potatoes, and so on, using a piping tube and bag. The tubes are sold in many sizes and designs.

POACHING

Cooking food, frequently eggs and fish, in water just to cover, and kept below boiling point. Poaching gives a more tender product than boiling and the food keeps a better shape. Many boiled foods are improved by more gentle cooking (see *Boiling*, page 220).

PORTUGAISE (À LA)

Means cooked with tomatoes.

POT AU FEU

Is boiled beef with vegetables, the stock being served as soup.

POT HERBS

A collection of vegetables used for flavouring soups and stews. They can be of any kind but are most frequently root vegetables, celery, and onion.

POT ROASTING

This is an old-fashioned method of cooking meat, game, and poultry, being a combination of frying and stewing or steaming. It requires a heavy pan and a gentle heat after frying. It can be done on top of the cooker or in the oven. The preliminary frying to brown the meat takes place on top of the cooker, then the meat is covered closely and cooking continued slowly until it is tender, allowing 40–45 mins. per pound ($\frac{1}{2}$ kg.). For cooking in the oven use a temperature of E.325–350° (160–180°C.), G.1–2.

It is a good method for tougher cuts of meat not suitable for ordinary roasting (see page 49). The result is similar to that obtained when meat is cooked in a covered roasting pan or in a parcel of foil or other modern wrapping.

PRESSURE COOKING (see page 37).

PROVENÇALE (À LA)

Usually means cooked with tomato and/or garlic and herbs.

PULSES

Usually means dried peas, beans, and other dried legumes, although the whole family of legumes is sometimes called the pulses.

PURÉE

A mixture which has been rubbed through a sieve to remove all lumps and fibre. Used chiefly for soups, sauces, fruit and vegetable preparations. The sieving can be done using a nylon sieve and a wooden spoon to rub the food through, or with a mechanical or electric sieve or an electric blender. With a blender, more *purée* is produced than when a sieve is used, but if the food contains small pips it will need straining after blending.

RAGOUT

A stew which begins with a sauce made by the *roux* method, then the other ingredients are added and cooking continued.

RAISING AGENTS

These are substances used to make baked mixtures light. Yeast makes doughs light by producing carbon dioxide gas, which gives a sponge-like texture.

Carbon dioxide is also produced by the use of baking powder, either added to plain flour or that already incorporated in self-raising flour. Some people mix their own baking powder with cream of tartar and bicarbonate of soda, and sometimes the soda is used alone.

Commercial baking powder is made from the alkali sodium bicarbonate, plus acids of various kinds. Those used are cream of tartar (potassium hydrogen tartrate), tartaric acid, acid calcium phosphate (calcium hydrogen phosphate), acid sodium pyrophosphate (disodium dihydrogen pyrophosphate).

Plain cakes can usually be made satisfactorily with self-raising flour, but there is too much raising agent in it for rich cakes, especially those with plenty of eggs, and particularly if they are mixed with an electric cake-mixer which beats in a lot of air. Too much raising agent spoils both the texture and flavour of a cake, and it is important to follow the advice of a good recipe.

When baking powder is added it should always be thoroughly sifted with the flour to get an even distribution. Bicarbonate of soda is usually dissolved in a little milk or water and added after the flour.

RASPINGS

Crumbs made by grating the brown crust of a loaf. Sometimes it also means crumbs made from dried bread (see *Breadcrumbs*).

RATAFIA

A liqueur, flavoured with the kernels of fruit such as apricots, peaches, or cherries. It has an almond-like flavour. Ratafias are small biscuits made from ground sweet and bitter almonds, sugar, and eggs and sold in small packets.

READY-MIXES

These are packet mixes for making cakes, batters, scones, breads, pastry, and other similar goods. They usually consist of the dry ingredients needed, plus fat, and sometimes dried egg and milk as well. In general the price of ready-mixes is much the same as when making the same quality of product for yourself, though sometimes the purchaser pays for the convenience of the pack. They do not usually produce such good results as a competent cook can achieve with better-quality ingredients, but they are a great help to the busy beginner.

Home-made ready-mixes are a time-saver – for example, a short pastry mix with the fat rubbed into the flour and the mix stored in a polythene bag in the refrigerator. The same idea can be applied to many cakes, scones, and similar items.

RECHAUFFÉ
A dish made using left-overs.

REDUCTION
Boiling a liquid to concentrate the flavour and reduce the volume. Use as wide a pan as possible because the bigger the surface of the liquid the more rapid the reduction.

REFRIGERATION
When the word 'chill' is used in recipes it means to put in the refrigerator until really cold (see also page 102).

RISSOLES
In English cookery these are similar to potato cakes or *croquettes*. In French cookery they are small turnovers of puff paste with a filling of forcemeat or minced cooked meat and are fried in deep fat. They are used for garnishing savoury dishes or in *hors-d'œuvre*.

ROASTING
Originally a simple method of cooking meat which was used before the days of efficient ovens. The meat was hung before an open fire and cooked by radiant heat. In order to prevent burning and scorching before it cooked through, the meat had to be kept moving, and the rotating spit was invented to do this. Recent times have seen a revival of this method. Enthusiasts claim that the meat is better than when oven roasted, which they label 'baked' and inferior.

However, oven roasting is still the simplest method, and has the advantage that other things can be cooked at the same time and less expensive cuts of meat can be made succulent and tender by means of slow oven roasting.

ROBE DE CHAMBRE (EN)

Means cooked in its skin, e.g. a potato baked or boiled without peeling.

RÔTI

Means roast.

RÔTISSERIE (see page 38).

ROUX

A mixture of fat and flour used for thickening sauces. The fat is melted, the flour stirred in, and the mixture cooked for a few minutes for a white *roux* or longer for a brown *roux*. After that the liquid is added, with flavourings, and the sauce cooked some more.

RUBBING IN

Used to mix fat into flour for pastry, plain buns, and cakes. The fat is cut into pieces and dropped into the flour. Then it is broken up further by using the fingers and thumbs and rubbing fat and flour together, continually letting the mixture fall back into the bowl and lifting up fresh fingerfuls. This continues until the mixture looks like fine breadcrumbs. As the flour and fat fall back into the bowl during the rubbing, air is mixed with it and this helps to lighten the mixture.

Rubbing in can also be done with an electric mixer.

SACCHARIN or benzoic sulphamide

A sugar substitute about 500 times as sweet as sugar. It is made from coal and there are a number of varieties, each with slight modifications, sold under proprietary names. Some modern varieties have no bitter after-taste which was a characteristic of the early forms.

Saccharin is not absorbed from the digestive tract, it has been in use for a great many years, and there is no evidence that it is in any way harmful to humans. The strength of saccharin preparations varies, and it is advisable to follow the manufacturer's instructions when using them. Saccharin has no carbohydrate or calorific value. It is sold in tablets, powders, and liquid form.

SALMIS

Pieces of game or wildfowl served in a rich brown sauce such as *Espagnole* sauce. The meat is roasted until partly cooked, cut up, and then finished in the sauce, sometimes at table, if suitable cooking apparatus is available.

SAUTÉ

Means fried in shallow fat. A special pan is used (see *Sauté pan*, page 39). The fried food is either served plain or, after removing the cooked meat, a sauce is made in the pan, the meat then returned and heated again before serving.

SCALD

To pour boiling water over. Scalding hot is boiling hot.

SCALLOPED

A method of preparing cooked fish, eggs, or vegetables by mixing with a sauce (usually white or *Béchamel*), and reheating in the oven with buttered crumbs as a topping. Special individual dishes shaped like escallop shells or cleaned escallop fish shells are used to hold the mixture.

SCORING

What the butcher does to the rind of a piece of pork for roasting. Parallel and criss-cross cuts are made.

SEAR

To subject to a very high temperature.

SEASONED FLOUR

  1 *Tbs. salt*   4 *oz. flour* (¾ *c. or* 125 *g.*)   ½ *tsp. pepper*
Sift these together and keep in a dredger for dusting meat and fish before cooking.

SEASONING

Most commonly means salt and pepper but can also include spices.

SHREDDING

Cutting in fine pieces either by knives or on a grater, e.g. suet is shredded on a grater, cabbage is shredded by slicing with a sharp knife or using a mechanical shredder.

SIEVING

Is rubbing through a sieve for the same purposes as sifting or to make a *purée* (see page 249).

SIFT

To pass through a sieve, either to remove lumps, or to mix dry ingredients such as flour and baking powder or spices.

SIMMERING

Cooking below boiling point, about 183° (85°C.). The surface of the liquid is agitated but not bubbling (see also *Poaching*, page 248).

SINEWS

Tendons in the legs of animals and poultry. They consist of connective tissue of the tough kind which does not soften with ordinary cooking methods. In poultry they are usually removed before the bird is cooked.

SINGE

To pass through a flame and burn the surface to remove hairs, feathers, e.g. with poultry. It is done with a gas flame, a lighted taper or paper spill, or with a spirit lamp.

SIPPETS

Thin slices of toast cut into small triangles and used for decorating soups and savoury dishes. They may also be made from fried bread.

SKIM

To scoop off the top layer, e.g. cream off the milk, scum from the top of jam and boiling meat or stock, or fat from a soup. A perforated spoon is the most useful tool for all except the fat, when an ordinary spoon is best and absorbent paper for the last traces of fat.

SLIVERS
Very fine strips, like splinters, and usually of vegetables.

SMOKING
A method used for preserving meat and fish, e.g. bacon, ham, kippers, smoked haddock. Wood smoke is used and this produces substances which have a sterilising and preserving action and give flavour and colour, but the main preserving is done by the salting which precedes the smoking.

SOUSING
This usually means cooking in a mixture of water and vinegar or wine, with spices and other flavourings.

STEAMING
This is cooking in steam, the food usually being placed in a perforated container which fits on to the top of a saucepan. Water is kept boiling in the saucepan and fills the pan above with steam which cooks the food. Small pieces of food like fillets of fish are sometimes steamed between two plates or on a plate covered with a saucepan lid, the plate fitting on top of a pan of boiling water. Food cooked in the top of a double boiler is also cooked by the heat from steam.

Steamed puddings are either put in a steamer, or else the pudding basin is stood in the saucepan with boiling water coming about halfway up the sides of the basin. The essential thing with all steaming is to keep the water boiling steadily and to replenish it before the pan boils dry. Steaming is an economical method of cooking because one boiling plate only is needed to cook a meal. It is useful for the bed-sitter, for camping, etc.

The sorts of foods most frequently steamed are suet and sponge puddings, fish, sometimes meat, potatoes, and other root vegetables. Steaming is not a good method of cooking green vegetables because it is slow and the loss of vitamin C is too great.

A complete meal can be cooked by steaming meat and root vegetables in the top compartment while a pudding is steamed below. Supply the vitamin C by serving some raw fruit at the end of the meal, or fruit juice or grapefruit at the beginning.

Cooking times for steaming are about half as long again as for boiling.

STERILISE

To heat to a high enough temperature to kill micro-organisms which cause food spoilage.

STEWING

This is cooking food in a liquid slowly at simmering temperature until it is tender. It is a method frequently used for cooking meats, fish, and fruit.

Today many stews are called 'casserole' dishes and are cooked in the oven, which is often easier to control at the low temperature required for good stewing.

There are some very famous dishes which are in fact basically stews, e.g. curries, goulash, ragouts, *navarin* of lamb.

STOCK

A flavoured liquid made by boiling meat, bones, fish, or vegetables in water. Stock is an important aid to making good sauces, soups, stews, and casseroles. Ready-prepared stocks are available as meat extracts (see page 243), meat and chicken cubes, and canned and bottled *consommé*.

In the days of universal solid-fuel cookers a stock pot was usually to be found in continuous use at the back of the stove, and into it went bones and trimmings of all kinds. Some people still do this, but for the majority the ready-prepared stock is more practical. But it is always worth while using a carcase of a chicken or other bird to make stock, and also to use any veal bones and trimmings. The pressure cooker is the simplest way of making it because the cooking time is so much less, $\frac{1}{2}$–1 hr. The bones are simply covered with cold water, or to about half fill the cooker, and after cooking the pressure is allowed to fall gradually. Then strain the stock, cool, remove fat from the top and store the stock in a refrigerator or freezer.

SUGAR BOILING

When sugar and water are boiled together the temperature gradually rises as cooking continues, until finally the sugar begins to caramelise and turn brown, and then chars or burns. Different kinds of confectionery are made by stopping the boiling at different temperatures. Although these temperatures may be guessed at, by various homely methods, it is much safer and more satisfactory to use a sugar thermometer.

Thread stage	230°F.	110°C.
Soft Ball stage	238°F.	114°C.
Hard Ball stage	254°F.	123°C.
Crack or Brittle stage	290°F.	143°C.
Caramel stage	350°F.	177°C.

If the sugar mixture is stirred during boiling it forms crystals, therefore all sweets are made without stirring once the solution has come to the boil.

Some syrup always crystallises on the sides of the pan and this can be washed down with a pastry brush dipped in water. When a very fine texture is wanted, as in fondants, a little acid such as lemon juice or tartaric acid is added. This hydrolyses some of the sugar to invert sugars which do not form crystals.

Fudges and similar sweets are stirred and beaten after cooking. If a fine texture is desired, such sweets should never be beaten during or immediately after cooking has finished, but allowed to cool for a few minutes.

SUPRÊME

This term is used for either special pieces of chicken such as the breast, or for food cooked in a special sauce usually containing cream and egg yolk.

SWEATING

Cooking vegetables slowly in a little fat in a covered pan so that they begin to soften without browning.

SYRUP

This may mean golden syrup or a solution of sugar and water used for making fruit compotes and fruit salads.

Bottled fruit syrups are made from fruit juices with sugar and preservative added. They are useful for making drinks and for cooking.

TABLE D'HÔTE

On a restaurant menu this means a set meal at a fixed price, as distinct from *à la carte*, which is a menu chosen by the customer according to taste and purse.

TARTARIC ACID

An organic acid commonly found in plants, especially in grapes and other fruits. A potassium salt of tartaric acid (potassium hydrogen tartrate) is known as cream of tartar. Both are used in raising agents (see *Raising Agents*, page 250).

They are also used in cooking where acid is required, e.g. in making certain sugar goods such as fondant; in making jam from fruit deficient in acid (see *Jam*, page 181); and to add acid to beverages.

TEMPERATURES, see *Thermometers and Thermostats*, below, and also pages 9 and 41.

THERMOMETERS AND THERMOSTATS

Many cooking processes depend for their success on using the correct temperatures, and the only way of ensuring accuracy is by using either a thermometer or the more modern automatic temperature regulator, the thermostat. This is a device which measures the temperature and raises or lowers the supply of heat as needed to maintain the predetermined temperature. This it does within a fairly narrow range.

The range of temperatures used in a kitchen is wide, from 0°F. (−18°C.) to 500°F. (316°C.). One thermometer will not usually cover this whole range and different ones are needed for special purposes.

Deep-freeze and refrigerator 0–50°F. (−18–10°C.). These are controlled by a thermostat, but a separate thermometer is useful to have for a check.

Yeast and Yeast cookery 70–120°F. (20–50°C.).

Deep fat frying and sugar boiling 212–500°F. (100–316°C.). There are some fat fryers which are thermostatically controlled and do not need a thermometer. Thermometers for sugar work usually have a clip to fasten them on to the edge of the pan. Not all sugar thermometers registerer as high as 500°, but a fat thermometer does and can be used for sugar work as well.

Roasting Meat 140–190°F. (60–88°C.). A special thermometer is needed for this as it has to have a metal end which will pierce the meat. Some modern ovens have a meat thermometer as a permanent fitting.

Simmering 185°F. (85°C.). An automatically controlled boiling plate will control at this temperature but some initial experimenting is needed to find the right setting for different pans.

Boiling 212°F. (100°C.). Does not need a thermometer when boiling is at normal atmospheric pressure, but at high altitudes water boils at lower temperatures.

Baking 200–500°F. (204–316°C.). Most modern ovens are automatically controlled by thermostats and a cooking chart is provided by the manufacturers to show the settings to use for different kinds of cooking.

Special oven thermometers are useful for older types of ovens. These are made to stand on the oven shelf, and the heat is adjusted to keep them at the temperature required.

TOURNEDOS

A special piece of steak for frying or grilling, usually a piece of fillet steak about 2 in. (5 cm.) square.

TRUSSING

This term is used for tying and skewering meat, poultry, and fish into convenient shapes for cooking.

TURNING

In cooking this has the same meaning as in woodwork, i.e. cutting into ornamental shapes. It is used chiefly for root vegetables to cut them all the same size and shape for garnishing purposes. The turning is done with a small vegetable knife or a special turning knife. The trimmings can be used for soups, stews, etc.

TURNOVER

A circle of pastry folded over to make a semi-circle with a filling in the middle.

VARIETY MEATS

American for Offal (see page 246)

VINAIGRETTE

A sauce consisting of oil, vinegar, chopped gherkins, parsley, onion, and other seasonings.

VOL-AU-VENT

A puff pastry case, individual size or a large one to serve several people. Usually filled with shellfish or meat in a rich sauce.

WHIP

The same as beating, but generally used for beating cream and eggs.

YEAST EXTRACTS

These are made from yeast with the addition of salt, vegetables, and spices for flavouring. They are concentrated dark-brown pastes used as spreads and for flavouring soups and sauces in the same way as meat stock or cubes. The best yeast extracts are good sources of vitamins of the B complex, especially of nicotinic acid and riboflavine.

ZAMPINO

A hand of salt pork, boned and stuffed, then boiled.

ZEST

The yellow part of the rind of oranges, lemons, and other citrus fruit.

INDEX

264

267

268

269